Building Competitive Gas Markets in the EU

LOYOLA DE PALACIO SERIES ON EUROPEAN ENERGY POLICY

Series Editor: Jean-Michel Glachant, *Holder of the Loyola de Palacio Chair on EU Energy Policy and Director of the Florence School of Regulation, European University Institute, Italy, and Professor of Economics, Université Paris-Sud, France*

The *Loyola de Palacio Series on European Energy Policy* honours Loyola de Palacio (1950–2006), former Vice-President of the European Commission and EU Commissioner for Energy and Transport (1999–2004), a pioneer in the creation of an EU Energy Policy.

This series aims to promote energy policy research, develop academic knowledge and nurture the 'market for ideas' in the field of energy policy-making. It will offer informed and up-to-date analysis on key European energy policy issues (from market-building to security of supply; from climate change to a low carbon economy and society). It will engage in a fruitful dialogue between academics (including economists, lawyers, engineers and political scientists), practitioners and decision-makers. The series will complement the large range of activities performed at the Loyola de Palacio Chair currently held by Professor Jean-Michel Glachant (Robert Schuman Centre for Advanced Studies at European University Institute in Florence, Italy, and Université Paris-Sud 11).

Titles in the series include:

Security of Energy Supply in Europe
Natural Gas, Nuclear and Hydrogen
Edited by François Lévêque, Jean-Michel Glachant, Julián Barquín, Christian von Hirschhausen, Franziska Holz and William J. Nuttall

Competition, Contracts and Electricity Markets
A New Perspective
Edited by Jean-Michel Glachant, Dominique Finon and Adrien de Hauteclocque

The Economics of Electricity Markets
Theory and Policy
Edited by Pippo Ranci and Guido Cervigni

Building Competitive Gas Markets in the EU
Regulation, Supply and Demand
Jean-Michel Glachant, Michelle Hallack and Miguel Vazquez

Building Competitive Gas Markets in the EU

Regulation, Supply and Demand

Jean-Michel Glachant

Holder of the Loyola de Palacio Chair on EU Energy Policy and Director, Florence School of Regulation, European University Institute, Italy

Michelle Hallack

Jean Monnet Fellow of the Loyola de Palacio Chair, European University Institute, Italy and tenured professor at Federal Fluminense University, Brazil

Miguel Vazquez

Jean Monnet Fellow of the Loyola de Palacio Chair, European University Institute, Italy

With contributions from Sophia Ruester and Sergio Ascari

THE LOYOLA DE PALACIO SERIES ON EUROPEAN ENERGY POLICY

Edward Elgar

Cheltenham, UK • Northampton, MA, USA

Published by
Edward Elgar Publishing Limited
The Lypiatts
15 Lansdown Road
Cheltenham
Glos GL50 2JA
UK

Edward Elgar Publishing, Inc.
William Pratt House
9 Dewey Court
Northampton
Massachusetts 01060
USA

A catalogue record for this book
is available from the British Library

Library of Congress Control Number: 2013935044

This book is available electronically in the ElgarOnline.com
Economics Subject Collection, E-ISBN 978 1 78254 064 9

ISBN 978 1 78254 063 2

Typeset by Servis Filmsetting Ltd, Stockport, Cheshire
Printed and bound in Great Britain by T.J. International Ltd, Padstow

Contents

Contributors

Sergio Ascari, Advisor, Florence School of Regulation, European University Institute, Italy

Walter Boltz, Executive Director of E-Control and Vice President of CEER, Brussels

Jean-Michel Glachant, Holder of the Loyola de Palacio Chair on EU Energy Policy and Director, Florence School of Regulation, European University Institute, Italy

Michelle Hallack, Jean Monnet Fellow, Loyola de Palacio Chair, European University Institute, Italy and tenured professor, Federal Fluminense University, Brazil

Sophia Ruester, Florence School of Regulation, European University Institute, Italy

Miguel Vazquez, Jean Monnet Fellow, Loyola de Palacio Chair, European University Institute, Italy

Foreword

Walter Boltz

Trading on Europe's gas wholesale markets or at hubs has made progress over the last decade, particularly in Northwest Europe. However, progress has not been the same in all parts of Europe and even where gas hubs have emerged, liquidity is still regarded by many as insufficient. Nevertheless, more needs to be done for European gas wholesale markets to be effectively connected to each other and to be sufficiently liquid to send reliable price signals – or in other words – to meet our goal of the Internal Energy Market.

The idea of the integrated energy market is to promote competition in the European wholesale markets and facilitate new entry to compete against the incumbents in supplying gas. A competitive wholesale market will need to be efficient, thereby delivering gas to where it is most valued while providing shippers with the right incentives to secure supplies to European consumers. An efficient market must also provide the signals for investment in both gas production and in gas network infrastructure, including transmission, storage and LNG (liquefied natural gas) facilities, in order to meet the demands of European gas consumers. There is also a strong need for non-discriminatory and fair arrangements for shippers to access the gas infrastructure in order for competition to develop and for the network to be used efficiently while guaranteeing adequate remuneration for investments. We need a regulatory framework that secures supplies in the long, medium and short term, which means making Europe, now and in the future, attractive to gas imports and taking account of seasonal and short-term fluctuations in gas demand.

One of the key challenges in creating an integrated market in Europe is to put effective rules in place for facilitating cross-border trading and market integration between Member States. As such, the Third Energy Package establishes a new regulatory framework for cross-border trade and provisions for legally binding European network codes to regulate cross-border aspects.

The European regulatory framework aims to improve efficiency in the use of cross-border capacity and to enhance competition through liquid wholesale markets. As part of the Third Energy Package the Gas Regulation[1] makes Transmission System Operator (TSO)-wide entry/exit systems obligatory by September 2011 and abolishes tariffs set on the basis of contract paths.[2] Measures are being pursued to open up network access to new entrants in a bid to foster greater competition. The Gas Directive[3] requires increased unbundling of the ownership and operation of gas networks from gas supply in order to remove potential for discrimination when granting network access.

European energy regulators have prepared, together with stakeholders, a vision for the European Gas Market with a view to completing the Internal Energy Market by 2014 as requested by the European Council and the European Commission. In our vision we suggest there be a series of liquid hubs across Europe where gas can be traded (these may be national or across borders) and that national markets are easily connected to these trading points. Gas will flow freely between these market areas and respond to price signals, that is, gas will flow to where it is valued most. It will also be important that sufficient and efficient levels of infrastructure investment take place to allow markets to integrate.

NOTES

1. Regulation (EC) 715/2009.
2. Recital 19 Gas Regulation.
3. Directive 2009/73/EC.

Introduction

Miguel Vazquez, Michelle Hallack and Jean-Michel Glachant

OPENING THE GAS INDUSTRY: USA VERSUS EU, AN OVERVIEW

Gas is a commodity and goes to the market. This should not astonish anyone since coal and oil, the two other fossil fuels, have been delivered by markets for ages. Natural gas is, however, less easily marketed because it flows inside closed pipes that have a 'big' efficient size and are very costly to replicate. The infrastructure of the gas network then operates as a barrier to open trade. With a small nascent gas demand the gas network is likely to be a natural monopoly and gas sources only one or very few. With a large, mature gas demand the gas network should encompass numerous facilities with alternative routes and several rival gas sources should candidate to feed consumption. In the latter case, opening demand to alternative suppliers is more easily feasible and makes sense. With nearly 600 million inhabitants and decades of gas usage in most of the Member States, the EU gas industry is not on average an infant industry and opening gas trade at the continental scale is not wrong, however, with different maturity levels of gas networks, gas sources and gas demand the grand opening of gas trade in the EU will not be simple. In practice, the institutional arrangements to opening trade in the gas industry are themselves various and numerous, and, unsurprisingly, the process for opening the gas sector has been significantly different among different regions of the world. Notably, the latecomer EU is not following the pioneering USA.

Opening Up US Gas Trade

The pioneer of gas liberalization decades ago was the USA. The liberalization was markedly characterized by the reliance on business forces to drive decisions in the production chain. Broadly speaking, the US gas sector is mainly organized around private companies who are in charge of deciding on upstream production, transportation, storage and downstream delivery of gas (while distribution to consumers can be regulated or public). In this context, gas transmission network investments and operations are mainly decided on by non-regulated agents, even if closely monitored in Washington by the Federal Energy Regulatory Commission (FERC).

This most liberalized setting has, by definition, the lowest requirements with regard to the design of the market. Hence, in such a setting, US wholesale gas markets are fundamentally based on bilateral contracts among producers and suppliers, without the need for any mandatory organized market to trade. These private contracts, in addition, are long term (10 or 20 years are usual horizons), which is related to significant aversion of bilateral traders to the risks of not injecting/withdrawing gas according to their initial business plan and capacity investment.

Following the same logic, transmission rights are also purchased long in advance. In this kind of transaction, producers and suppliers enter into contracts that provide the right to use the network to transport gas from one point to another, and whose counterparts are the owners of the infrastructure involved in the path between both points. In this regard, shippers decide on the physical path that the gas will follow, and pay for the use of the associated infrastructure. In addition, under this organization, the investment in network infrastructure is largely driven by those long-term contracts, and hence decisions on network planning are directly taken in the interaction between non-regulated network investors on the one hand and consumers and suppliers on the other.

Nonetheless, gas supply and demand patterns are highly volatile, and the balance of flows in the gas system must be coordinated in shorter terms. Hence, in the short term, shippers will face frequent imbalances, which must be dealt with by considerably complex combinations of gas trade arrangements and the associated transmission rights changes. Consequently, the above wholesale markets are typically associated with the definition of a place where the physical delivery of the commodity takes place: the physical hub. A hub is a place where gas wholesale trading is facilitated by the conjunction of several transmission facilities and services. It is, under this scheme, a junction of pipelines where a significant number of gas sales and purchases take place, and where sellers and buyers can also obtain storage and flexibility services. Serving as marketplaces, hubs have often been seen as a prerequisite for gas pricing through gas-to-gas competition in the sense that they are a key element to facilitating the coordination of gas systems in the short term.

These particular transactions largely aim at adjusting shippers' portfolios in the short term. They can be thought of as secondary transactions, as most gas trading is done in the long term. But these secondary short-term transactions are 'central' in the functioning of gas markets, as many delicate technical issues concerning the allocation of physical transmission rights are organized around them.

As in the case of long-term contracting, the US gas sector has not considered it necessary to centralize these transactions and has left them to bilateral arrangements. In that situation, the coordination of players in the short-term operation of the gas networks is facilitated by bilateral agreements between gas arbitrageurs and network operators (who are often owners of the infrastructures). These kinds of arrangements and trade platforms arise as a 'natural' need of the market participants, without particular push for a reference market design or for standardized contracts.

Finally, in this 'spontaneous market' context the price coordination between long- and short-term decisions is completed through financial contracts, where the underlying asset is usually the gas delivered in the hub. Such trades are often made in organized financial markets (NYMEX being the biggest in the USA). The function of these organized markets is to contribute to the inter-temporal coordination of the gas industry.

Opening Up EU Gas Trade

The liberalization of gas industries in Europe came after liberalization in the USA, so one might think that the USA was somehow the model for the European liberalization. However, when looking at the previous elements of US gas industry organization, EU and US markets have few common factors. In fact, the design of EU gas markets seems to be closer to the design of EU electricity markets than to the US gas markets. It is very likely that these differences arise largely from the fact that the EU prefers to organize gas network activities in each Member State as a 'nationally centralized' and regulated business.

The logic for this decision might have been the consideration that EU gas network activities have the structure of a natural monopoly or a too-concentrated oligopoly and thus were recognized as the main barrier to the opening of the commodity market. In such a situation, as in the electricity sector, the activities related to production and supply are considered as open businesses that may benefit from a market arrangement, whereas network activities must remain subject to public regulation regarding their operation and investment. From a different viewpoint, it might also be possible to support a regulation of network activities, arguing that too decentralized decisions in the operation of the network would lead to inefficiencies. The efficient option is then to design a centralized operation by means of a Transmission System Operator (TSO), coordinating the gas system interactions as much as possible. In practice, so far, it has been centralized only at the national level, even if some countries such as France and Germany still have several separated areas. This suggests that European Member States' institutional powers (i.e., their veto power in any EU common gas arrangement) heavily influenced the EU choice set.

In any case, new markets created in Europe rely on the regulation of network activities (from capacity booking and allocation to congestion management, from cross-border trade to entry/exit pricing). In practice, these EU markets build on the strong separation – unbundling – of the business of transmission networks from the business of trade in the commodity market (again, in this regard, closely related to electricity market rationale). With such a choice, the regulation of the rights of commodity buyers and sellers for using the regulated network becomes a central part of the market design.

From a long-term perspective, the rights for using the network closely interact with the negotiation and implementation of any long-term commodity contract between suppliers and demanders. The contracts that allocate transmission capacity and frame the actual capacity usage become a platform of interactions between market players and a central architecture in this 'centralized' gas system. Thus, the market design must contain enough elements to coordinate the contracts of capacity with the commodity contracts. From a short-term perspective, where the arrangements to manage congestion or imbalances take place, the market design must take into account the way in which the regulated network operator allocates transmission rights among market players. It is in the process of designing those mechanisms where most of the differences between US and EU gas markets appear.

THE LOGIC FOR VIRTUAL HUB REGULATION IN THE EU

In the EU the seller of transmission rights is a regulated player. Thus, a first choice for the market designer arises: should allocation of transmission rights be explicit (capacity only) or implicit (capacity and commodity are traded together)? The advocates of implicit allocation build their case on two ideas. The first is that combining two trades (capacity and commodity) made separately in a very short period of time (day or intra-day) causes significant transaction costs for traders, ending in an inefficient use of transmission capacity signalled by significant trade in the 'wrong' direction. The second is that gas market structure is characterized by significant horizontal concentration and vertical integration. Consequently the market designer must take potential strategic behaviour into account.

A key is the strategic use of network 'congestion': incumbents may have the incentive to over-contract network capacity to foreclose short-term markets for small competitors, and hence to induce effective entry barriers. When the commodity market 'implicitly' allocates the rights to use the network, the gas can be traded without the need for ex ante contracting of network services. Thus, the opportunities to foreclose contracting of network capacity disappear (Joskow, 2003). Although other measures to mitigate this kind of strategic behaviour have been considered, the implicit auctioning has been favoured as a solution to deal with strategic behaviour in network capacity contracting.

The comprehensive approach to implementing the implicit allocation would have been to consider the physical network in full detail, where all physical injection and withdrawal points may have a potentially different gas price. These detailed pricing points would also correspond to the actual gas network flows. However, following the design in the UK, EU gas markets did not go so far into the network details and favour organizing gas transactions around a virtual hub.[1] Such a virtual hub is not a physical junction of pipelines, but instead a regulated set of delivery points with a very simplified representation of the actual physical characteristics of the network. Virtual hubs avoid consideration of the actual physical network that will be ultimately used by the commodity transactions. To do so the market designer defines a 'commercial' network, that is, a few network characteristics that will be taken into account in wholesale commercial transactions. That market design is close to that of European electricity markets, where detailed market clearing based on nodal pricing (with the representation of all nodes of the physical network) was substituted by relatively simple commercial networks (in most cases, made up of a single node). The fundamental logic for virtual hubs is to increase the market liquidity associated with the simplification of the network. As the number of delivery points is highly reduced, the network specificities of the commodity are markedly reduced and thus the gas-to-gas competition is enhanced at the expense of a more efficient operation of the network.

VIRTUAL HUBS IN THE SHORT RUN

The virtual hub approach implies that the market uses a commercial network for most of the transactions of the commodity, which is different from the physical network. The European standard approach to the definition of the commercial network is entry/exit regulation. There the market players have the right to inject gas in a gas system at any entry point, and to withdraw gas from any exit point. Therefore, this market design requires a set of additional elements to bridge the gap between the commercial and the physical gas networks, which are usually grouped under the header of balancing mechanisms. When the design of the market is built on the definition of a commercial network, additional transmission activities arise in the short term to coordinate the operation of the commercial and the physical networks.

In a system like the USA's, with network services directly organized by competition, market forces determine the kind of contract that can be found, according to the preferences of players. In the EU regulated environment, it is, on the contrary, necessary to define by means of a set of centralized rules how the network can be used by gas commodity players. This necessity is amplified by the potentially conflicting usages that users may back on their 'Third Party Access' (TPA) rights to the same infrastructure. Therefore, the rules governing these usages influence market outcomes and their potential efficiency. The effects of such design rules are at the core of market activity, as they implicitly pre-define the network services made available to market participants.

In the short term on the one hand, market players must make arrangements to manage their gas injection/withdrawal imbalances; on the other hand, the network operator must allocate network rights in a way that will make all commercial commodity transactions physically feasible.[2] The usual approach in the EU electricity market is defining a gate closure as a certain time horizon after which the commodity market has no further decision right on network capacity allocation. Hence, a regulation defines a certain time scope (such as hour ahead, day ahead, or week ahead) where the role of the commodity market to manage its own imbalances ends. In EU natural gas markets the right of players to change their physical portfolio is defined by the re-nomination right.[3] As the players can re-nominate within the balancing period, in the current regulatory frame there is no clear period separation between the TSO balancing actions and the shippers' secondary arrangements.

In this context, the obligation of the TSO is to allow real time flow and the obligation of the shippers is to have equal injection and withdrawal at the end of the balancing period. The guarantee of physical flows is, thus, the responsibility of network operators, and the cost to keep the flows balanced is taken by the network if at the end of the balancing period the shippers' portfolios are balanced. Nevertheless, if at the end of balancing period the shipper has an open position, they are obliged to pay the cost or even some penalties.[4]

In the entry/exit regime most gas transactions are determined with reference to the commercial network. However, the process of actual network service allocation is the responsibility of the transmission operator. Of course, the rules governing network usage should allow the efficient use of the transmission network. This, conversely, is not straightforward in an entry/exit scheme as the network operator is obliged to take a bunch of 'ex ante' decisions to be able to allow the physical flow in real time. However, as the flow decisions taken by shippers are unknown to the TSOs, it is difficult to guarantee an efficient use of the infrastructures.

In an entry/exit system the commercial network capacity is a calculation made by the transmission operator. In this calculation, the transmission operator must take into account the fact that market participants own the right to carry gas from the entry points to any exit point. Hence, the operator must reserve not only the network required to carry gas from an entry to a defined exit, but also the network required to carry gas to all other exit points of the system. Therefore, a congestion in the network from an entry point and one exit point might cause congestion in the network to other exit points. This problem is often called 'contractual congestion'[5] (the network is not necessarily congested, but the system operator cannot allow more injections into the system given the existing set of rights). The direct consequence of contractual congestions is that the network is not efficiently used.

The design of other rules for possible network services may have consequences on the ability of market players to express their preferences. A typical case is the allocation of line-pack. Pipeline line-pack is the possibility of storing (de-storing) gas inside the pipes by decreasing (increasing) the pressure differential between successive compressors. As the gas pressure differential is the factor making both the gas move and be stored, it determines the resulting transport capacity and pipe congestion. In fact the line-pack of a pipeline is a substitute service of its transportation capacity. However, as 'entry/exit' markets refer to commercial networks without any accurate representation of the physical pipelines, these markets cannot reveal any order of preferences regarding the various possible combinations of line-pack and transportation capacity. The fact that the ultimate decision on such combinations is taken unilaterally by the regulated transmission operators may have a significant impact on market outcomes.

Another important consequence of the current EU regime is that the costs of the network cannot be allocated according to the detailed actual use of the network (for instance, precise locational signals cannot be given in the short run). The costs of the decisions taken by the transmission operators in the process of matching commercial and physical networks within the balancing period are socialized among network users. The use of different prices for certain entry and exit points of the commercial network cannot reproduce the real flow paths, just an approximation of network costs based on flow simulations.

The actual consequence of simplifying the physical network in a commercial network depends markedly on the nature of the gas transactions in the corresponding wholesale market. Actually, the rules to allocate network services in current EU regulations are somehow conceived for relatively flat patterns of gas flows. The logic for this is that, when flow patterns, or equivalently, the market participants' needs for variable injection and withdrawal patterns (both time and spatial variability), are relatively flat the rules for using the network are easier to define, as the simulation of cost sharing just takes into account the location of the players. However, if the need for a different and more flexible use of the network increases, the gap between the commercial and the physical network has a larger impact on market outcomes. Hence, the simulation of cost should take into account the diverse patterns of network use to better evaluate the trade-off between line-pack storage and the available transport capacity.

This fundamental change in usages of the gas network happened on the demand side with the massive introduction of CCGT (combined cycle gas turbine) gas-fired power plants, as well as with the flexible gas supply brought through LNG (liquefied natural gas). A massive introduction of gas-fired power plants in electricity generation created a new group of gas consumers in the gas market. On the supply side, LNG trade has increased in volume and in flexibility, allowing more arbitrage between players. LNG flexibility allows the gas supply to change according to gas price arbitrages, playing a key role in this world where demand (including CCGT) has a higher elasticity. Moreover, LNG has also been a new type of gas supply, responding easily to gas demand increases as re-gasification technology is modular and has lower scale economies (Jarlsby, 2004). The delay between investment decisions and infrastructure operation is lower than with most other gas sources.

As a consequence of growth of the gas industry centred on LNG and gas-fired power plants, supply and demand patterns are dramatically changing and both are more volatile than in the past. Thus, the storage component of the gas system has dramatically increased its technical and economic value. Today, among gas system users, some key players would give a high value to system flexibility while other key players would give it a much lower value. It becomes more difficult to use simple regulations that do not reflect what real network use has become.

VIRTUAL HUBS IN THE LONG RUN

From a long-term standpoint, assuming that most of the commodity transactions take place through bilateral contracts, a commercial network reduces transaction costs. As with short-term transactions, the number of contracts associated with the network is reduced, as the commercial network is simpler than the physical network. Reduced transaction costs in turn provide increased liquidity. Implicitly, this approach leaves the matching between commercial and physical networks for the short term. This implies that fewer transactions can take place in the long term, as many of the contracts associated with transmission rights will be left to short-term capacity allocation. Consequently, many of the signals associated with the inter-temporal allocation of network rights are distorted.

Closely related to this is the organization of investment decisions, as they strongly depend on the signals associated with the use of network services. Traditionally, the most important investments in gas systems are network and field investments. Actually, both businesses are closely related as the value of a gas field changes significantly according to its access to networks. Correspondingly, network investments are affected by the actual requirements of producers to have their gas delivered to certain consumption points. For decades investment in transmission facilities has largely been driven by the needs of gas producers. Lastly, this link between gas production and transmission investment has notably weakened. A key factor is a marked increase in demand uncertainty, the best example of which is the uncertainty associated with the actual consumption of gas-fired power plants. Massive renewables with priority of dispatch amplify the uncertainty of gas demand. In this new context, the combination of the requirements for network services of both sides of the gas industry (the upstream and the downstream) is a challenge.

In a market like the USA's where network activities are themselves liberalized, all investments, including those corresponding to network infra-structures, are decided by market forces through long-term contracts. In the EU where the network is regulated under TPA (Third Party Access), a kind of network planning is needed. Of course, any central planner is likely less informed than producers and consumers about the possible future gas flows and the various business models that support them. The most direct way for the planner to decide on the required investment is to look at market outcomes to identify the actual system needs. In a market characterized by long-term, bilateral contracts this task is not always straightforward. Moreover, in a commodity market that refers to a virtual commercial network, as with entry/exit schemes, the investment signals delivered by the market are necessarily limited. In this case, an important signal for the planner is the outcome of the commodity balancing market (including congestion management). It is where the commercial network is confronted with the requirements of the physical network. Therefore, the design of the balancing mechanism is not only key from a short-term standpoint, but also to providing the planner with information required for investing in gas networks.

SECURITY OF SUPPLY

Security of supply is the most controversial aspect from the viewpoint of market design because it fundamentally encompasses different issues, including economic and non-economic ones, that cannot all be easily or clearly defined in engineering or economics. In our view, there are two different levels of regulatory intervention under the heading of security of supply. On the one hand, in many gas systems some key players or public decision-makers advocate having some particular geopolitical profile to build some bargaining positions in external relationships. This has little to do with European market design, except for the fact that all measures targeted at choosing some suppliers above the rest may significantly impact the market. Therefore, the decisions regarding political or political economy aspects of security of supply are exogenous to the market design, and thus are constraints put on the possible market solutions. On the other hand, from an economic perspective, when one has a well-functioning market, security of supply is in fact a part of bearing market risk. If the European Union has an efficient internal gas market it means the gas may flow among the EU players according to their preferences. As a result the risk of any individual player having a physical supply disruption decreases. That is, the security of supply discussion regarding the main effect of an external disruption is about price risk. However, the determination of the market willingness to bear risk may not be an efficient process (Grossman and Stiglitz, 1980). This is closely related to problems of information. Markets may fail to coordinate inter-temporal decisions given the difficulty of market players to deal with a highly complex and uncertain future. In turn this means that they do not have (or do not reveal) clear preferences about highly uncertain events, and therefore markets are often incomplete (as they cannot cope with all possible contingencies).

In the case of gas industry security of supply one would assume that consumers are poorly informed about the characteristics of the supply patterns in wholesale gas markets, and thus cannot provide the market with their risk aversion profiles. This would result in inefficient market risk bearing. The solution could be to complete these markets, using the fact that the regulator can be better informed about possible contingencies of gas supplies. The role of regulated security of supply measures is to complete the wholesale gas markets with an estimation by the regulator of the risk preferences of gas consumers.

In summary, one might say that markets are not the best adapted mechanism to deal with 'un-contractual' scenarios (i.e., scenarios of cold or hot war, or any other international diplomatic concern) where there is no enforcement mechanism or self-enforcement corresponding to the obligations to be fulfilled in such rare occurrences. However, a well-functioning European market will always decrease the existing informational risk. It should also decrease many minor disruption risks, transforming them into mundane price risk.

INTEGRATION OF SEVERAL ENTRY/EXIT SYSTEMS

The logic for a single European market based on entry/exit regulation is the rationale behind gas market design in the EU. The integration of numerous 'entry/exit markets' has no analogue in international experience (ERGEG, 2010; ACER, 2011a). In practice, however, in the task of integrating these numerous markets, the design decisions to be taken follow a sequence similar to a single entry/exit market.

One of the very first decisions to be taken is whether an explicit allocation or an implicit allocation of the interconnection capacity should be used. The same arguments already seen may be applied: the transaction costs of combining capacity and commodity traded separately, and the possible strategic use of interconnection contracts. In this context, the design for integrating the European markets could be radical: a single entry/exit market in the whole EU and the definition of a single EU commercial network as distinct from the various existing physical networks. This single entry/exit system would contain all existing national markets that are interconnected. With this approach, however, the difficulties and the costs of the decisions required to bridge the gap between commercial and physical networks would be extensive.

An alternative approach would be to design the pan-EU commercial network with more keys: as a representation of all the critical physical characteristics of actual interconnections, leaving the existing national markets unchanged. In this approach, one can rely on the explicit allocation of the interconnection capacity. This would require, in addition, some effective measures aimed at preventing the possible strategic behaviour (for instance, it is not clear that the use-it-or-lose-it conditions could effectively prevent this kind of behaviour).

It is also possible to implement the implicit allocation with much less simplification in the definition of the commercial network. One could implicitly allocate the interconnection capacity without simplifying the physical characteristics of existing interconnections too much. Such a 'detailed' implicit allocation would come from the combination of the gas pricing of the connected markets by means of an algorithm of zonal pricing (such as 'market splitting', 'market coupling'). Moreover, when this solution is adopted, it is possible to reach a halfway point between implicit and explicit allocation. The 'strategic behaviour' problems of explicit network allocation has to do with the strategy of contracting large amounts of capacity that foreclose the short-term capacity market in the long term. But as soon as the short-term capacity is implicitly allocated by the commodity market, this strategy is no longer possible. However, the long-term allocation of interconnections can still alternatively be done through explicit auctions.

One faces two opposite forces when confronting a tight single entry/exit market for Europe with a loose and light wholesale market made up of interconnections between existing national entry/exit markets. On the one hand, with tight single entry/exit the gap between commercial and physical networks may be too large in terms of both efficient use of the network and cost allocation to beneficiaries. On the other hand, its opposite, being the coexistence of several entry/exit zones, creates other cost allocation problems related to cross-border transactions. It is because, besides the cost of the interconnection, cross-border transactions need to pay the entry and exit price of each corresponding zone. Therefore, some trades that would be economically efficient between the two ends of the interconnection, from the one with lower gas prices to the one with higher prices, will not occur if this price difference cannot compensate for the extra cost associated with the entry and exit prices (which represented the network price of each entry/exit zone). Ultimately, when the interconnection capacity is contracted in advance, this may result in reversed flows (from the high- to the low-price zones).

From the investment viewpoint, a single EU entry/exit market would share the characteristics described for the case of a national entry/exit market, except that the hypothetical European planner would face a larger number of missing market signals. Conversely, the loose integration scenario between existing national markets would require additional mechanisms to decide on and build the required interconnections. Interconnections are the core gates of the European Internal Energy Market, but who will develop them, why and how? This could typically involve some kind of public consultation, in either an auction or an open season process.[6] Would it be enough to build a competitive and open bridge between the existing key EU markets? Would it compromise the vested interests of the existing incumbents too much?

OVERVIEW OF THE BOOK

This book focuses on market design issues common to most EU gas markets, and especially the European integration of those markets. National gas markets in Europe are already built as virtual hubs based on entry/exit schemes. This is made legally binding by European law (Third Energy Package) and therefore already enacted by the new European regulatory agency ACER (Agency for the Cooperation of Energy Regulators) in its Framework Guidelines (ERGEG, 2010; ACER, 2011b). Thus this book takes this as a given for European gas market integration, and examines the subsequent characteristics and requirements of such a European design strategy.

A sensible way to begin an analysis of the design of a European gas market is to identify the current characteristics of the gas flow patterns in European gas systems. This is, hence, the motivation for the first part of the book. After the introductory chapter, in Chapters 2 and 3, Michelle Hallack and Sophia Ruester, respectively, analyse the demand and supply patterns in the EU, showing that both have changed after the introduction of the growth of gas-fired power plants on the demand side and liquefied natural gas on the supply side.

One of the main features of the 'new' demand and supply in the EU is the larger variability of injections and withdrawals (hence the gas flows) and the higher flexibility required from gas systems. These characteristics are already impacting the integrated European market. On the one hand, the range of possible suppliers has increased significantly. Consequently, the formerly efficient contracting patterns and the currently efficient combination of gas suppliers should not be the same any more. This is why (and where) markets may be of help: to reconfigure all this accordingly. On the other hand, the expansion of gas-fired power plants (the main factor in gas demand growth) increases the time variability of gas demand. Actually, gas-fired power plants often create both higher peak demands and lower annual cycles, and both these changes bring new usages of infrastructure. In that view, again, markets are useful tools to implement all the needed adaptation.

European integration is targeting national gas markets that are already being organized around entry/exit zones. It is thus necessary to have a close look at the repeated interactions between transmission operators' activity and gas commodity markets. This is done in the second part of the book. After the introductory chapter, in Chapter 5 Michelle Hallack addresses the actual design of commercial networks in EU markets. How does the relationship between the commercial and the physical networks work regarding the 'new' flexibility requirements of network users? In practice they are the existing operation rules applied to the existing infrastructure that frame the flow's variation management. Consequently the precise design of the bridge between the commercial and the physical networks is at the core of the functioning of gas markets already being based on entry/exit regulation.

The last part of the book presents two proposals for the EU gas target model. These two models tackle the fundamental questions (from the standpoint of the overview provided above). They regard both the organization of short-term transactions and the mechanisms for investment in new long-life infrastructure needed to integrate the EU markets. Both models build on the idea of designing gas markets around an implicit allocation of network capacity in the short run. Following the EU Third Energy Package, they start from an entry/exit regulation as the basis for European market organization. Under this scheme, several integration issues must be addressed. From the short-term perspective, the most important elements for market integration are the coordination of several entry/exit markets and the organization of cross-border transactions.

Several possibilities are investigated. After the introductory chapter, in Chapter 7 the director of the Florence School of Regulation, Jean-Michel Glachant, proposes an option aiming at merging neighbouring markets to obtain competitively viable and tightly unified entry/exit zones. He reveals another option that leaves other markets as independent entry/exit zones connected by means of an implicit auction algorithm, along the lines of market coupling. To implement the network allocation in cross-border transactions, both options propose relying on hybrid mechanisms (explicit and implicit). In particular, both propose using implicit allocation in the short term, and leaving the long-term allocation to explicit auctions.

The gas sector advisor of the Florence School of Regulation, Sergio Ascari, offers a third possibility in Chapter 8. It is a 'free' market option that does not prescribe any size or shape for the virtual hubs. Market forces are left free to ultimately decide the most convenient number, location and size of European hubs.

When it comes to defining a set of more closely unified entry/exit zones or to using some algorithm for looser zonal pricing, Jean-Michel's model leaves the choice to a public authority, as both strategies are possible. Nonetheless, Jean-Michel gives criteria as the gas volume traded (around 20 billion cubic metres) and the number of alternative gas sources (at least three). Sergio, for his part, claims that a tight coordination of short-term transactions is not especially important in the design of the target model, as a more spontaneous coordination will emerge from market interactions.

These two target models are less convergent when it comes to the design of investment mechanisms in new infrastructure. Jean-Michel relies on a planning scheme where TSOs call for auction to organize new investments and regulators can intervene to review. Sergio highlights the benefits of a purely merchant investment scheme.

Security of supply is dealt with by Jean-Michel by giving a say to regulators in supply infrastructure diversification. Sergio does not give any particular recommendation in this regard. Building his proposal on a wider reliance on market forces, he assumes that the security of the European gas markets will be ultimately determined by the preferences of market players.

ACKNOWLEDGEMENT

The editors would like to thank Alice Morin for her perfect editing of the manuscript.

NOTES

1. It is worth highlighting that the regulation of network operation does not require the design of a virtual hub, but it is just a design choice aimed at allocating the network implicitly.
2. In a pure liberalized environment, infeasible transactions are not offered in the market. When there are several non-regulated operators competing among them, it is not necessary to organize markets to combine the technical characteristics of the network and market preferences.
3. The re-nomination is the last moment when the shipper is allowed to inform the network operator of how much gas it will actually inject into the determined entry point.
4. It is important to note that some countries, such as the Netherlands, Belgium and Germany have some kind of hybrid balancing period. In these cases other obligations to keep flows balanced are established inside the balancing period.
5. It is worth noting that the Third Directive (EC, 2009b) states that contractual congestion means 'a situation where the level of firm capacity demand exceeds the technical capacity' and physical congestion as 'a situation where the level of demand for actual deliveries exceeds the technical capacity at some point in time'.
6. The differences between open seasons and auctions strongly depend on the definition of open seasons. Here, an open season is a consultation that does not imply firm contracts.

PART I

The new European gas market: increased flexibility in both demand and supply

1. Introduction to Part I

Michelle Hallack, Miguel Vazquez and Jean-Michel Glachant

Traditionally in the gas industry both supply and demand patterns were rather flat, so the short-term flexibility of gas delivery was not a scarce resource and so markets or network regulation did not need advanced tools to deliver and to price pipeline flexibility. This part of the book will show that this is not the case any more, as both supply and demand sides are changing with regard to flexibility while transport capacity and pipeline flexibility are competing for the use of the network.

Chapters 2 and 3 show how 'new' patterns have made gas flows more variable in the last two decades. The development of the gas commodity market in a 'dash for gas' (Winskel, 2002) refers to the strong increase in gas demand (Heather, 2010). This change should not be understood just as a variation in traded volumes; it also accounts for a change in gas demand and supply profiles. Electricity power plants as gas consumers have changed the profile of gas usage. In the same way, the increasing use of liquefied natural gas as a flexible supplier has changed the supply portfolio.

Until the massive introduction of electricity generation the main drivers of gas demand had been industrial and household consumers. On the supply side, European gas originated from national fields, and from gas pipeline importation through ship-or-pay contracts. Thus, both for the demand and supply sides, the gas industry historically developed based on flat flows with seasonal (winter) peaks caused by the household heating demand. Consequently, gas transport services were largely based on flat flows and seasonal cycles, with some weather-related daily volatility. The network built to deal with the low flexibility required by 'traditional' gas demand started to encounter shorter-term flexible flows as a consequence of the 'electricity gas demand' boom after the 1990s and the increased introduction of flexible LNG.

Chapters 2 and 3 analyse how gas-fired power plants and liquefied natural gas link with flexible flows, which in turn require a flexible use of the network. Chapter 2 describes changes in the demand side of the market. With the massive introduction of gas-fired power plants in most power systems the gas demand tends to react in the time frame defined by electricity markets (as the gas consumption of gas-fired power plants is defined by those markets), which in turn significantly increases the need for flexibility. Chapter 3 describes how the structure of gas supply has dramatically changed recently with new supply tools introduced in the market. The most prominent is associated with LNG, which in turn has also motivated a change in contracting practices with shorter commitments between buying and selling parties.

2. Gas demand: the role of gas-fired power plants

Michelle Hallack

One of the most important incentives for developing gas-fired power plants (GFPPs) was the matching of the features of recent gas and electricity markets and the flexibility of GFPP technologies. In short, we could say that the operational flexibility of the GFPP is a consequence of its technical feature of allowing fast start-up and shutdown. Thus, flexible GFPP operation is able to fulfil short-term electricity demand (Espey and Espey, 2004; Roques et al., 2008). In this chapter we will show what the flexibility offered by GFPPs means to the electricity market through the perspective of the gas market dynamic.

Traditionally, natural gas demand used to be characterized by seasonal cycles. Each group of gas consumers has a typical demand profile, and they interact in the gas market in order to form the gas flow profile. 'Traditional' gas consumers were household and industrial consumers, the main drivers of demand until the 1990s. The massive introduction of GFPP gas demand in the gas market and the increased importance that it took in the total gas demand portfolio has changed the gas demand profile.

This chapter first analyses the GFPP demand profile and the impact of the GFPP in the entire gas demand. In the second section we investigate how the characteristics of GFPP gas demand interact in the gas market with gas supply and storage. We argue that these interactions change the observed and the expected gas flow.

GFPPs represent a new gas demand, which is driven by a demand for flexible power generation. GFPP gas demand depends on the electricity demand profile and the electricity generation portfolio. For this reason it is quite specific to each electricity market. Roughly, it is impacted by daily cycles, extreme weather impacts (colder or warmer), 'exogenous environmental impacts' (such as wind velocity) and fuel spark prices. In the short term (intra-day) GFPP gas demand may be characterized by high peaks if they run as last resort power plants.

As long as these 'new' demand features in the current and expected gas flows interact with the other 'traditional' gas demand profiles, their interaction shapes gas demand as a whole. The new gas demand interacts with gas supply and storage and, as a consequence, there is a new gas flow characteristic. GFPP gas demand tends to increase some peak demand and decrease the traditional annual cycles. The change in gas flows, in fact, interacts with physical infrastructures: on one hand it changes the use of installed infrastructures; on the other hand the flow variation is constrained by the possibilities allowed by the existent infrastructure.

1   The New Gas Demand as a Function of Electricity Demand

This section focuses on describing the meaning of electricity flexibility requirements and how these requirements interact with the gas demand profile. In this regard, it is important to highlight that power markets are characterized by the short-term price inelasticity[1] of electricity demand, and by its non-storability. Both characteristics explain the observed high peaks in electricity demand, as well as the variability of electricity production. Since production must be in balance with demand in real time,[2] electricity production has variability characteristics that are similar to the electricity demand, which varies according to days, hours, temperature, income and so on (Labandeira et al., 2009).

In the typical electricity market, GFPP loads depend on electricity demand and electricity generation dispatching orders. This dispatching order largely depends on the variable costs of installed generation capacity, which in turn are mainly defined by the cost of the fuels used to fire the units. Thus, the position of the GFPP in relation to other available technologies impacts on the GFPP gas demand price elasticity. In this view, it is important to note that this gas demand elasticity depends on the whole dispatching order of the system: if it is the only plant able to generate electricity to meet the demand at a specific moment the GFPP gas demand would be inelastic; however, it may present higher elasticity if it is possible to substitute GFPP generation for other technologies. Such substitution can be related either to the possibility of using other fuels to run the same plant or to the possibility of running other units fired by other fuels. Hence, the gas price elasticity of GFPP gas demand will strongly depend on fuel price differentials. The first part of this section is devoted to describing such characteristics of GFPP gas demand.

The second part of this section details the interaction of GFPP gas demand features and traditional gas demand. In other words, it describes how the increase in the GFPP gas demand may change the dynamics of gas demand as a whole. One of the most important issues raised throughout this study is to observe that GFPP can be, depending on the period considered, both complementary and substitutive to industrial and household demands. In this study, we have stressed the relation between household demand and GFPP demand, because they present more complex interactions. Industrial demand is mainly flat on weekdays, and thus the interaction with GFPP demand will be typically low, even if it exists in particular periods of increases in gas market liquidity. On the other hand, household demand presents more variability. Moreover, it is sometimes complementary to GFPP gas demand, as in the case of winter/summer seasonality, and hence the interaction between both demands is relatively high. However, in some periods, household and GFPP gas demands are competing, as in the peak winter demand when the two demands become inelastic in the short term. Consequently, the interaction of GFPP and household gas demand tend to be lower in such periods.

1.1 THE HETEROGENEOUS IMPACT OF ELECTRICITY DEMAND INELASTICITY ON THE GAS-FIRED POWER PLANT PROFILE

The inelasticity of electricity demand may be transmitted to gas demand through GFPP gas demand, as the electricity generation profile must follow electricity demand. However, the reliance of electricity generation portfolio on GFPP determines the price elasticity of GFPP gas demand. The price elasticity of GFPP gas demand may change over time, whether or not the generation portfolio changes over time.

1.1.1 Electricity Demand Short-term Inelasticity

The GFPP gas demand profile depends both on electricity demand and on the load of the GFPP. Consequently, in order to understand the GFPP gas demand, it is important to analyse the electricity demand profile as well as the GFPP position dispatching order.

Power plants are dispatched according to their marginal costs, so the plants with lower marginal costs often produce for more hours throughout the day.[3] GFPP technologies have been especially adapted to produce as load-following units.[4] Thus, they are usually intended to produce during periods with high electricity demand, and, consequently, the electricity demand variation strongly impacts on the GFPP gas demand.

The electricity demand mainly changes according to household habitudes and industrial production:

> Electricity demand is subject to fluctuations both on a seasonal basis, across the week, and during the day. Demand can also be influenced by irregular events, such as particularly extreme weather or television programmes (known as 'tv pick-ups'). These demand peaks and troughs are met by different types of generation, according to their different characteristics. . ... Typically, electricity demand is higher between Monday and Friday, the normal working week, and lower during Saturday and Sunday. The peak demands on Saturday and Sunday are usually much lower than during the week, while the low demands are also lower. Demand for electricity also fluctuates quite strongly across the day, according to human activity. . ... Electricity demand is typically low during the night hours, with little domestic or industrial/commercial consumption. Demand falls more quickly during the early hours of Saturday morning, with less demand from industrial/commercial premises through the night, reaching a lower floor at around 6:00am, compared with an hour earlier on the weekday. From here on, demand gradually picks up. There is usually a large surge in demand around 7:00am, when most people arise and begin using electrical equipment – for example lighting, kettles, toasters and power showers. . ... During the week, from around 9:00am, demand continues to rise, until around lunchtime, as offices, shops and industrial premises open and electrical equipment such as computers are increasingly utilised. It then falls off from around mid-afternoon, as the population begins to leave work premises for home. At around 5:00–5:30pm, the second demand surge of the day usually occurs, as people arrive back home from work/school, and begin using electrical equipment – lighting, kettles, and cooking equipment for dinner. This surge is even more pronounced in the winter, when heating is switched on. From this point on, demand usually slides over the course of the evening as people finish dinner, before dropping off substantially in the late evening as people retire to bed.[5]

In the shortest term, there is an information problem where most consumers do not know the real electricity price. Second, there is a real question regarding the value consumers give to using electricity at specific hours of the day. Other authors argue that consumers may react to electricity prices not through marginal electricity prices, but through mid-term average prices (Van Helden et al., 1987). It means that consumers do not stop using electricity during a peak hour because there is a higher marginal price, but they may change their habits in the mid- and long terms if the average price rises. In other words, they may change their lifestyle if they see their monthly electricity bill increasing.

So far, the idea that the electricity demand does not decrease with price increases in the short term (intra-day) seems to be widely accepted. Such demand inelasticity causes a high variability of electricity demand, and as a consequence of GFPP development the increase in electricity demand means increasing electricity prices and frequently means increasing gas demand peaks.

1.1.2 Short-term Price Response of Gas-fired Power Plants' Gas Demand

Contrary to electricity, which is hard to substitute in the short term, gas as the fuel to run power plants may be not so difficult to substitute. Nonetheless, the possibility of producing electricity from gas or from other fuels depends mainly on the electricity generation portfolio. The price elasticity of power plant gas demand is a consequence of the possibility of inter-fuel substitution. High power plant fuel substitution means higher gas demand elasticity. According to Patrik (2001) this can be achieved in two ways: switching the input fuel in the same plant or switching the plant. This subsection will describe the first option, leaving the description of the second for the next. Switching the input fuel consists of switching the input fuel of dual-fuel-fired generators, which have some flexibility to switch between natural gas and alternative fuels in power generator boilers. These plants may take advantage of relative fuel price changes, though this capability varies across countries. Actually, the substitution of gas for other fuels (e.g., oil products), may be profitable even if these plants run with higher operational costs because of their higher flexibility.

A number of gas-fired power plants are able to substitute the combustion fuel. Both oil and natural gas liquid can be used as feedstock if the plants have the equipment that gives them the capability to switch quickly between fuels. Such units will optimize their use of the two fuels according to the operating costs, principally fuel costs and efficiency. The most suitable equipment for fuel switching is a boiler.[6] In order to be able to change combustible fuel the power plants need to be technically adapted to fuel switch. As explained by the Interstate Natural Gas Association of America (INGAA, 2001), the most frequent substitute for gas is a fuel derivative of petroleum.

The decision to invest in dual-fuel projects depends on expected costs and expected profits. When providing back-up fuel capability, the GFPP capital cost increases. The ability to change fuel depends on the installed technology and on the access to the substitute fuel. The expected profits of back-up investment depend on the gains related to the decrease in gas supply risks and the possible penalties. In addition, the risk associated with the opportunity cost corresponding to the expected spark prices should be considered. It means that the investment depends on the expectation that the cost is lower than the profits of fuel flexibility, according to the reliability criterion and the possibility to arbitrage prices.

As Table 2.1 shows, gas multi-fired production corresponds to 19 per cent of the total share of generating electricity production in the EU-15.

Table 2.1   IEA EU/multi-fired electricity-generating electricity production

IEA Europe Multi-fired Electricity-generating Electricity Production[a]	
Electricity production GW	129.4
% Gas multi-fired/total generating electricity production	19%
% Gas multi-fired/thermal-generating electricity production	37%

Note: a. IEA (International Energy Agency) EU is the EU-15 plus Czech Republic, Hungary, Iceland, Norway, Poland, Slovak Republic, Switzerland and Turkey.

Source: Author elaboration, data from IEA (2002).

This means that 19 per cent of the electricity-generating electricity production is technically able to switch fuel if the marginal cost of running the power plants with gas is higher than the cost of running with substitute fuel.[7] Concerning only thermal-generating electricity production,[8] the multi-fired plants achieve 37 per cent. Moreover, regarding the impact of multi-fired technologies on gas demand, the IEA (2002) survey found that in Europe nominal short-term fuel-switching capability by industrial customers and power generators amounts to about 12 per cent of the daily average of the total gas consumption.

1.1.3   Fuel Prices Impacting Power Plants' Dispatching Order

The second mechanism to substitute the gas demand of power plants, as shown by Hartley et al. (2007), is related to the ability of power plants to shut down and start up the plant according to gas and electricity prices. It means that the ability to respond to the cost differences depends on plants' technology:

> Coal and gas generation are more flexible, and adjust according to the level of demand (and thus price). Coal generation is especially responsive, with coal prices currently high relative to gas, and limited hours available under the Large Combustion Plant Directive, making it economical to generate only at higher wholesale prices.
>   Wind generation is utilised whenever it is available; however, the intermittency of it means it does not always contribute to meeting demand, particularly in the summer months. This was particularly the case with the low wind speeds experienced in the first half of 2010.
>   Hydro generation is very flexible plant, and can start generating quickly, so long as there is water in the reservoirs.[9]

The power plant fuel elasticity does not depend directly on the fuel price, but is mainly based on the price difference between competitive fuels that

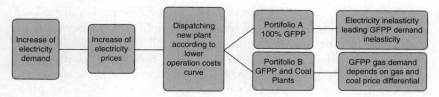

Source: Author elaboration.

Figure 2.1 Impact of electricity peak demand on GFPP gas demand according to electricity generation portfolio

may operate at a specific moment. Therefore, it is important to consider not only the relative position of a power plant in the dispatching order of the whole generation portfolio, but also if there is a possible substitute fuel and what fuel is to run another plant to cover the same demand.

The dependency between gas and electricity is conditional on the electricity generation portfolio. If the dependency is high, the impact of inelasticity, characteristic of gas demand, will probably be higher. To see this it is possible to consider a situation where, given the installed capacity and input conditions, no other fuel is able to produce more electricity in a specific moment (the case of Portfolio A represented in Figure 2.1). In this case, the electricity demand inelasticity pushes up electricity prices and the higher price is transferred to gas power plants. Thus, if the marginal electricity generation depends on gas, GFPPs should run even with high gas prices, so the GFPP gas demand presents quite low elasticity.

In the other case, the GFPP gas demand tends to have higher elasticity. This situation is represented by Portfolio B in Figure 2.1, where the electricity generation portfolio allows marginal electricity to be produced by gas or another fuel (in Figure 2.1 represented by coal). The choice of the power plants that should operate depends on their marginal costs, which are highly dependent on fuel costs. Thus, the GFPP gas demand will depend on the price differential between gas and the competing fuel. In this case, assuming that other fuel prices are independent of gas prices, an increase in gas prices will decrease gas demand, if it makes GFPPs' operational cost higher than their competing plants' marginal cost. In this case, GFPP gas demand is highly elastic to gas prices.

In the case where GFPPs have an elastic gas demand, the differential between marginal costs of alternative plant generations results in price arbitrages, allowing gas to be traded on the market. This mechanism often allows customers to switch more easily from gas provider to gas provider, making the gas markets more short-term responsive.

As seen before, the GFPP has been greatly used for peak and back-up electricity demand. In the short term (a few hours), there is almost no availability of other plants able to meet demand with the same start-up timing and short-term efficiency. In these cases, even with high gas prices, peak electricity demand tends to be met by GFPPs. Thus, in the short term there is a tendency to lower gas price elasticity because of the low probability of having competitive fuel turbines available.

With horizons of several weeks the use of GFPPs to generate electricity decreases if gas prices are high. In the context of high gas prices, the possibility of having available capacity to run with competing fuels is better. So, if the operational cost of gas plants is higher than the competing fuel, the GFPP is shut down. Therefore, there is a tendency for higher elasticity, but it actually depends on the fuels' price differential and the available generation capacity in the electricity market.

With horizons of several months to several years, GFPP gas demand is more elastic to gas prices. But the gas prices considered in the long term are the forecasted gas prices, or the prices of long-term contracts. More precisely, the most important forecast concerns the difference in operational costs between running plants and competing fuels.[10]

1.1.4   Gas-fired Power Plant Interruptible Contracts

Interruptible contracts enable gas customers to be cut off in situations of high demand, so they enable customers to pay lower prices. These kinds of gas contracts are mainly used in industry and power generation, so they are especially suitable for the consumer who has back-fuel technology (enabling the use of different fuels) or the consumer who is able to shut down gas turbines. Voluntary interruptible contracts are typically written on average daily prices, so the gas is cut off if daily prices are higher than a specified price level.[11]

The number of interruptible contracts is an indicator of the inclination of gas consumers to decrease demand when gas prices increase. Therefore, it can also be seen as an index to measure the price elasticity of consumers, as it shows the willingness to pay for gas by consumers with higher propensity to change the demand volume according to price variations.

The European Commission Security of Supply Report (EC, 2009a) analysed interruptible contracts of EU-14 members, and its results indicated that power plants are the main gas consumers entering into interruptible contracts. In 2007, industrial gas consumers contracted 14 bcm (billion cubic metres) of gas through interruptible contracts while power plant gas consumers contracted around 25 bcm of gas through interruptible contracts. The ability to switch fuel inputs is quite different depending on the electricity market considered, and in the absence of integrated markets we can assume that it varies according to the generation portfolio in each country.[12]

Accurate measurement of gas price elasticity is complex because of the role played by other factors in actual gas demand. It is not easy to separate the influence of gas prices from other exogenous variables in observed gas demand (such as changes in income, climate, lifestyles, investment cycles, technology, price expectations and government policies). Elasticity also varies according to the actual level of competing fuel prices. In other words, the shape of the demand curve may be far from linear. In some contexts the price of gas in a particular market may rise significantly without choking off much demand if the cost of the cheapest competing fuel (which determines the market value of the gas) is already much higher.[13]

Despite national diversity, in the EU-15 portfolio, the peak-load plants have mainly been run by coal or gas. Thus, in the majority of cases the dispatching order power plant depends on the relationship between spark prices of gas and coal. In this view, GFPP demand tends to present high price elasticity. However, this GFPP tendency differs depending on the relation of the GFPP and the other power plants. The use of GFPP depends on the whole generation set. First, demand elasticity does not depend just on gas prices, but also on price differentials between substitute fuels. Second, the elasticity exists only if there is free capacity on the generation portfolio to run with a substitute fuel when electricity generation is demanded. It means that in some peak situations, when the generation capacity to run with other fuels is not available, the GFPP gas demand is highly inelastic.

1.2 THE IMPACT ON THE WHOLE NATURAL GAS DEMAND PROFILE: LESS SEASONAL CYCLES AND NEW SHORT-TERM VOLATILITY

The growth of residential and commercial gas demand has been relatively modest. With the introduction of GFPPs, residential demands for gas and electricity have become closely associated. This drove a process that placed the gas and electricity markets closer to each other. The convergence carried some features of the electricity demand profile to the gas market:

> The concept of convergence of gas and electricity has emerged in recent years, mainly as a result of the increasing use of gas for power generation and the perception of growing inter-dependencies between gas and power markets.

This concept has remained somewhat ill-defined and is widely used in many different contexts and in multiple meanings. A useful distinction can be made between convergence at the 'commodity' level, referring to inter-dependencies between gas supply and power generation activities, and convergence at the 'retail' level, referring to inter-dependencies between gas and power supply to final customers.[14]

According to this definition, we focus on the convergence of GFPP activities and the gas supply. It is shown that convergence between gas and electricity markets, on the one hand, increases short-term volatility of the gas market, as the electricity volatility is passed to gas demand. On the other hand, such convergence decreases the typical volatility of household heating gas demand.

Gas and electricity are sometimes complementary markets and sometimes competing markets. As electricity production can consume gas at rather short notice, traditional gas demand is lower, being a complementary profile. But the decrease in gas demand to end users can coincide with the increase in power plants' gas demand, and in this case the utilization of gas by GFPPs and by traditional gas consumers compete in the gas market.

Traditionally, gas and electricity demands had different profiles. The analysis of these profiles helps us to understand the possible complementarities between gas and electricity demands. In order to simplify the analysis we will first underline the role of household demand cycles. It is possible to assume that industrial electricity and gas demands tend to be relatively independent of the weather. They may change with respect to economic cycles but in this case, gas and electricity demands for industrial consumption should change similarly, according to economic production levels. Another factor that can alter industrial gas and electricity demands is the change in the fuel price differential. The change in fuel prices may bring some demand volatility; however, these variations cannot be characterized as normal demand cycle profiles (so they will be discussed separately). Then, in order to consider and compare the expected cycles of gas and electricity demand profiles, we consider the captive consumers, which represent mainly household and commercial demands.[15]

Three major cycles affect the gas demand. The first cycle observed is the seasonal variation, from winter to summer. The second cycle is the demand variation from one day to another (inter-day variation). The third is the hourly consumption during the daily cycle (intra-day variation).

Looking at the hourly, daily and seasonal demand variations of gas and electricity we can observe that the intra-day cycles are much more pronounced for electricity demand than for gas demand, especially if we observe the residential demand. The seasonal impact on gas demand is

Table 2.2   The comparison between electricity and gas demand intra-day, inter-day and seasonal cycles

Period	Cycles
Intra-day (hourly)	Gas < Electricity
Inter-day (daily)	Gas ≥ Electricity
Seasonal (monthly)	Gas > Electricity

Source: Author elaboration, data from NPC (1999).

much higher than the impact on electricity (see Table 2.2). For instance, in the UK between January and July in 2009, the increase in total gas demand was around 75 per cent, whereas the increase in electricity demand was around 25 per cent.[16] This shows how seasonality tends to impact on gas demand much more than on electricity demand.

The differences between gas and electricity daily volatilities are quite dependent on market specificities, and thus it is more difficult to arrive at a general tendency. However, the temperature, one of the main drivers of daily cycles, impacts on electricity and gas demand differently. While gas demand is affected by low temperatures because of heating demand, electricity demand is impacted by low and high temperatures, because of heating and cooling demand. In the short term, intra-day cycles are traditionally more pronounced in electricity demand than in gas demand. The variation in electricity demand over the day is related to household routines, with large consumption differences between night and morning, and some peak hours such as the beginning of the day and of the evening.

This subsection details the impact of the interaction of gas and electricity demand. It will be shown how electricity cycles may sometimes reinforce gas cycles, and sometimes may smooth them out. First, we discuss the impact of increased dependence between gas and electricity through GFPPs on the seasonal profile of gas demand. Next, we point out the impact of electricity and gas dependency on inter-day cycles. Finally, we indicate the expected impact on the intra-day gas demand profile.

1.2.1   Decreasing the Amplitude of Seasonal Cycles

Seasonal variation is caused by the residential and commercial segments of the market. The decrease in participation of residential and commercial consumers would decrease the seasonal cycles of gas demand. As the industrial demand is flat throughout the year, if the decrease in residential and commercial gas demand participation is a consequence of an increase in industrial demand participation, it would be characterized by the addition of flat demand decreasing the volatility of the whole gas market. However, the same effect is not observed in cases where the decrease in household demand participation is caused by an increase in GFPP gas demand.

The increase in GFPPs in gas demand participation means a development of different demand volatility. GFPP volatility is less dependent on weather and more dependent on fuel prices. In this way, GFPP electricity production means the decreased participation of seasonal demand, and the decreased participation of flat demand means more volatility.

Residential and commercial consumers rely on natural gas for space heating, water heating, cooking and other purposes. The most important component is often the space heating, being around 70 per cent of the residential and commercial load. Consumption of space heating, however, is closely tied to the winter heating season.

Residential, commercial and small industrial customers have traditionally made up the market core of the EU. It is the market served by the natural gas local distribution companies (LDCs). Nowadays, demand growth in these sectors has tended to occur roughly in proportion to increases in population and economy activity. Though yearly variations can occur due to weather, the growth in these sectors is gradual and relatively easy to anticipate.

Industries use natural gas both for process heat and, in some cases, as a direct input to manufacture of substances such as plastics and fertilizers. In the early years of natural gas availability, the vast majority was used by industrial processes, substituting for petroleum. Industrial use dropped off dramatically in the decade after the Arab oil embargo, as price-controlled domestic supplies of natural gas were unable to keep pace with demand. This meant that supplies of natural gas were unreliable for many industrial customers. Since industrial customers purchased their own supplies of natural gas and relied on the gas distribution company (LDC) only for transportation services, the importance of historical industries, such as pulp and paper, has declined over time. Moreover, the plants have become more efficient, which results in a tendency to reduce the participation of flat gas demand. As the industrial demand is the most stable, the decrease in industrial demand participation means a decrease in gas demand stability.

Looking at the increase in demand for natural gas as fuel to produce electricity, and knowing that this demand depends on spark prices, it is possible to conclude that the natural gas surplus during off-peak would decrease. If natural gas prices become more sensitive to the price of electricity, this may mean that natural gas will no longer be significantly

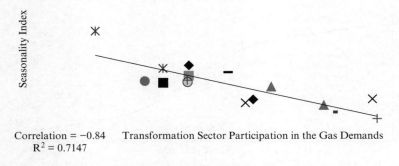

Correlation = −0.84   Transformation Sector Participation in the Gas Demands
    $R^2 = 0.7147$

Source: Author elaboration, data from IEA (2008) and Platts (2009).

Figure 2.2   EU-15/correlation between the degree of seasonality and the participation of the transformation sector in gas demand

cheaper in the summer months. As long as gas-fired electricity generation is added to regional natural gas demand, the risk management strategies, historically used by local gas distribution utilities may need to be revised. Whether or not gas-fired electricity generation is added to regional natural gas demand, distribution utilities need to revise their supply portfolio in order to include the idiosyncratic features of GFPP demand.

The seasonality in gas demand is highly correlated to its use for household and commercial heating, which means that gas demand of householders has higher seasonal volatility than the industrial and transformation sector (the transformation sector includes GFPP, co-generation and industrial gas demand in the transformation process as energy).

The GFPP is a key player in the transformation sector, either for an independent producer or for an industrial producer. The increase in GFPPs drives the increase in the transformation sector total gas demand and it attenuates the seasonal changes on gas demand, by means of the decrease in gas over-supply in summer and of the decrease in gas over-consumption in winter.

As we can see in Figure 2.2, among the EU-15 there is a strong correlation between the magnitude of the difference in demand between winter and summer and the participation of the transformation sector in total gas demand. The difference between gas demand in winter and summer presents a correlation of −0.84 with the participation of the gas transformation sector. Moreover, through a linear regression we found the value of 0.7 for R^2. At the two extremes are France and Greece with largest and lowest demand seasonality respectively. The gas demand in France, where 37 per cent of gas demand is residential and 1 per cent is demanded by the electricity sector, presents the highest demand seasonality. In Greece,

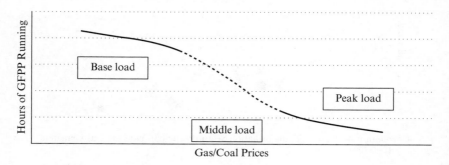

Source: Author elaboration, data from Honoré (2006).

Figure 2.3   UK/the impact of gas/coal prices on the number of hours of
GFPP running

where just 5 per cent of total gas demand is residential and 56 per cent
of gas is demanded by GFPP consumers, there is the lowest demand
seasonality.

The increase of GFPPs in the total gas demand portfolio tends to
decrease the difference in average gas demand between summer and
winter.[17] There are two main reasons: first, the decrease in residential
and commercial heating participation, which decreases the gas demand
participation of consumers with higher weather dependency; and second,
the impact of plants' fuel price arbitrage on demand. The latter is a consequence of the GFPP gas demand ability to respond to prices. The price
difference between gas and competing fuels is a key aspect to determining
the GFPP load, as observed in the UK example in Figure 2.3

As explained by Honoré (2006), and illustrated in Figure 2.3 regarding the UK portfolio in 2005, when gas/coal prices were lower than 2, the
GFPP ran more than 7000 hours per year. If gas/coal prices were between
2 and 2.5 the GFPP ran around 4000 hours per year. And if gas/coal prices
increased more than 2.5, the GFPP began to run around 2500 hours per
year or less, to meet the peak load demand. The impact of plants' fuel
price arbitrage tends to decrease the seasonal cycle (Honoré, 2006). So if
market mechanisms are in place, in summer, when gas is less utilized for
heating, gas prices tend to decrease and so increases the incentives to run
the installed GFPP for longer.

In summary, GFPPs have represented a counter-seasonal demand.
The GFPP changes the traditional seasonal cycle of natural gas demand
because of the impact of electricity demand profile features, and because
of the electricity generation diversity.

Weather impact on the electricity demand profile is different from the weather impact on the gas demand profile: first, because of the importance of the variation regarding the whole demand; and second, because the impact on natural gas is especially related to heating, but the impact on electricity depends on heating and cooling demand. It is worth noting that the electricity cooling demand complements the gas heating demand, whereas the electricity heating demand competes with gas heating functions.

The second motivation of GFPP modification of gas seasonal effects has to do with the use of gas to generate electricity. It depends on the electricity generation portfolio and inter-fuel prices. It means that the demand of electricity does not always directly affect gas demand, since gas demand of GFPPs is more elastic than residential gas demand in most cases. This elasticity, however, depends on the electricity generation portfolio and the availability of other power plants to run when gas prices increase more than other fuel prices.

1.2.2 Ambiguity of Daily Cycles

Concerning daily cycles, on the one hand the increase in peak days can occur by demand accumulation. In the winter, the peaks can be provoked by accumulation of weather conditions added to electricity market peaks. On the other hand, a decrease in amplitude can be observed when the increase in gas prices drives the decrease in volume demanded of GFPPs, and it cancels or attenuates the effect of weather or seasonal demand peaks in gas. But the decrease in gas demand (residential and industrial) may also push the gas prices down, and it may drive an increase in GFPP demand. The actual impact, thus, depends on the electricity generation portfolios (along the same lines of discussion on peak demand represented in Figure 2.1).

Table 2.3 describes the use of line-pack (the actual amount of gas stored in a pipeline or distribution system) for CCGTs and local distribution zones (LDZs) in the UK's winter and summer. It can be considered as a proxy of unexpected gas demand, because the unexpected gas demand is covered by line-pack.

The days with the highest unexpected peaks are a result of cumulative effects between gas and electricity, and they are characterized by days when the demand is higher than expected. The reasons are the extremely low temperature and the increase in the electricity generation demand. In summer, the average unexpected increase in gas demand for CCGTs is higher than for LDZ consumers. It can be explained by weather constraints and by the lower importance of gas heating demand in summer.

In addition, electricity demand in summer may also be affected by daily

Table 2.3   UK/maximum daily line-pack depletion by season (2001–02)

UK – Maximum Daily Depletion Statistics (mcm/d) 2001–02			
		Max	Average
LDZs	Winter	8.02	2.93
	Summer	4.03	0.66
CCGTs	Winter	3.90	1.41
	Summer	3.21	1.57

Source: Author elaboration, data from Ofgem (Office of Gas and Electricity Markets) collected in Lapuerta (2003).

variations. Therefore, the gas-fired electricity production may be affected by fuel prices and electricity portfolio features. As we can see, the elements affecting gas demand and unexpected demand are quite similar and independent of the season.

Roughly, the short-term elasticity of electricity production is often higher than that of LDZ consumption. Consequently, the importance of peak days tends to decrease in response to the increase in GFPP participation in the gas demand. Nevertheless, this tendency is not necessarily a rule, depending on the electricity generation park (the set of plants that supply a region) and the real substitutability of gas by other fuels or of GFPPs by other plants.

In the UK, between 2000 and 2008, the increase in GFPP electricity production was reflected in the tendency to decrease the average peak demand, as shown in Figure 2.4

Figure 2.4 compares the daily peaks in several years, in two different seasons, winter and summer. First, we can observe a linear tendency to

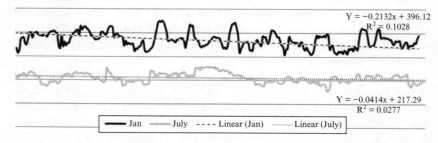

Source: Author elaboration, data from Platts (2009).

Figure 2.4   UK/average peak daily demand (mcm)

decrease the daily peak demands between 2000 and 2008. Second, we observe that the tendency to decrease peaks was stronger in January than in July. It means that GFPPs shut down more often during winter peaks than during summer peaks. It may be explained by the fact that the gas daily peak results in higher prices in winter than in summer, and so in winter there is a higher increase in marginal costs and larger changes in the dispatching order. Therefore, Figure 2.4. shows an example of the hypothesis that increase in GFPP gas demand tends to decrease peak days' demand, largely because of the price elasticity of GFPP gas demand.

1.2.3 Increasing the Magnitude of Intra-day Peaks

The arbitrage possibility coming from the convergence of electricity and gas markets may decrease some of the daily peaks and some seasonal cycles, but it increases hourly peaks. It is explained by the electricity daily profile and the low elasticity of GFPP gas demand in the short term. It is frequently observed that in the short term (hourly horizons) the GFPP cannot be substituted by another plant running with a competing fuel.

Moreover, the presence of intermittent generation such as wind power plants, which need to be quickly replaced, may also contribute to the need for running GFPPs in the context of high gas prices for a short period. As a consequence of the short-term importance of GFPP production, there is a high increase in intra-day gas demand peaks.

The inability to predict demand with precision is especially true for electricity generation customers, since electricity generation must meet swing requirements of residential electricity consumers and back-up requirements of renewable generators. It can be more pronounced in the winter, as the residential consumers have peaks of gas and electricity demand at the same time. Even if the peak of residential consumption is moderate in the usual peak hours, it exists and it is added to the peak hours of electricity.

To show the impact of GFPPs driving the increased magnitude of the peaks over the day, we compare the magnitude of intra-day consumption in Spain for two years, 2004 and 2006. The choices of 2004 and 2006 are explained by the fast increase in GFPP electricity production in Spain between these two years as observed in Tables 2.4 and 2.5.

As we can see in Table 2.4, GFPP electricity production increased by about 35 TWh (terawatt hours) between 2004 and 2006, which means an increase of 10 per cent in GFPP participation in the total electricity generation in Spain. The importance of this new GFPP electricity production

Table 2.4   Spain/the participation of gas-fired power plants in national electricity generation (2004–06)

Spain – Electricity Generation (TWh)

	Gas-fired power plants	Total	Gas-fired power plants/Total
2004	31.63	280	11.30%
2005	53.56	294	18.22%
2006	66.22	303	21.85%

Source: Author elaboration, data from IEA (2008).

Table 2.5   Spain/the participation of gas-fired power plants in national gas demand (2004–06)

Spain – Electricity Participation on Gas Demand Portfolio (mcm)

	Gas demand to the electricity sector	Electricity sector demand/total gas demand
2004	5 479	20.28%
2005	8 684	27.24%
2006	11 196	34.04%

Source: Author elaboration, data from IEA (2008).

was not only observed in the electricity generation portfolio but also in gas demand.

The increase in GFPP electricity production between 2004 and 2006 drove a huge increase in gas demand, around 6000 mcm (million cubic metres), and a consequent increase in the electricity share in gas demand, an increase of around 14 per cent. Observing Table 2.4 and Table 2.5 we can conclude that there was a significant increase in GFPP participation in these three years, and we observe that it strongly changed the magnitude of gas consumption during the day, represented in Figure 2.5.

In Figure 2.5 we can observe that the increase in the magnitude between the hourly consumption of gas during the day in 2006 is more dispersed regarding average consumption. The hourly peak consumption in 2004 in January was on average 10 per cent higher than the daily average of gas consumption. In 2006, this difference increased to 20 per cent.

Comparing the information observed in Table 2.4 and Table 2.5 and in Figure 2.5, we can observe that the increase of GFPP participation in the total gas demand is related to the increase in the magnitude of intra-day

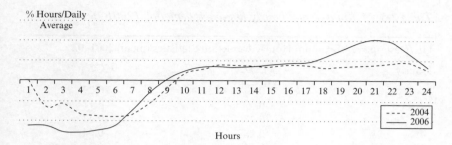

Note: a. Hourly gas demand/average of the hourly gas demand during the day = [(Monthly average of hourly gas demand) − (Monthly average of daily average of hourly gas demand)]/Monthly average of daily average of hourly gas demand.

Source: Author elaboration, data from Platts (2009).

Figure 2.5 Spain/average hourly gas demand[a] January 2004 and 2006

consumption. The component of the electricity demand in gas demand is emphasized by the coincidence between the hour of peak and dip in gas demand and the typical schedule of electricity. The lower gas demand occurs between 2am and 5am; the higher gas consumption is achieved between 7pm and 10pm.

GFPPs have introduced higher peaks in intra-day demand in Spain. It can also be observed in the UK, based on the data from Lapuerta (2003), which shows that the CCGT largest demand of line-pack per hour is larger than that of LDZs.

We also use line-pack depletion as an index to measure unexpected demand, assuming that gas supply corresponds to the expected demand of gas. We can assume that line-pack use derives from the difference between supply and demand, so we can call it unexpected demand covered by line-pack.

As we can see in Table 2.6, the change of hourly gas demand of CCGTs is much higher than LDZ demand. The CCGT largest negative imbalance (larger withdrawal than injection) was 0.82 mcm, whereas the LDZ was 0.37 mcm. The largest positive imbalance is the CCGT's, 1.06 mcm, whereas LDZ presents 0.42 mcm. It means that the hourly magnitude (the difference between peaks and average) was 1.88 mcm for CCGTs, and 0.79 mcm for LDZs. Thus, we can conclude that the difference between actual hourly gas demand and the average gas demand is larger for CCGT consumers than for LDZ consumers. Moreover, it is possible to observe that the peak combinations may increase more than the total gas demand peak. We can also see that, in these cases, only in the first hour are there

Table 2.6   UK/maximum hourly line-pack depletion (2001–02)

UK/Descriptive Maximum Hourly Depletion Statistics (mcm) 2001–02

Hourly	LDZ	CCGT
1	–0.13	0.29
2	–0.37	–0.11
3	–0.27	–0.43
4	–0.28	–0.64
5	–0.14	–0.76
6	–0.17	–0.58
7	–0.16	–0.4
8	–0.08	–0.33
9	–0.05	–0.18
10	–0.07	–0.35
11	–0.18	–0.76
12	–0.22	–0.82
13	–0.18	–0.63
14	–0.07	–0.28
15	–0.01	–0.06
16	0.09	0.2
17	0.14	0.27
18	0.2	0.51
19	0.16	0.65
20	0.25	0.7
21	0.36	0.79
22	0.42	0.89
23	0.37	0.97
24	0.38	1.06
Daily	–0.010	0.0

Source: Author elaboration, data from Ofgem collected in Lapuerta (2003).

complementary effects between the two kinds of imbalances, CCGT positive and LDZ negative. It may be underlined that the hourly peak is larger in CCGT demand. The presence of gas-fired power plants may increase the intra-day peak, especially if there is an additive effect between residential and gas-fired power plants' demand peaks.

2   New Gas Demand Changing Gas Flows

This second section focuses on the change of gas supply and storage respectively. It describes how the new gas demand profile interacts with the gas market, impacting on the gas supply side and storage, which is the traditional tool to deal with the household demand variations.

Regarding the supply side, special attention is paid to liquefied natural gas (LNG), as it has been a flexible source that has been highly developed in the last two decades. LNG flexibility allows the gas supply to change according to gas price arbitrages, playing a key role where demand has higher medium-term elasticity. It has been also a tool for new gas supply (when the GFPP gas demand increased). As LNG re-gasification technology is quite modular and with low-scale economies (Jarlsby, 2004), the delay between investment decision and infrastructure operation is lower than most of the other gas supply sources. In addition, the next chapter of the book will deal with the contracting dynamics of LNG.

Storage has been the preferred tool to accommodate traditional gas demand variability, as this variability has been highly seasonal. Thus, storage had mainly been built to deal with seasonal changes in gas demand. Recently, with the increase in GFPPs, gas demand and demand variability have changed, and arbitrage has important roles. Thus, storage has started to play a new role in the gas market, operating infrastructures differently in order to adapt to the new gas market's variability.

We saw in the previous section that the inclusion of GFPPs in the gas market drives the attenuation of seasonal cycles and the increase in the short-term peaks. In this section we will show how the insertion of large gas demand that requires flexibility changes gas flow characteristics and increases the demand for flexible gas services.

2.1 NATURAL GAS SUPPLY: NEW FLEXIBILITY SOURCES DRIVEN BY LNG DEVELOPMENT

Electricity markets have a profile driven by their electricity consumers and require instantaneous response by gas suppliers. Historically, gas suppliers have mainly provided flat gas provision, with some seasonal cycles, so a tendency was observed for a mismatch between electric load and short-term variations of gas supplies. This mismatch increased gas peak prices, and consequently increased the value of flexible supply.

Moreover, the demand for flexibility is stressed as a consequence of the decreased participation of EU swing production. The role of LNG becomes central in this context where there is a need to increase gas importation, supply flexibility and source diversification.

Natural gas has traditionally been traded in regional markets like the European, the North American and the Asia-Pacific markets. Most of the international gas trade to and within Europe has been transported via pipelines. However, after the 1990s the participation of LNG in the gas supply portfolio of EU countries strongly increased. As forecasted by EIA (2007), in ten years the LNG supply to Western Europe will have increased more than 300 per cent. The increased participation of LNG can be seen in many countries such as Spain, Portugal, Turkey, France and Italy, and more recently the UK and Greece have entered this group (Jensen, 2007b; IEA, 2008).

These trends reflect the fact that gas resources, to a large extent, are located far from the main consuming regions, increasing the attractiveness of LNG. Liquefied natural gas is actually a physical form of gas that permits a new mode of transportation, such as by ship. An LNG facility chain brings, besides the traditional aspects of the gas industry (exploration, production, transport, storage and distribution), a new set of facilities, those of gas liquefaction, gas shipping, gas re-gasification and gas storage.

The decrease in the cost of LNG observed over the last two decades was also another factor that pushed the development of LNG in Europe and worldwide. The most expensive part of the LNG chain is liquefaction and shipping (Rosendahl and Sagen, 2009). Liquefaction costs reduced between 35 and 50 per cent between the 1990s and 2003, and shipping costs reduced around 40 per cent between 1996 and 2006.

LNG terminal usage patterns differ by region, reflecting the structure of LNG demand in various markets. In the countries where LNG is generally used as the main gas source and without large underground gas storage, gas demand fluctuations are absorbed by redundancy in LNG terminal capacities. Such redundancy also provides flexibility to meet unforeseen demand increases. In the countries where large quantities of gas can be held in the system, which includes more underground gas storage facilities, LNG terminals can enjoy higher utilization rates. In the countries where LNG plays a marginal role, LNG deliveries vary depending on price differences with other fuel markets. In these markets, the utilization of re-gasification is frequently rather low. LNG absolute volume is still low if compared with pipeline gas importation, though it has increased its importance, as we can see in Figure 2.6 Moreover, LNG has been shown to be the most dynamic section of the gas market (Keppler, 2007).

In 2007, LNG participated in 15 per cent of total European Union importation, which is significant considering the level of volume flexibility and price arbitrage allowed by this new supply source. In Figure 2.7, we observe increasing LNG participation. Moreover, the LNG participation is still increasing.

The other key change in the LNG market is the introduction of new gas suppliers, as we can see if one compares the LNG exporters to Europe in 1993, Figure 2.8, and in 2007, Figure 2.9. We observe a decrease in

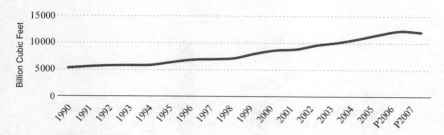

Note: P = Preliminary data.

Source: Author elaboration, data from EIA (2008).

Figure 2.6 EU-15/volume of gas importation (between 1990 and 2007)

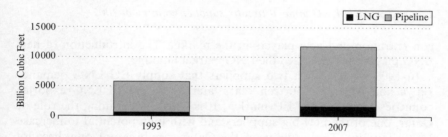

Source: Author elaboration, data from EIA (2008).

Figure 2.7 EU-15/volume of gas importation by pipeline and LNG (in 1993 and in 2007)

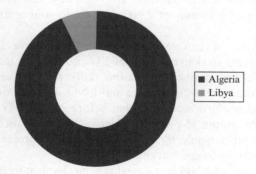

Source: Author elaboration, data from EIA (2008).

Figure 2.8 EU-15/LNG importation by supplier country in 1993

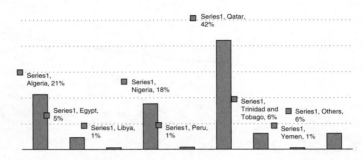

Note: 'Others' includes non-specified exporters and exporters providing less than 1% of
           EU LNG.

Source: Author elaboration, data from IEA (2011).

Figure 2.9   EU LNG importation by supplier country in 2007

concentration and new players in the market. The introduction of new
LNG players has increased the LNG market liquidity.

In 1993 we have just two suppliers that supply EU LNG demand,
Libya and Algeria. Fourteen years later, there are 13 LNG exporter
countries attending the EU market. It is worth underlining the role of
Qatar, one of the new big suppliers and with high potential to increase
LNG liquidity. The liquidity of the Qatar supply is not only because
of the size of its natural gas reserve (900 trillion cubic metres) but
also because the model of development of its reserves, which has been
flexible and based on short-term trade (Bartsch, 1998; Ledesma, 2009).
The tendency observed in Europe for decreasing participation of EU
production seems likely to continue over the next few years, as well as
the increasing participation of LNG as supply source and of storage
deliverability.

In Figure 2.10, we can see that Gas Infrastructure Europe (GIE)
forecasts a decrease in deliverability of EU production, maintaining the
same tendency observed over the last few years; this deliverability will be
substituted by the increase in storage and LNG. Pipeline deliverability is
predicted to increase around 10 per cent before 2018, LNG almost 20 per
cent and storage around 15 per cent. Briefly, the importance of LNG and
storage deliverability would likely increase in the future and it would be
even more important to gas market flexibility.

The introduction of LNG as a gas supply mechanism technically allows
location flexibility for transportation. However, the real flexibility is
achieved only when there is also time flexibility. In other words, LNG
can be delivered to different points as well as at different points in time.

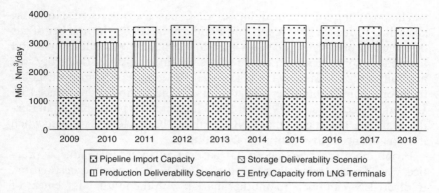

Source: Author elaboration, data from EIA (2008) and GIE (2009a).

Figure 2.10 EU-27/gas deliverability scenario

Thus, the possible existence of spot markets drives the increase in price and volume arbitrage.

LNG facilities are modular, which means that they can be operated separately from the rest of the gas network and that they can be plugged into different places. A given LNG ship, with some technical restrictions, can come from different exit points and can arrive at different entry points. The LNG chain provides interconnection among different networks, having no connection node and no common infrastructure.

In relation to the location choices of LNG terminals, it depends on the existing available transport infrastructure and the location of consumers. The terminals located near to old producers' areas can be viewed as providing supply replacement for declining domestic production. These terminals are usually located in regions where there is free gas transport capacity. In this case, they would demand just incremental investments. The terminals developed in new areas tend to be closer to the consumer areas, but greenfield pipelines need to be constructed to link the new gas supply to the rest of the grid.

The time flexibility to buy and sell gas depends on the existence of a spot market to allocate gas according to the different values of consumers. A decade ago, when the LNG industry was based exclusively on long-term, take-or-pay contracts and the number of market players was limited, the impact of price signals was weak. The liquidity of the flexible LNG market has increased as a consequence of the increasing number of LNG-producing and -consuming countries. Moreover, the emergence of some uncommitted volumes of LNG and the development of arbitrage activity has also improved LNG flexibility.

The possibility of real flexibility of LNG has always existed. However, according to Jensen (2003), until the middle of the 1990s the number of gas liquefaction platforms and re-gasification terminals was quite small and focused on some rigid markets, and the potential physical flexibility was not fully utilized. Ships were contracted for long-term transport, going from one point to another for 20 years.[18] The flexibility introduced by LNG only became a reality when LNG increased its participation in flexible markets. This means that LNG flexibility begins to be exploited when it meets the necessary institutional conditions.

From about five years ago it has become an acceptable industry practice, even for contractually committed LNG with a specified destination, to divert LNG shippers to another market with the mutual agreement of the seller and the buyer. The financial incentives to deviate shippers are consequences of profits resulting from price arbitrage between markets.[19] The profits resulting from the arbitrage are usually shared by the seller and the initial buyer. The participants of the deal can be the seller, the initial buyer, the end buyer, or an independent trader/trading team (intermediary). LNG arbitrage implies that more than two parties are involved in the transaction and it often consists in a number of trading operations in order to deliver the cargo to another market, and to organize the replacement of the diverted cargo if required. However, without a price spread that allows the trader to profit, no arbitrage transaction can take place (unless it is a diversion for operational reasons, to reduce costs). This barrier is the most critical among those considered. Price spread must be large enough to cover the transaction costs and be a sufficient incentive for the aggregator, who often has to share the profits with another party.

As soon as there are more than two buyers in the market, an arbitrage deal should be possible. The number of players does not really predetermine the number of arbitrage transactions. The quality of players is critical; traders should possess divertible cargoes, buyers must offer a competitive price, and both parties have to be able to organize logistics (decreasing transaction costs).

Nevertheless, besides the traditional destination clause and the availability of non-committed shipping capacity, there are other barriers to LNG price arbitrage. Factors such as technical and market restrictions, high transaction costs or tight LNG supply can hinder LNG diversions. The significance of these barriers varies over time and differs from market to market.

LNG and its infrastructure are still far from standardized, and they complicate the arbitrage to a significant extent. Recent LNG industry investments have involved long-term agreements, especially to build re-gasification plants and liquefaction terminals. These agreements determined LNG specifications, prices and volumes, which have decreased transaction costs, even if we can still observe LNG quality heterogeneity (Zhuravleva, 2009).

Ship–shore compatibility and the compatibility of offloading and receiving equipment must be taken into account as well. This means that technical issues still restrict diversions of LNG vessels and this barrier is considered one of the most critical constraints regarding arbitrage growth. Thus, the existence of a spare re-gasification capacity will not attract a diverted cargo unless a competitive price is offered and technical and regulatory restrictions do not hinder it.

The compatibility of LNG supply and GFPP demand is remarkable for different reasons. First, the GFPP is the main driver increasing gas demand, and LNG is one of the gas sources meeting the increase in gas demand; second, because LNG supply and GFPP are potentially highly elastic regarding the gas price. The third variable of GFPP and LNG compatibility has to do with the flexibility to choose the localization of future gas demand and supply. And last, LNG is especially interesting because of the low period required for infrastructure development, which is a consequence of its technical modularity.

However, LNG flexibility is limited because of transaction costs, some physical specificity, and the limited participation in the total gas supply.[20] On the other hand, GFPP flexibility may also be limited because of its participation in the power generation portfolio.

2.2 SHORT-TERM TOOL OF FLEXIBILITY: THE NEW ROLE OF STORAGE IN THE EQUILIBRIUM OF OFFER AND DEMAND

As described above, on the gas demand side we can identify three major consumption cycles: seasonal, daily and hourly. With regard to the offer, the upstream of gas is not flexible enough to face demand cycles. It explains why increased short-term volatility of demand increases the importance of, and confers new roles to, storage infrastructure.

In the EU, gas storage has been mainly developed to manage seasonal gas demand. In vertically integrated industries, gas storage was an important optimization tool for gas suppliers. Traditionally, gas has been injected into the storage reservoirs in summer and withdrawn in winter. This allows pipelines and well-head production to operate at a more consistent and more efficient annual level.

Storage can be built to meet different kinds of time arbitrages (Esnault, 2000). Nowadays, with EU liberalization, we can see the development of new roles for storage. These new roles are to cover demand peaks, to enhance cost efficiency of gas, to balance seasonal variations in consumption, to secure emergency gas supply and to benefit from trading opportunities. In other words, in the recent EU market-oriented gas industry:

> [S]toring gas becomes an instrument for prices arbitration. Price differential can be exploited in a tighter timeframe than the seasonal one (with daily, monthly, quarterly injections or withdrawals) or between the electricity and gas markets. In the latter case, if prices soar at power exchanges utilities can obtain rents from gas-fired power plants by resorting to gas in storage instead of buying it in the spot market at a higher price, provided that the cost of access to storage is not too high.[21]

With regard to technical features, there are four different available storage technologies: depleted field, aquifer storage, salt cavern storage and LNG peak shaver (GIE, 2009b). The choice of efficient storage technology depends on the expected use of the storage (withdrawal and injection rates) and the geological conditions of the region. The first two underground storage technologies are indicated for medium- and long-term storage, and they are dependent on geological conditions. Cavern storage is more utilized to offer medium- and short-term flexibility; it is also dependent on geological conditions. LNG peak shaver is storage dedicated to the short-term flexibility, and it is not dependent on geological pre-existent conditions.

2.2.1   Change in Storage Withdrawal and Injection Rate Patterns

Given the strong variation between summer and winter residential and commercial gas demands, the industry has traditionally used storage fields to manage large seasonal differences. The economic logic has been to inject gas into storage reservoirs in summer and to withdraw it in winter. This allows pipelines and well-head production to operate at a more consistent and a more efficient annual level. The segment from supply to storage is typically designed based on average daily levels, while that from storage to the market is based on a peak-day requirement. This design is based on the idea that the transport capacity from storage to final consumer needs to be large enough not to inhibit long-haul transport from the supply regions. And storage localization would be determined based on physical possibilities and the trade-off between storage cost and the cost to build larger transport pipelines from supply to demand, or to build smaller transport capacity between supply entry point and storage.

In order to deal with gas demand seasonal cycles, infrastructure investments may consist of peak transport capacity through long-haul pipelines directly from the supply region to the demand region, or to include storage and peak transport capacity through short-haul pipelines linking storage to final demand.

The most important parameters to define the working capacity of a given storage facility are the working capacity and the withdrawal rate. The working capacity is the maximum volume of gas that can be withdrawn during a season of operation. Actually, it is said to be the difference between the total capacity and the volume of cushion gas (the gas being used to push the working gas outside). The withdrawal rate is the maximum volume that can be withdrawn during a given time, usually a day or an hour. These two parameters summarize the characteristics of the storage facility: 'On the one hand its size and on the other hand the maximum and minimum pressure authorized during the operation. It is crucial not to go below a specified pressure, compliance can cause storage reservoir to collapse and destabilize the subsoil'.[22] The highest load periods of gas consumption still correspond to the heating season, and the peaks in storage demand would be extreme in the event of very cold weather. However, the summer peak is a recent phenomenon that has been observed due to the increase in GFPPs. Demand for GFPPs, which is the main forecasted demand, is also highly variable on hourly and daily bases.

GFPPs change the storage demand. First, they create an hourly demand profile and it is even more pronounced than the traditional volatilities of residential and commercial gas consumers. Second, the summer peak is shorter than the gas injection period, as it allows the injection only in the off-peak electricity demand hours of the day, and thus requires more volume to be injected into the shoulder (historically lower demand) months, usually from April to June and from September to October. Each time that new GFPP facilities are added to the infrastructure, supply dedicated to serving this market will compete with supply intended for storage injections. In environmentally constrained supplies, the decrease in storage injection time may push up summer gas prices, as the gas consumed in the power generation sector competes with gas intended for storage.

2.2.2 Incentive to Invest in Short-term Storage

In the economic literature there are three main motivations to explain the benefits of storage for firms: arbitrage, precaution and seasonal production smoothing (Baranes et al., 2009). In order to invest efficiently in gas storage, a key issue is to consider the features of storage demand.

Table 2.7   EU/selected countries/storage seasonal variation

Country	Stock Change/Consumption (Oct to March %)
Germany	11.6
France	21.4
Italy	9.9
UK	3.9

Source: Author elaboration, data from Bonacina et al. (2009).

In the last decade, storage has become a priority for both gas companies and governments. Spurred by declining national gas reserves, inflexible production patterns and expensive alternatives to balance supply and demand in the yearly gas cycles, storage is vital to the effective and efficient functioning of national gas markets (Bonacina et al., 2009).

The difference in storage usage in the countries represented in Table 2.7 reflects different consumption patterns. For instance, seasonal consumption is much larger in France than in the other three countries. It can be explained by the high participation of residential consumers in the France portfolio. In Italy, Germany and the UK, gas consumption includes the important participation of the electricity sector, and so gas demand in these countries is smoother over the year, and it is also more elastic than residential demand for home heating.

The changes in the traditional seasonal demand of the gas industry based on residential and commercial consumers have increased the need for daily and hourly storage deliverability, and so the need for investment in storage with higher deliverability. The increase in summer gas demand can interrupt storage refill and increase summer gas prices. If the seasonal spread prices are not high enough to remunerate the storage, seasonal storage can start to become uneconomical. In addition, the gas market's fluctuations on a day-to-day, week-to-week and month-to-month basis require a quick adjustment of storage inventories. Moreover, with regard to the credit cash flow, a market environment has a need for faster cash flows, as there is a higher credit risk in gas storage for six or eight months.

In the EU context, the development of markets for gas storage is a tool to drive increased EU market liquidity. Most of the EU gas markets are still illiquid, and developing a real third party access to storage capacities could increase the liquidity of the supply and enable shippers to discriminate between their gas supply sources in the short term: 'Given that storage capacities have transferred to third parties since August

2004, it is obvious that storage will become a significant flexibility tool when choosing a gas supply portfolio as it is observed in many American states'.[23] Furthermore, gas storage development is also a tool to manage the demand of gas market flexibility, coming especially from the GFPP gas demand and the need for load management in daily and intra-day bases.

3 Conclusions

The impact of GFPPs in the gas market can be seen as a consequence of the interaction between new gas demand and traditional gas demand, as well as gas supply and gas storages. GFPP gas demand may behave as complementary or/and competing gas demand. In both cases, the intro-duction of massive GFPP gas demand changes the dynamic of countries' demand. In the interaction between household and GFPP demand, the latter tends to decrease the seasonality of total gas demand but increases the amplitude of its short-term volatility. In interaction with flat gas demand, GFPP demand tends to increase seasonal volatility as well as short-term volatility. In that view, GFPP gas demand introduces two main variables to the gas market: short-term peaks, which are charac-teristic of the electricity demand profile, and increased elasticity of gas demand.

With regard to gas supply, GFPP gas demand relied on increasing European imports, which have been partially supplied by LNG. LNG interacts with GFPP gas demand because of flexibility characteristics and price elasticity. Thus, the introduction of GFPPs into the gas market has valorized the flexible gas supply, also being an incentive driving European LNG supply. On the other hand, the introduction of LNG has increased the flexibility of gas supply and has tied at least part of the gas supply to gas prices.

Storage dynamics have been also affected by the introduction of GFPPs in the EU. In fact, storage has been a tool to balance gas offer and demand. As the volatility in gas demands has become more important in the short term, storage has assumed a new role. However, this new role in the short term impacts the performance of storage to react in its long-term traditional role.

The interaction of all these factors shows that the introduction of GFPPs in the EU has contributed to a change of gas flows. Gas flows, however, depend on network infrastructure services. The rest of the book will deal with the consequences and challenges associated with these effects in the EU network regulation.

NOTES

1. 'Price elasticity of demand' is a measure of consumers' sensitivity to price. It is the proportional change in demand given a change in price. A good with a price elasticity larger than -1 is said to be 'elastic'; goods with price elasticity smaller than -1 (closer to zero) are said to be inelastic.
2. There are also some other technical features that make the instantaneous matching between electricity demand and production more complex. These characteristics require balancing tools to allow the electricity network to work properly.
3. Loosely, the base load the plants dispatch is around 5200 hours/year, the middle load plants run around 2600 hours/year and peak load plants run around 900 hours/year.
4. But, depending on the country's electricity generation portfolio there are some GFPPs running on base load, especially when gas prices are low. For instance, we can observe GFPPs running as base load plants in the UK in 2010 (UtilityWeek, 2010).
5. DECC (2010a).
6. Switching fuel is simpler and cheaper in open cycle gas turbines than in combined cycle gas turbines (CCGTs). Therefore, the increase in CCGTs increases the cost of installing fuel switching equipment.
7. In the USA the scenarios are different. According to the International Energy Agency (IEA, 2009), about one-third of US power plants that use gas as the primary fuel (mostly steam boilers) were also able to run on oil products in 2008, even though most of the new gas-fired electricity production (largely CCGT) added at the beginning of the current decade cannot use oil as a back-up or alternative fuel.
8. Thermal-generating electricity production excludes nuclear, hydro and other renewable power plants.
9. DECC (2010b).
10. Expected operational costs include expected CO_2 prices.
11. There are also interruptible contracts allowing shippers to be cut off under some contractually specific circumstances such as gas supply disruption (EC, 2009a).
12. This tendency of the higher importance of gas interruptible contracts of GFPP gas consumers is not homogeneous in all countries. For instance, it is not observed in countries like Italy and Denmark (EC, 2009a). The heterogeneity may be explained by electricity generation portfolios highly dependent on gas, different incentive tools offering reliable electricity production, among other institutional specificities.
13. This is more frequent in countries that regulate gas prices on the basis of cost of supply or the ability of consumers to pay (which may result in a price well below the market value of the gas). Once the price of gas rises above the threshold of its market value and the logic of conservation or efficiency measures becomes clear-cut, demand may fall off quickly.
14. Offant (2002), accessed 16 March 2013 at http://www.onepetro.org/mslib/servlet/onepetropreview?id=WPC-32319.
15. The gas market can be divided into the captive segment and the non-captive segment. The demand on the captive segment varies according to climate conditions. The variation of gas demand from the non-captive segment is correlated with the economic growth and relative price between gas and its substitute fuels.
16. Calculated based on National Grid (2010b).
17. The impact of electricity sector demand and industrial demand on decreasing the seasonal cycle is shown by Read (2007) in the USA. Read shows that the decrease in gas demand by industrial demand has increased the seasonal cycle, but that GFPPs increasing demand has decreased the seasonal cycle.
18. 'Asian customers in particular have been complaining about the rigidities inherent in the traditional LNG contract and welcome the possibility of negotiating for more flexible supplies' (Jensen, 2003, p. 4).
19. As defined by Zhuravleva (2009), LNG arbitrage can be defined as a physical cargo diversion from one market to another that offers a higher price. The diversion of the

cargo can be regarded as arbitrage if the cargo was initially committed to the first market and to the initial buyer in a commercial contract. The two key drivers for arbitrage are commercial and operational respectively. The commercial driver has the ability to take advantage of price differentials between the markets, which arise due to differing pricing structures, variations in the relative balances between supply and demand and market inefficiency.

20. Spain is the country with largest participation of LNG as gas supply in the EU.
21. Creti (2009, p. 2).
22. Bourjas (1997, p. 199).
23. Creti (2009, p. 32).

3. Gas supply: the role of liquefied natural gas

Sophia Ruester

1 Introduction

During the last decade, the LNG industry altered substantially. Traded volumes increased by an annual average of 7 per cent from 2000 on. New players entered the market and new trading patterns evolved. On the one hand, vertical and horizontal integration have become more common, with traditional oil and gas majors investing in a portfolio of LNG export, transport and import capacities, which enables flexible trades. On the other, new business models of non-integration emerged. Long-term contracts with a duration of more than 20 years co-exist with short-term agreements. Recent developments in unconventional gas resources change the global supply picture. The past economic crisis still entails short-term over-capacities in the global natural gas export market and supports the development of a buyers' market at least for the medium-term future. The survival of incumbents and new entrants strongly depends on their ability to operate economically and adapt to the changing market circumstances. This chapter therefore discusses recent dynamics in the liquefied natural gas market as well as changing corporate strategies regarding contracting patterns, horizontal integration (i.e., investments in various export and/or import markets) and vertical integration along the LNG value-added chain.

2 Recent Dynamics in the Liquefied Natural Gas Market

Converting natural gas to LNG for transportation by tanker has been utilized for more than 40 years, but the industry achieved a remarkable level of global trade only recently. Since 1964, the technology of natural gas liquefaction enabled commercial transport in tankers, but transport remained expensive and natural gas markets stayed regional in nature until the 1990s.

The North American market, including the USA, Canada and Mexico, has traditionally been highly self-sufficient, with substantial domestic production in all three countries and some intra-regional pipeline trade. The USA opened its first LNG receiving terminal in 1971 to import additional volumes from Algeria. However, due to a surplus in domestic supplies in the mid-1980s two of the four import terminals (i.e., Elba Island and Cove Point) were mothballed in 1985 and contracts with Algerian Sonatrach were terminated before their official end. In Europe, indigenous natural gas supplies and imports via pipeline were available to meet demand and LNG capacities grew relatively slowly. Spain opened its first LNG import terminal in 1969; Italy and France followed in 1971 and 1972, respectively. In contrast, traditional Pacific Basin natural gas importers such as Japan, South Korea or Taiwan lack domestic supplies and are beyond the reach of any pipeline sources. They are highly dependent on imports in the form of LNG and dominated the LNG industry during its first decades.

During this early stage, most of the world's LNG export infrastructure remained under state control and private or foreign companies were involved only with minority shares. Inflexible bilateral long-term contracts with take-or-pay and destination clauses secured the capital-intensive infrastructure investments and reliable supplies for import-dependent buyers. Nissen (2004) calls these early trading structures the 'project-utility chain model' where the export project (typically a joint venture between a national oil and gas company [NOC] and a private oil and gas major) functions as the seller and a monopoly franchised utility or a merchant trader as buyer. Downstream competition in most importing countries was not encouraged. For example, buyers in South Korea and Taiwan were state entities, the Japanese natural gas sector was highly regulated without any foreign participation and Japanese utilities controlling all imports; and also in European countries such as France, for example, a state-owned monopoly was responsible for all imports and natural gas transmission. Capacities along the whole value chain, including shipping, have been bilaterally committed and each supply project was linked by technical and commercial design to a specific market.

Since the 1990s, investments in LNG infrastructure grew rapidly as worldwide natural gas demand increased significantly, leading to substantial economies of scale throughout the value chain. New entrants include Turkey (1994), Greece (2000), Portugal (2003), India (2004), China and Mexico (both 2006). The UK re-emerged as an LNG importer in 2005 to substitute for declining domestic production. Significant expansions and new investments have been realized in Spain and the USA re-opened its mothballed terminals since domestic supply sources no longer appeared adequate to support the expected increase in demand. South American countries received their first LNG in mid-2008.

The LNG industry has altered substantially during the last decade. Re-gasification capacities increased from 251 mtpa (million tons per annum) in 1999 to 462 mtpa at the end of 2009 (+84 per cent), liquefaction capacities from 108 to 229 mtpa (+112 per cent) during the same period and the number of operating LNG vessels augmented from 106 to 337 (+218 per cent). Atlantic Basin LNG trade gained in importance (Figure 3.1). After nearly 20 years without any export capacity extensions, Trinidad/Tobago and Nigeria opened their first liquefaction trains[1] in 1999, Egypt followed in 2005, and Equatorial Guinea and Norway in 2008 and 2009, respectively. The Middle East, accounting for more than 40 per cent of worldwide proven natural gas reserves, is becoming the largest regional exporter of LNG. With Qatar and Oman, two additional suppliers started deliveries in 1997 and 2000. The region is currently evolving into a swing producer;[2] deliveries to European and Asian markets and even to North America are feasible without a significant difference in transportation cost. Jensen (2007b) even argues that Qatar, the largest LNG exporter since 2005, may become the 'Henry Hub' of global LNG pricing.

In today's LNG market, new flexibility in trading patterns comes from (1) changes in the structure of long-term contracts, (2) a small but growing short-term market and (3) a trend of suppliers towards self-contracting with their own downstream marketing affiliates. Changes in contract terms have taken several forms: average contract duration as well as contracted volume is decreasing, take-or-pay requirements are reduced, destination clauses are eliminated and buyers increasingly conclude for free-on-board agreements enabling cargo diversions. Long-term contracts are accompanied by flexible short-term agreements as well as vertical integration and strategic partnerships. Today, spot[3] and short-term trade account for about 20 per cent of total LNG trade. Arbitrage trade in the Atlantic Basin is increasingly linking North American and European markets. The first liquefaction projects without having sold total volume based on long-term contracts are moving forward.

Changes in the institutional framework, that is, the move from monopolistic structures to competition, in turn demand fundamental changes in the organizational behaviour of market participants. More competition, mirrored by evolving spot markets, a gain in contract flexibility and increasing international trade, exposes traditional players to greater pressure. Global mergers and acquisitions, integration and strategic partnerships have become routine today and the LNG industry is dominated by a small number of large players. Global oil and natural gas producers and distributors are frequently engaged in all stages of the LNG value chain. In addition, export projects are increasingly financed and developed by private (and foreign) interests. Former downstream monopolists

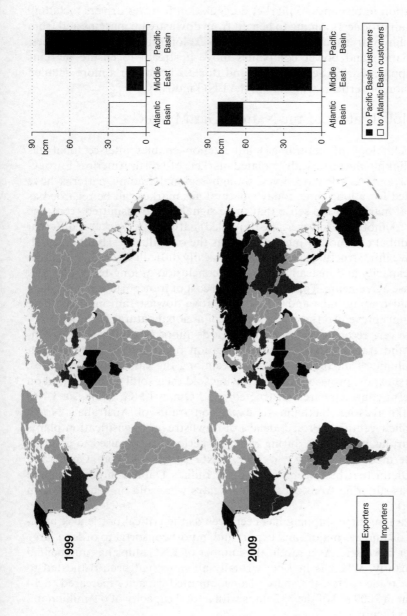

Source: Own depiction based on data from BP *Statistical Reviews of World Energy* (2000, 2010).

Figure 3.1   Countries participating in LNG trade and inter-regional trade volumes 1999 vs 2009

of natural gas are finding their traditional markets challenged by the intrusion of oil and gas majors integrating into import markets. Vertical integration in response to market deregulation features drivers including upstream producers aiming to benefit from downstream margins and from ownership of transportation capacities to exploit arbitraging possibilities. Distribution and power companies move upstream to ensure margins and supply security. See Section 4 and Box 3.2 below for a more detailed discussion of vertical structures in the LNG industry.

3   Globalization of the Natural Gas Market?

The technology of natural gas liquefaction enables inter-regional gas trade, linking the historically isolated markets of North America, Europe-Eurasia and Asia-Pacific. Even though regional trading patterns have prevailed for a long time, today's natural gas market can be regarded as a global market in the sense that price signals are transmitted from one region to another. However, the (liquefied) natural gas market is different from global commodity markets such as the oil industry. Highly capital-intensive infrastructures make it economically difficult to hold permanent spare capacity and instead support the conclusion of long-term sales and purchase agreements. Together with high cost of transportation and a lack of liquid trading hubs and fully competitive downstream markets these conditions prevented the establishment of a global natural gas price.

However, recent developments towards more flexibility within contracts and trades support the globalization of the natural gas market. The volume of uncommitted capacities along the value chain increases. The first export projects, without having sold their total volume based on long-term contracts, are constructed (e.g., Oman LNG, Malaysia LNG Tiga, the Russian Sakhalin II, expansion trains of Australia's North West Shelf venture). Project delays of downstream re-gasification plants or a surplus in capacity during ramp-up periods can be used to conduct short-term deliveries (e.g., in 2002, LNG shipments from Oman and Abu Dhabi that had been destined for India's Dabhol import terminal that was suffering from construction delays were sold on the short-term market).

For a long time shipping has been seen as the critical bottleneck motivating oil and gas majors and export and import consortia to order a large number of vessels. As a result, the number of LNG ships has augmented significantly. Whereas in 1999 virtually all ships had been dedicated to specific trade routes, the share of uncommitted capacity increased to 14 per cent in 2009 (49 of the 337 ships with a total capacity of 6.9 million m³; see also Figure 3.2).

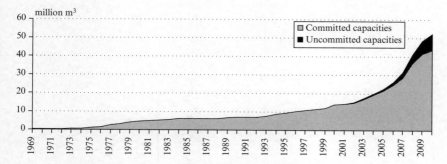

Source: Own depiction based on data from http://www.shipbuildinghistory.com.

Figure 3.2 Development of shipping capacities

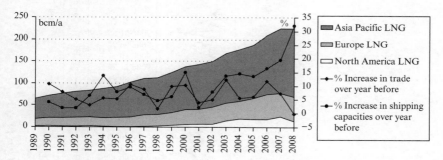

Source: Own depiction based on data from http://www.shipbuildinghistory.com and BP *Statistical Reviews of World Energy*.

Figure 3.3 Development of LNG trade and shipping capacities

Free transport capacities are also available due to recent delays in the start up of liquefaction projects. In addition, the economic crisis reinforced this imbalance between LNG production and transportation capacities at least for the medium-term future. Whereas LNG trade ceased growing in 2008, the number of LNG ships still increased by 32 per cent from 2007 to 2008; another 35 ships were in the shipyards' order books at the end of 2009 (see Figure 3.3). It is likely that this surplus will support the future expansion of the short-term and spot markets. LNG vessels could also be employed as temporary floating storage and sellers, thereby taking advantage of short-term and seasonal price differences.

Figure 3.4 shows the historical natural gas and crude oil spot prices observed on both sides of the Atlantic. Whereas oil prices (i.e., the US

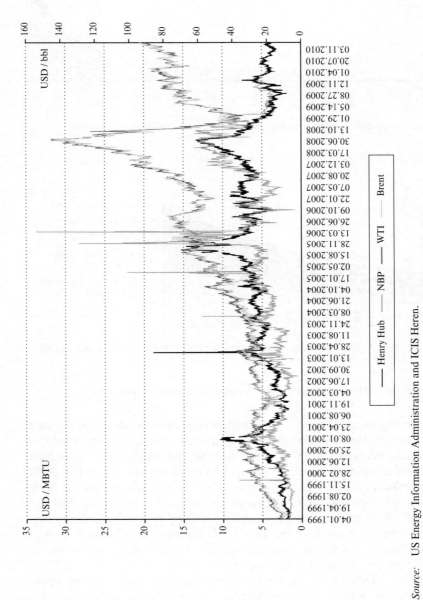

Source: US Energy Information Administration and ICIS Heren.

Figure 3.4 Development of crude oil and natural gas prices

West Texas Intermediate [WTI] and North Sea Brent) move quite parallel, reflecting a global oil price, natural gas prices (i.e., US Henry Hub and UK National Balancing Point [NBP]) clearly diverge. For the major part, they reflect region-specific, instead of global, supply–demand conditions. Using spot data for the USA, the UK and Continental Europe from 1999 to 2008, Neumann (2009) confirms the non-convergence of international natural gas prices. However, she shows that formerly regionally isolated markets are becoming more integrated and that convergence is higher for winter months when markets are tight and natural gas spot prices tend to be more volatile, supporting the redirection of LNG spot cargoes.

Tight supply situations in Asian importing countries regularly mirror in high prices for short-term deliveries too, despite the absence of liquid natural gas markets and import prices being determined based on oil price indexed pricing formulas within long-term contracts. The short-term price differences between regions provide economic incentives to redirect flexible cargoes and to deliver additional spot volumes to higher-value markets. In the period from 2000 to 2001, for example, the USA faced higher price levels than Continental Europe, which led to cargoes being redirected from Europe to North America. A similar price relationship and trade pattern was observed in 2003.

During the winter of 2005–06, a severe competition for LNG spot cargoes within the Atlantic Basin and sharp price spikes occurred. In North America, hurricanes Katrina and Rita severely affected production; in the UK, the transition from net exporter to net importer created additional import demand; Spain suffered from poor hydro conditions, raising the demand for gas-fired power generation; and demand in Continental Europe was high due to a cold winter.

In early 2008, cold weather pushed Japanese power consumption to record levels at the same time when a major share of the country's nuclear capacity was offline. Tokyo Electric Power shut down its 8.2 GW Kashiwazaki-Kariwa power plant after an earthquake in July 2007. Hence, natural gas demand from the power sector increased substantially, which was mirrored in prices of up to 19 USD/mbtu (million British thermal units) that were paid for LNG spot cargoes at a time when average import prices were in the range of 9 USD/mbtu. In April 2008, China bought an LNG spot cargo at 14 USD/mbtu. Similar prices were paid for other spot shipments in spring 2008. Energy giant RWE contracted for the delivery of eight cargoes to be delivered to the UK from December 2009 to January 2010. Due to recent price increases in the USA, however, these volumes had been planned to be redirected towards the North American market.

Theoretical and empirical studies of arbitrage trade in the LNG industry are rare. Hayes (2007) simulates the value of the option to conduct flexible LNG trades, developing a mean-reverting model to represent the stochastic evolution of gas prices in regional markets and the resulting price spreads. Obviously, larger price differences will be observed for a low correlation between regional prices. Zhuravleva (2009) provides a qualitative discussion of different arbitrage models (i.e., initial seller-arbitrageur, initial buyer-arbitrageur, and independent trader-arbitrageur).

4   Changing Corporate Strategies Along the LNG Value Chain

The development of the global LNG market has been accompanied by far reaching dynamics in vertical structures within the industry. The following subsections discuss the changing role of traditional long-term contracts and the increasing relevance of short-term and spot trade. A number of oil and gas majors follow a strategy of vertical and horizontal integration investing in a portfolio of export, shipping and import capacities at the same time that other companies choose a strategy of non-integration, operating LNG terminals as 'tolling facilities'.

4.1   THE CHANGING ROLE OF LONG-TERM CONTRACTS

Investments in LNG infrastructure, especially in upstream exploration, production and liquefaction, are very capital intensive. Therefore, financing traditionally required the conclusion of long-term sales and purchase contracts before the construction process was initiated. Sellers typically have been state-owned oil and gas majors (e.g., Algerian Sonatrach, Indonesian Pertamina, Malaysian Petronas) and for a minor share, joint ventures of private companies (i.e., USA's Phillips and Marathon) or of private and state companies (e.g., Brunei Coldgas, a partnership between the state of Brunei, Shell and Mitsubishi). Buyers have typically been downstream state-controlled utilities (e.g., Gaz de France, Japanese Tokyo Gas and Osaka Gas, Korea Gas Corporation, Turkish Botas, or Spanish Enagás).

The traditional contract was a rigid take-or-pay contract in which the buyer accepted to take off a certain minimum level in the range of 90 per cent of the nominal contracted quantities (CIEP, 2003). The seller in turn accepted a price escalator related to some measure of competing energy prices. Thus, the buyer took the volume risk whereas the price risk was transferred to the seller. Restrictions in destination limited arbitrage trades.

Within the three importing regions, alternative contracting patterns and pricing structures were established. Prices for LNG are thereby set either by price competition with domestic gas (mainly USA, UK) or by the operation of pricing formulas. When the first LNG contracts were negotiated with Japanese buyers in the 1960s, Japanese power generation was heavily dependent on fuel oil. Pricing clauses therefore tied the price escalation to the Japanese Customs Clearing price, an index of Japanese crude oil import prices. This pricing scheme was later adopted for other Asian contracts too. In the mid-1990s, the oil linkage of LNG prices in Asian contracts was softened. So-called 'S-curve' formulas guarantee the interest of the seller if the price of the benchmark crude oil index drops below a certain threshold and protects the buyer from oil prices rising above a certain ceiling.[4] Asian importers were traditionally willing to pay a price premium of about 1 USD/mbtu as compared to LNG buyers in Europe and North America, reflecting their concerns about supply security (EIA, 2003; IEA, 2009). Continental European pricing structures were effectively originated by the Netherlands' pricing policies for domestic natural gas produced from the Groningen field since 1962. The natural gas price was indexed to light and heavy fuel oil. This pattern was also later adopted for export contracts. More recent (liquefied) natural gas contracts also include prices of other relevant energy sources such as coal, natural gas or electricity (Stern, 2007).

The improvement of gas-to-gas competition and increasing liquidity in natural gas hubs should support the establishment of gas market indicators. In contrast, North America and the UK today are characterized by a functioning gas-to-gas competition with long- and medium-term contracts being to a large extent tied to gas market indicators. Suppliers adopt their contracts according to the common pricing structures in the import market; for example, Qatar links the price for LNG deliveries to crude oil prices in Japan, to fuel oil prices in Continental Europe and to natural gas spot prices (Henry Hub and NBP) in the USA and the UK (Dorigoni and Portatadino, 2008).

As the LNG industry has expanded during the past decade, terms of long-term supply contracts started to change and trade became more flexible (see Box 3.1). Average contract duration as well as contracted volumes are decreasing in both Atlantic and Pacific Basin markets (von Hirschhausen and Neumann, 2008; Ruester, 2009). Destination clauses are eliminated, take-or-pay requirements are relaxed and options for additional cargoes are included in recent contracts, for example, in a recent contract between Korea Gas Corporation and Qatar's RasGas venture. Whereas deliveries in the early years of the industry have typically been ex-ship sales, free-on-board (fob) agreements are becoming more common (Nissen, 2007). For

BOX 3.1   OPTIMAL CONTRACT DURATION OF LNG SUPPLY CONTRACTS – A TRADE-OFF?

Ruester (2009) provides an empirical analysis of long-term LNG supply contracts investigating the trade-off between contracting costs and flexibility as discussed in theory and investigated in a number of empirical papers (Gray, 1978; Crocker and Masten, 1988; Klein et al., 1990). On the one hand, transaction cost economics predicts that investments in idiosyncratic assets result in ex post bilateral dependency and lead to a lock-in situation where the investor faces the hazard of post-contractual opportunism and strategic bargaining by the counter-party. In such settings longer-term agreements attenuate those costs by stipulating the terms of trade over the life of the contract. On the other, contract duration is limited due to uncertainty about the future and the hazard of being bound by an agreement that may no longer reflect market realities (e.g., demand levels, input and output prices, changes in the institutional environment, technological innovations). Obviously, spelling out every contingency is costly or even impossible. Hence, the trade-off lies in choosing 'terms that maintain incentives for efficient adaptation while minimizing the need for costly adjudication and enforcement' (Crocker and Masten, 1988, p.328). The optimal level of contract duration corresponds to a situation where the marginal costs and marginal benefits of contracting equalize.

   Using a unique dataset of 224 LNG supply contracts, the study tests, based on a simultaneous equation model, propositions (1) on the above-mentioned trade-off with long-term contracts securing durable investments but forgoing some flexibility, and (2) on the influence of transaction frequency (within the relationship as well as between the trading partners) on contract duration. Estimation results show that the presence of high dedicated asset specificity in LNG contracts results in longer contract duration, confirming the predictions of transaction cost economics. At the same time it can be shown that the increasing need for flexibility in today's 'second generation' LNG industry reduces contract duration, as does the presence of high price uncertainty. Concerning transaction frequency one has to distinguish between a 'within' perspective (i.e., transaction cost economics view) and a 'between' perspective (i.e., organizational learning and reputational effects view). Firms experienced in bilateral trading are generally able to negotiate shorter contracts. Countries that rely heavily on LNG imports are often willing to forgo some flexibility in favour of supply security. Deliveries to competitive downstream markets typically take place under shorter-term agreements.

fob contracts, the buyer takes ownership of the cargo once it is loaded and has complete flexibility over a potential redirection or resale. For example, Korea Gas Corporation traditionally procured LNG ex-ship but enlarged its tanker fleet recently and now concludes for fob contracts. In 2007, Equatorial Guinea sold its entire LNG output on an fob basis to BG. In 2008, a re-loading facility was inaugurated at the Zeebrugge import terminal. Once a cargo is discharged to the storage tanks, the LNG belongs to the importing company and re-export is feasible without violating the contract. Cargoes sourced originally from Qatar have already been delivered to South Korea, India, Portugal and Spain.

Contract flexibility has also been a major target of buyers when renegotiating existing contracts. The Japanese importers Tokyo Gas and Tokyo Electric Power, for example, have renegotiated a Malaysian contract to supply a part of the volume fob rather than ex-ship, enabling the buyers to resell some cargoes. It is also becoming common practice to divert contractually committed LNG volumes to third markets given a mutual agreement between seller and buyer. This increased contract flexibility gives security since it permits adaptations to short-term changes in the supply–demand balance. The netback[5] value will determine the most attractive market in those cases where LNG shippers are free in the choice of destination.

Long-term supply contracts allowing the financing of new infrastructures are increasingly accompanied by short-term agreements (less than three years) and spot transactions balancing supply and demand in the short to medium term. For example, a consortium of Japanese buyers signed contracts with Malaysia to buy 0.68 mtpa (million tons per annum) for a period of 20 years and an additional 0.34 mtpa for a single year beginning in April 2004. The short-term component is updated annually. This combination of short- and long-term provisions provides much higher volume flexibility than conventional take-or-pay contracts.

The short-term market was not established before the 1990s, with the first arbitrage trades and swap agreements appearing in the early 2000s. Electricité de France (holding 3.3 mtpa at Zeebrugge and 0.7 mtpa at

Montoir) has signed a swap agreement with the US-based Dow (3.75 mtpa at Freeport) offering each party a slot of 1 bcm (billion cubic metres) per month of import capacity at the other company's import terminals. The additional margin is shared among Electricité de France, Dow and the supplying company. A similar transatlantic swap agreement involves Suez and ConocoPhillips. Major short-term and spot volumes today are supplied by Qatar, Algeria and Oman; main buyers have been the USA, Spain and South Korea.

However, there may be technical and economic constraints limiting arbitrage activities. First, free capacities have to be available along the value chain, including liquefaction plants (sellers may utilize volumes during the ramp-up period of a contract), shipping, and storage at the downstream re-gasification plants. Second, gas quality differs by natural gas source and import facilities constructed during the early years of the industry have been designed to receive LNG of a certain composition. However, it is technically feasible to endow import terminals with natural gas adaptation equipment, allowing for a decrease (i.e., nitrogen injection; mainly necessary in the UK and the USA) or increase (i.e., propane injection; mainly Asian importers) of natural gas quality in order to meet grid requirements. Third, during the loading and shipping period, typically between four days (e.g., Trinidad/Tobago to the US Gulf Coast) and two weeks (e.g., Qatar to Japan), spot prices in the destination country may change.

For the near-term future, the outlook for spot LNG trade is quite modest and will critically depend on how quickly the global economy recovers from the recession. Many buyers that have been active in spot and short-term trade can currently meet their gas requirements by their long-term contracts and some even have to demand downward adjustments in volume flexibility due to weak consumption levels. For the longer term, the outlook is more optimistic. LNG exporters increasingly dispose of uncommitted liquefaction capacities. The overhang in re-gasification capacities facilitates downstream market access for non-incumbents and the increasing liquidity of European trading hubs enhances price transparency.

4.2 TRENDS TOWARDS VERTICAL AND HORIZONTAL INTEGRATION

Joint ventures always have been a common form of organization within the LNG industry for two main reasons. First, the large investment costs associated with upstream exploration, production and liquefaction ventures make it difficult for one single company to develop and finance the project on its own. Joint ventures are set up in order to share the risks and financial burden. Partnerships between private oil and gas companies have formed: for example, for Alaska LNG (ConocoPhillips and Marathon) or for the North West Shelf venture in Australia (BHP Billiton, BP, Chevron, Mitsubishi/Mitsui, Shell and Woodside Energy). Second, a joint venture with the incumbent NOC is likely (e.g., Abu Dhabi, Egypt, Indonesia, Nigeria, Russia or Qatar). On the one hand, NOCs seek to retain control over natural gas reserves; on the other, private majors contribute technological knowledge and marketing channels to the partnership. In summary, at the end of 2009, 15 per cent of the existing nominal liquefaction capacities have been owned and operated by joint ventures between private majors, the majority of 76 per cent is controlled by partnerships between NOCs and private partners, and the remaining 9 per cent of the capacities is operated by NOCs without any third party (i.e., Algeria, Libya).

Forward integration from the upstream to the downstream sector is a governance form that has become characteristic for the industry, with players controlling capacities along successive stages of the value chain. Upstream producers aim to benefit from downstream margins. One recent phenomenon is the increasing employment of 'self-contracting'. Thereby the seller concludes for a sales-and-purchase agreement with its own marketing affiliate, as has been realized at Qatar's Qatargas and RasGas liquefaction projects (Exxon Mobil, Qatar Petroleum and Total), in Trinidad/Tobago (BP, Repsol and BG) and Norway (Statoil and Gaz de France). In Nigeria, the first three trains of the Bonny Island venture were dedicated to traditional long-term take-or-pay contracts concluded between the venture and European buyers. For trains four and five in contrast, Shell and Total (holding equity shares in the liquefaction plant) self-contracted certain volumes. In total, 11 companies have self-contracted for about 1660 bcm of LNG over the period from 2009 to 2025 (IEA, 2009).

In one version of this commercial business model, the LNG export project is operated as a 'tolling facility' selling the services of liquefaction, storage and loading to the LNG merchant (see also Nissen, 2004, 2006) and natural gas producers rather than the venture become the sellers of natural gas (Nissen, 2006). This structure has been adopted, for example, in Egypt where the BG Group and BP act as merchant traders at the Idku plant and the Spanish Union Fenosa at the Damietta facility. Alternatively, the venture's project partners buy the LNG from the project.

The unbundling of transportation assets and services from rigid export–import project relationships is a major precondition for flexible trade and the control of non-committed shipping capacities has become of strategic value in today's LNG market. Private players have invested in a significant number of vessels during the last decade: Shell controls 30 carriers through joint ventures and direct ownership. Exxon Mobil and Qatar Petroleum have a fleet of 27 ships. The BG Group owns eight vessels and recently ordered another four ships. Several other companies entered the midstream shipping stage during the 2000s (e.g., BP, Gaz de France and Osaka Gas). As already discussed above, the number of uncommitted ships has increased from approximately zero before 2000 to 49 in 2009 (of a total of 337 ships representing 14 per cent of total shipping capacity).

Self-contracting accompanied with investments in a portfolio of upstream and downstream positions and uncommitted ships enables the players to decide where to send LNG cargoes on a shorter-term basis and to take advantage of favourable price conditions. Three case studies will demonstrate the successful employment of this strategy: Shell disposes of LNG export positions in Australia, Brunei, Malaysia, Nigeria, Oman and Russia at the same time as the company holds capacity rights at import terminals in India and Mexico. It will continue its expansion within the industry and participate in projects proposed for France, Italy and Brazil. Similarly, Total has built up a portfolio of export positions in all three exporting regions and import positions in India, Mexico and France. Exxon Mobil and Qatar Petroleum entered a partnership in the late 1990s. In order to mitigate supply costs given the long distance from the Middle East to consuming centres, they constructed the largest liquefaction facilities (7.8 mtpa trains) and ordered the largest vessels ever (>210000 m³), thus realizing substantial economies of scale. At the same time, the partners secured capacity rights at import terminals on both sides of the Atlantic (South Hook in the UK, Rovigo in Italy and Golden Pass in the USA).

Backward integration from the downstream to the upstream sector can be observed too. Traditional natural gas distributors increasingly participate in LNG export ventures, motivated mainly by supply security considerations: Gaz de France holds shares in Egypt's Idku project and Norway's Snovhit LNG; Union Fenosa participates in Oman's expansion train; and Tokyo Gas in Australia's Darwin project. Also, electricity companies, forming part of the extended value chain including natural gas-fired power production, enter the stage. Whereas Spain's first LNG terminals were operated by Enagás, traditional electricity companies (Union Fenosa, Endesa and Iberdrola) are now the dominant investors. AES Corporation, the operator of a 319 MW gas-fired power plant in the Dominican Republic also owns and operates the country's LNG import terminal. Electricité de France proposed a re-gasification facility in the

Netherlands. Some Japanese power producers even integrate further upstream: Tokyo Electric Power holds a share in Australia's Darwin project and Kansai Electric will participate in the Pluto venture.

In contrast to these integrated players there are also some new entrants into downstream LNG markets, which follow a strategy of non-integration: with the upcoming enthusiasm for LNG needs within North America in the early 2000s, Cheniere Energy entered the market and applied for the construction of four onshore LNG import facilities at the Gulf Coast, which should be operated as tolling facilities. The Freeport LNG and Sabine Pass projects were commissioned in 2008. However, as discussed above, the USA's supply–demand balance altered throughout the last few years. With the development of substantial unconventional resources, increased domestic production is outstripping higher-cost LNG supplies. Thus, the two terminals suffer from low utilization rates. Plans to build the additional facilities are dormant at the moment and it is very unlikely that these projects will be realized in the next decade. In fact, recent developments have resulted in liquidity problems for the company and Cheniere had to lay off more than half of its 360 employees in April 2009.

Another entrant is Excelerate Energy, founded in 1999. In 2008, the German RWE acquired a 50 per cent stake in the company. Excelerate employs an innovative technology of offshore, onboard re-gasification. Five import facilities have already been built with the Gulf Gateway (start-up 2005) and Northeast Gateway (2008) in the USA, Teesside GasPort in the UK (2007), Bahía Blanca GasPort in Argentina and Mina Al-Ahmadi GasPort in Kuwait (both 2008). An additional facility is proposed for German offshore Wilhelmshaven. However, industry experts report that up to today only minor deliveries took place through these facilities. The non-integrated players still have to prove to be successful in an industry that for a long time has been a sellers' market without major uncommitted export capacities, and in which also in the longer-term future, once the economic crisis is overcome, importers are expected to continue to compete for global supplies.

5 Conclusions

This chapter has given an overview on recent dynamics in the global LNG market, which had, and continue to have, important impacts on contracting patterns and corporate strategies. The global natural gas market is changing both in quantity and quality. Natural gas hubs gain in liquidity. Long- and short-term contracts co-exist. On the one hand, joint ventures, strategic partnerships and vertical and horizontal integration become common practice and enable arbitrage trades and the realization of swap

---

BOX 3.2   VERTICAL INTEGRATION ALONG THE LNG VALUE CHAIN – AN EMPIRICAL ANALYSIS

Ruester and Neumann (2009) provide an empirical study investigating vertical integration along the LNG value chain. The study builds on recent theoretical developments that propose the so-called positioning-economizing perspective linking Williamson's transaction cost approach (Williamson, 1975, 1985) and Porter's strategic positioning framework (Porter, 1996). Based on a two-step decision-making process, the authors test two propositions on corporate strategies in the LNG industry. First, based on the strategic positioning framework, three possible target market positions are identified: chain optimization (investments in infrastructure along a single value chain) versus a flexibility strategy (investments in a portfolio of LNG export and import positions) versus national oil and gas companies. Empirical results confirm the industry-specific predictions and support the positioning-economizing approach hypothesis of an interrelation between the three strategic choices of target market position, resource profile and organizational structure. They show that NOCs rely on less idiosyncratic assets than companies following a flexibility strategy and that those companies following a flexibility strategy rely on less idiosyncratic assets than chain optimizers. Second, based on transaction cost economics the determinants of vertical integration are investigated. Estimation results confirm the theory's predictions and show that idiosyncratic investments in uncertain environments lead to a motivation to organize transactions within a firm's own hierarchy.

---

agreements; on the other, some new entrants invest in non-integrated commercial LNG import facilities.

The survival of incumbents and new entrants strongly depends on their ability to act economically; strategic decisions (of private sector players) are driven by cost minimization. The heterogeneity of transactions in terms of varying levels of relationship-specific investments, external uncertainty, downstream competition, or dependence on natural gas imports in the form of LNG of natural gas importing countries is matched by diversity in governance forms (varying levels of vertical integration, varying characteristics and duration of supply contracts, etc.). See Ruester (2010) for an in-depth empirical analysis of changing corporate strategies in this industry based on the concept of transaction cost economics and recent developments thereof.

NOTES

1. LNG plants' liquefaction and purification facilities.
2. Supplier controlling its global deposits and possessing large spare production capacity. A swing producer is able to increase or decrease supply at minimal additional internal cost, and is thus able to influence prices and balance the markets, providing downside protection in the short to medium term.
3. The spot energy market allows producers of surplus energy to instantly locate available buyers for this energy, negotiate prices within milliseconds and deliver actual energy to the customer just a few minutes later.
4. The first 'S-curve' formula was applied within a contract concluded between the Australian North West Shelf venture and Japanese customers in 1994. The floor price was set at 16.95 USD/bbl (dollars per barrel) and the ceiling price at 26.95 USD/bbl (Chabrelie, 2003).
5. A summary of all the costs associated with bringing one unit of oil to the marketplace, and all of the revenues from the sale of all the products generated from that same unit.

PART II

The role played by networks regulation

4.   Introduction to Part II

Michelle Hallack, Miguel Vazquez and Jean-Michel Glachant

In the EU gas industry, the technical constraints of gas flows are a key to actual operation, and a challenge for academic understanding. In order to build markets and to achieve efficient market clearing, networks' constraints are simplified. We then obtain a 'commercial' and a 'technical' definition and measurement of gas networks. In this view, market design, and especially the definition of network use rules, should always take account, at a certain time horizon, of the physical reality of the network. If the incentives for network use defined by the rules make a market participant under-use the network, then the rules are implicitly defining the network.

The development of gas-fired power plants and the introduction of liquefied natural gas impact gas flow dynamics, and gas market flows (gas demand and supply) shape the demand side of network services. But, on the other hand, the offer of network services is constrained by both the physical characteristics of the network and by the definition of rights to use the infrastructure. As a result, gas market changes compel networks to adapt to new flexibility requirements.

Under a liberalized regulatory system, different shippers with different needs may use the infrastructures. The network adaptation choice is strongly dependent on the infrastructure usage rules. In the short term, the rules of network use define the set of feasible gas flows, as they determine the kinds and volumes of services that existing infrastructures may offer. In the long term, network rules impact the network investment incentives and so the network architecture. Thus, they determine the kinds and volumes of infrastructures that may efficiently respond to new service demand.

The second part of this book shows how network regulations, which frame the rights to use infrastructures, have affected the offer of flexibility. We focus on EU network regulation because the demand for flexibility has strongly increased, and because of an increased concern about the rules framing the use of network infrastructures. Chapter 5 is devoted to analysing whether the rules defined by the present EU regulatory framework are providing the right signals to market participants, and to show the influence of these rules on actual network use. The access to gas transport networks plays a key role in developing gas markets, as actual physical or contractual barriers may increase the costs, or block trade among national markets. Commercial arrangements to access networks are not sufficient to promote markets just by themselves, but they are a central part of the industry chain where gas markets operate.

5. Opening a market for gas flexibility?

Michelle Hallack

This chapter shows that, in a context of highly heterogeneous supply and demand patterns, the cost of inefficient regulation is significantly higher than in the past. The offer of gas network services is the outcome of infrastructures' rules and already installed infrastructures. Decisions concerning how to use these installed infrastructures are the central variable determining the portfolio of services offered. Thus, the kind and the number of flexibility services provided by the network are a consequence of infrastructure use, as with any other network service. In Chapters 2 and 3 we showed that gas-fired power plant (GFPP) gas demand and the increased participation of liquefied natural gas (LNG) supply increased the demand for flexibility services. In turn, this chapter shows that provision of flexibility to deal with GFPP and LNG demand necessarily implies the flexible use of networks.

In Europe, the use of network infrastructures is constrained by a set of rules defining rights and duties of shippers and pipeline operators.[1] These rules define the services that installed infrastructures may, must and must not offer. Thus far this set of rules delineating the possible uses of infrastructures have been national ones, but based on EU-wide principles. The EU defines the directions that national regulators should follow to achieve a liberalized gas market.[2]

Historically, the gas sector in Europe was characterized by state-owned vertically integrated monopolies.[3] In Europe, the network's regulations determine what services may be offered by network infrastructures and how the services should be offered. Notwithstanding the EU requirements at the European level, national transpositions of EU rules have been quite diverse, even if nowadays there are new policies that are trying to homogenize the national rules.

National network rules actually determine the set of services that the use of infrastructures should offer (Codognet, 2006). The set of network services may be separated into two clusters: simple transport services and storage flexibility services provided by networks. This split is central to all analyses to clarify the production of two goods by the same infrastructures:

storage services organized around market arrangements, and mobility, which are a de facto monopoly, at least in Europe (ERGEG, 2005, 2008).

First, transport service can be defined as the capacity to carry gas between two geographical points when the price differential between these points is higher than the transport costs (Micola and Bunn, 2007). This has been the traditional core of services offered by networks (Codognet, 2006; Glachant and Hallack, 2009).

Second, the flexibility service offered by the network may be defined as the service that allows shippers to wait and see (Smith and Trigeorgis, 2004). Or, we can define flexibility as a service that allows shippers to alter operating decisions and change flow decisions as circumstances arise (Boot and Thakor, 2003). In this chapter, flexibility services are defined as services that change the timing of shippers' decisions, decreasing the lag time between the shipper decision and the real use of natural gas. In other words, flexibility allows shippers to wait and see before taking a decision; consequently, shippers may change their decision concerning the gas destination according to circumstances.[4] A network flexibility service is the offer of an option to use gas at different geographical sites and/or at different points in time.

According to the network's technical properties, we can observe that network infrastructures are able to provide two kinds of flexibility services: flexible mobility and flexible storability.

Flexible mobility

Flexible mobility depends on the flexibility of transport service. In operational terms, flexible mobility depends on the delay between decisions on transport services and real network operation. Smaller delays (shorter notice) means a higher level of flexibility. Thus, flexible mobility is characterized by the ability to change the location and the volume of gas flowing between entry/exit points at short notice. Thus, it decreases the site specificity[5] of gas consumers, suppliers and storage sites. The possibility to change the volume and path of gas transported at short notice depends not only on services' characteristics but also on the approach utilized to require the services. Following the EU gas network regulatory framework, the network services bid depends on the capacity allocation mechanism, the capacity nomination rules and congestion management procedures.

Furthermore, flexible mobility services are necessary to allow any other player to offer flexible provisions of natural gas. In other words, flexible mobility is necessary to allow gas consumers or suppliers to respond to market incentives at short notice. Thus, it is a complementary service required to allow any other gas flexibility tool to reach consumers. For instance, gas supply, storage or even gas trades cannot be offered at short notice if transport services have not been offered at short notice, or if transport services do not allow path changes. The access to gas transport is a sine qua non condition to allow gas exchangeability, as the gas demand and offer can vary only in cases where they are able to access gas transport capacity in a flexible way (Codognet, 2006).

Flexible storability

The second kind of flexibility that networks may offer is storability: the capacity of the network to keep the gas inside the pipeline over a certain period. The storage capacity of networks is achieved by changes in pressure differential, that is, changes in pipeline line-pack (the actual amount of gas stored in a pipeline or distribution system). As with any other storage, it decreases the temporal specificity[6] of gas as a commodity. Contrary to flexible mobility, line-pack storage competes with the rest of the tools offering flexibility.

The access to storage services of network infrastructures depends on the one hand on the installed physical infrastructures; on the other, on the network offer of line-pack storage. In Europe, the rules to offer line-pack flexibility are defined by means of network balancing rules.[7] Moreover, the access of network storability depends on the set of rules for line-pack bids.

These two kinds of services that increase flexibility are valuable services, however, because they have costs. The number of flexibility services offered by a network alters the amount of available transport capacity that is offered to shippers. In other words, high flexibility means a lower amount of transport capacity. The allocation rules that allow more flexibility lead to the reduction of the transport capacity available to market players (Lapuerta and Moselle, 2002; Lapuerta, 2003). Therefore, analysis of flexible services and the methodology of cost allocation are central to determining the economic efficiency of network activities.

Hence, the first section of this chapter details the services that increase flexible mobility, which is complementary to other available flexibility tools. We describe how this kind of flexibility is set by national Network Codes.[8] The second section focuses on network storability in order to explain how it is produced and why it competes with other available or potential flexibility tools. We also point out that the use of pipeline line-pack flexibility has been regulated by balancing rules.

1 Complementarities Between the Flexibility Provided by Gas Transport Network and Gas Market

In Europe the network system operator is the market player responsible for guaranteeing the efficient performance of the network. As is defined

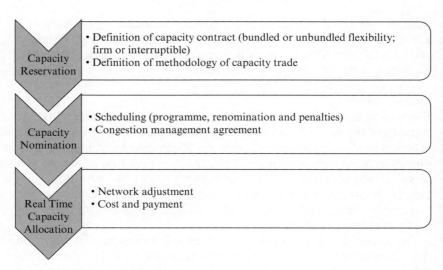

Source: Author elaboration.

Figure 5.1 The sequence of transport infrastructures allocation

by the Third Energy Directive: 'Each independent system operator shall be responsible for granting and managing third party access, including the collection of access charges and congestion rents, for operating, maintaining and developing the transmission system'.[9] Service outcomes of network operation, however, depend on the existent physical assets and the rules of asset utilization. Transport services can be grouped into three sequential actions: capacity reservation, capacity nomination and capacity final allocation (Figure 5.1).

The features of these stages, on the one hand, change how much transport capacity infrastructure operators can make available to shippers; and on the other, they change the flexibility offered by the infrastructures.

Capacity definition is the first and main tool able to change available capacity; it defines the right to use the infrastructures, the geographical flexibility and the temporal requirements that come with those. Different degrees of flexibility can also be offered according to the methodology of capacity reservation. Some capacity reservation methodologies prioritize long-term contracts, whereas others allow short-term reservation. Clearly, short-term reservation tends to be more flexible, as it allows players to 'wait and see' before taking the final decision.

After the capacity requirement stage, the specification of the nomination scheduling confirms the shipper's injection and withdrawal timetable.

During the nomination, the possibility of nomination at short notice improves flexibility because it allows better visibility of real demand. In addition, the nomination may also have different frequencies. The same volume over large nomination periods means greater possibility of adjusting the use of infrastructures to its market value. On the other hand, in cases where there is higher service demand than the capacity that the infrastructure is able to offer, the services are allocated according to congestion management agreements.

The third stage is the real-time operation, when the network has the adjustment responsibility. The larger the period of adjustment the higher costs to networks and the lower shippers' adjustment responsibility. This step is detailed in the next section, as network adjustments are largely provided by means of line-pack storage use.

We can observe that flexibility associated with gas mobility complements most of the gas provision tools. Thus, the offer of adequate flexible mobility is an essential step in allowing other parts of the gas industry to provide flexibility. Comparing the main driver of gas flexibility, that is, electricity sector operation, and the level of flexibility offered by the gas transport capacity in Europe, we observe a mismatching in both sets of rules. Specifically, we underline the difference between the timing of decisions in these two industries. The decision of electricity players to consume gas may be taken over shorter terms than the gas shippers' decision to demand transport services. Such mismatch may block the development of short-term gas provisions. The absence of transport services compatible with short-term demand for gas flexibility slows or impedes the development of tools that may provide gas flexibility, as storage, LNG supply or spot markets.

1.1 TRANSPORT CAPACITY DEFINITION: THE EU REGULATORY FRAMEWORK

The available transport capacity of a network depends on its physical characteristics, but also on its allocation rules. The capacity available to market participants should be the maximum capacity at all entry and exit points, up to the limit of being able to ensure system integrity. In this view, efficient network operation and capacity allocation must provide the maximum use of capacity allowed by system integrity. The rules of capacity allocation define the possibility, the timing and the localization of possible injections and withdrawals by shippers.

Given the existing network, the flexibility of network use faces variable costs and fixed costs. The variable costs are easy to define and depend mainly on the fuels to run compressors to add flexibility to the existing network. The fixed costs of flexibility are more difficult to measure by means of traditional production function, as production function of pipeline flexibility services and pipeline transport actually uses the same infrastructure. It can be classified by the classic microeconomics theory as a multi-product monopoly with independent demand for each product (as both have different substitutes and elasticities) but the service costs of product A are dependent on the production of product B (Tirole, 1988).

Lapuerta and Moselle (2002) have proposed the use of the opportunity costs mechanism to measure network geographical flexibility costs. These authors use opportunity costs to compare different capacity systems with regard to flexibility rights and tariffs, and to evaluate market consequences. Following Lapuerta and Moselle (2002), the opportunity cost approach may be used not only to measure the cost of geographical flexibility of network capacity systems, but also the other flexibilities. This methodology takes into account the physical characteristics of the networks and can be calculated through simulations of how much capacity may be offered with and without flexibility. The difference in the available capacity in the two situations actually represents an estimation of the fixed costs of flexibility. In this view, the increase in flexibility means a decrease in transport capacity.[10]

To allocate flexibility efficiently, it is necessary to build price mechanisms reflecting fixed and variable costs. It is why under-regulated tariff settings are likewise a tool to increase or to limit the ability of transport operators to offer an efficient amount of flexibility. In Europe, the network capacity allocation should be guaranteed to all shippers under the same conditions; however, these conditions may allow different levels of flexibility. There is higher flexibility when shippers are able to allocate and/or nominate capacity at short notice. Current capacity allocation and nomination procedures prioritize long-term decisions and obstruct short-term decisions regarding efficient gas allocation. Natural gas trades between consumers, suppliers and storages are mainly dependent on the availability of transport service. Thus, short-term flexibility regarding gas decisions needs to be complemented by the short-term flexible mobility services offered by networks.

1.1.1 Transport Capacity Definition: Transport Services Decreasing Natural Gas Specificity

The transport capacity definition may provide different degrees of geographical flexibility: defining the capacity of transport services as specific paths; or as a specific entry or exit point; or as a volume that may be transported to any place in the network. As explained by Lapuerta and Moselle (2002), the transport capacity definition specifies the rights acquired by the shipper when they sign the contract.[11] The characteristics of capacity contracts actually define the rights of use and determine the way that shippers may use capacity. Thus, they delimit the level of flexibility. The flexibility offered to shippers in terms of location of injection and withdrawal is a key issue in developing gas trade. Since it allows swaps between different traders, it may encourage secondary trade of capacity and it may allow small shippers to attain flexibility at small costs, increasing their competitiveness.

There are three typical kinds of capacity definition: postal,[12] point-to-point or entry/exit, which offer different degrees of mobility to shippers: 'Each involves a different bundle of rights and obligations between the TSO and the shipper. These contracts entail different trade-offs between the goals of fostering competition, promoting liquidity, and managing congestion'.[13] According to the types of contract capacity, the flexibility given to shippers is different. More flexible contracts mean that the shippers have more decision rights to change how to use network capacity without incurring additional costs. On the other hand, contracts giving more flexibility rights to shippers are more costly to networks. In flexible contracts, the network operator needs to take into account the possibilities of the infrastructure's uses, and make them available to each shipper.

Table 5.1 compares different degrees of flexibility between three types of capacity contracts. Postal capacity is the most flexible type as it gives

Table 5.1 Transport capacity types and shipper costs to change

Transport Capacity Type	Definition	Shipper Costs to Change
Postal	It gives the shipper the right to enter gas at any entry point and take it out at any exit point	No costs to change exit and/or entry points
Entry/exit	It ties shippers to specific entry points, but gives them access to customers who have booked exit capacity at any exit point	Cost to change the entry (exit) point and no cost to change exit (entry) point
Point-to-point	It gives shippers the right to enter gas at a particular entry point and to take it out at a particular exit point	Cost to any changes in the gas flow

Source: Author elaboration, data from Lapuerta and Moselle (2002).

the right to the shipper to use the network capacity linking any entry and any exit point. In a flexible capacity type, such as postal, if demand of gas decreases, the shipper can resell its capacity to any other shipper who wants to use the network, regardless of the entry or exit points used. Or the shipper can sell the gas to other consumers (using other exit points) without any extra transport cost. It means the capacity right does not have site specificity.

The entry/exit capacity type gives the right to shippers to use one entry or exit point, so different combinations can be made by the combinations of rights to use the entry points and the rights to use the exit points. With entry/exit contracts, if the shipper wants to sell un-needed capacity, in a point-to-point system, they need to find a buyer who has the same entry and exit point.

The point-to-point capacity type is the least flexible, as capacity contracts give the right to the shipper to use only one specific entry point and one specific exit point, and any change of these points demands a different contract.[14] In the point-to-point system, there is considerably higher site specificity in the capacity contract, as the contracted capacity is attached to a specific path.[15] Or, if shippers want to change the gas's final consumer, they need also to incur costs to change the capacity contract. It may be noted that (physical or virtual) hubs address this point by referring contracts to hubs where title transfer is easy, hence reducing transaction costs.

The different kind of flexibility represents a trade-off for the networks system. On one hand, more flexibility allows more possibilities of short-term trade and shippers' flow adaptation. It is especially valuable in contexts of volatility and uncertainty. On the other hand, the increase of flexibility represents an increase in the costs. The use of homogeneous capacity contracts actually socializes the flexibility cost among all consumers, independently of their real needs for flexibility.

As shown by Lapuerta and Moselle (2002), the flexibility provided by capacity contracts, such as the postal system and entry/exit system, can affect the amount of firm capacity available. The simple example developed by those authors shows that, in the same network, the available capacity according to a point-to-point type is six times larger than the capacity of a postal type, and 1.2 times larger than an entry/exit type:

> This hypothetical example illustrates that the amount of firm capacity the TSO can sell depends on the type of capacity contracts it offers. Allowing greater flexibility in capacity contracts may reduce the amount of firm capacity the TSO can sell. The postage stamp capacity definition is the most flexible

possible, but allows the TSO the least amount of firm capacity. Point-to-point is the least flexible type of capacity contract. It allows the TSO the largest amount of firm capacity, but at cost in terms of flexibility and liquidity.[16]

This exercise using the UK network data in the beginning of the 2000s is an example of how the fixed costs of flexibility services can be calculated. Actually, the economic concept behind this exercise is the classical opportunity cost definition. Assuming that the same infrastructure may offer 1 unit of transport capacity with flexibility type A (complete geographical flexibility), or 1.2 units of transport capacity with flexibility type B, or 6 units of transport capacity without any bundled flexibility, we conclude that actually the fixed cost of flexibility type A is equivalent to 5 units of transport capacity without any flexibility. And the flexibility cost type B is equivalent to 0.2 units of transport capacity without any flexibility.

In a system whose geographical flexibility is bundled to transport capacity by means of homogeneous services, different kinds of distortions can be observed. First, in cases in which high flexibility is guaranteed to all consumers, cross-subsidies by shippers who do not use geographical flexibility to shippers using flexibility will incentivize players to use more geographical flexibility, and so will make actual network costs higher than the efficient costs.

In the case where geographical flexibility is not allocated, the inefficiency comes from the obstruction of gas market development. In fact, the definition of capacity contract types strongly impacts the rest of the gas industry, including non-regulated segments of the industry chain.

1.1.2 Capacity Timing: Period and Regularity Also Play a Key Role in Flexibility Level

The capacity involves different periods and frequencies. Periods refer to how long shippers and network operators should respect the agreement. Frequency refers to the time interval during which the capacity volume can be utilized. Different capacity periods are often available, for example, daily, weekly, monthly, yearly contracts and even multi-year contracts. In Europe, the different capacity periods are set through different procedures, but there are usually some regulatory constraints concerning the capacity volume associated with each period, and the contracts may present different tariff structures.

Flat consumers tend to prefer longer-term capacity, whereas more volatile consumers tend to prefer shorter-term capacity. Shorter capacity periods actually mean higher flexibility, as the shippers' commitments are shorter. In fact, it gives shippers higher capacity to wait and see before making flow decisions.

Regarding frequencies, the capacity contracted ($m^3/\Delta T$) means different services: it is a volume (m^3) that may be used during a specific period (ΔT), for example, an hour or a day. Shorter periods to use the capacity contracted (ΔT) decrease the shippers' flexibility. In Europe, the frequency of capacity services is regulated, and the network operators are rarely allowed to offer different kinds of frequencies.

1.1.3　Capacity Allocation Methods: The Shippers' Ordering Mechanism

The access to capacity depends on the access right guaranteed by 'Third Party Access' (TPA) rights, but also on the conditions and the methods of capacity allocation. In Europe, there are various methods to define and to allocate the available capacity. Nevertheless, this allocation may be divided into two main groups: auction methods and regulated methods. In an explicit auction,[17] the price starts at a minimum price; if there is more demand than available capacity, the prices rise until the demand decreases enough to be equivalent to the available capacity (Beckman, 2010).

Among the regulated methods, the two frequently used methods in the EU are pro rata and first-come-first-served. The pro rata allocation is a non-market mechanism in that, if the demand exceeds the maximum available capacity, the request of market participants will be curtailed through a specific mechanism. Two persistent problems of pro rata methodology is the incentive to shippers to overbook capacity in order to guarantee a big share of supply rate, and the risk of supply restriction to a level that makes the capacity no longer commercially interesting.

The first-come-first-served mechanism consists in fulfilling the capacity requested according to the order of receipt. The drawback of this mechanism is the high risk of capacity hoarding through shippers' overbooking, especially by the incumbents, which would create barriers to entry.

Table 5.2 shows that market-based capacity allocation is only applied in the UK and in Germany (in the case of congestion), even if it is the mechanism recommended by the EU Commission. Most of the EU countries still allocate their capacity based on the first-come-first-served principle. The pro rata mechanism is used in France in the case of congestion. In the absence of a secondary market, the first-come-first-served methodology encourages decisions to be taken in advance, and thus it allows lower short-term flexibility (KEMA, 2009). The back-pack principle actually bundles gas and transport capacity. Hence, if the gas is traded among gas shippers who have had prior access to the pipeline, such trades can be made at short notice, as the transport capacity is bundled too. In this

Table 5.2   EU-15/transport capacity allocation

Allocation of Transport Capacity	
First-come-first-served	BE, DK, FR (TIGF), DE, IT, NE, LU, ES
Back-pack principle[a]	AT, FI
Open subscription period[b]	FR (GRTgaz)
Pro rata	FR (congestion)
Explicit auction	DE (congestion), UK

Notes:
a. The back-pack principle follows the same logic of first-come-first-served, but it links the transport capacity to the gas as commodity, so the contract of gas also automatically transfers the capacity of transport.
b. The open subscription period is a similar mechanism to pro rata. In a situation where demand for capacity is smaller than capacity offered, all shippers can subscribe to transport capacity over a certain period.

Source: Author elaboration, data from Lapuerta and Moselle (2002) and KEMA (2009).

view, there is transport flexibility among existing gas traders, but not for new entrants.

The pro rata mechanism does not prioritize long-term capacity allocation over short-term capacity allocation.[18] However, it may impede flexibility, as it does not allocate capacity according to its value. Thus, the short-term demander can end up with just a part of the demand in the case of congestion.[19]

The capacity of auctions to offer flexibility depends on the auction scheduling. Auctions that take place long before transport use are less flexible than short-term auctions. Short-term auctions have been highlighted by the European Regulators' Group for Electricity and Gas (ERGEG) as an exemplar for the design of allocation mechanisms that drive efficiency and flexibility in transport capacity allocation: 'Flexibility can be provided by short-term capacity products offered though flexible Capacity Allocation Mechanism (CAM) such as day-ahead auctions. Flexibility can also be achieved by means of firm and interruptible short-term UIOLI [use-it-or-lose-it]'.[20]

1.1.4   Capacity Nomination Processes

In Europe, system operators must be given advanced notice of flow reservations by shippers by means of nominations. The nominations are checked before the flow reservation is made. Initially, the nominations for flow into or out of the networks must not exceed the shipper's capacity, and they must work within the networks' limits. Ideally, nominations should be supplied at least one day in advance. However, shippers have asked for greater flexibility to modify nominations at short notice. This has led to, in some systems, the creation of shorter-term nominations. Nevertheless, in Europe, short-notice nomination of firm capacity is still rare.[21]

In Europe, TSOs have implemented standardized nomination and re-nomination[22] procedures (including lead times). The nomination, when close to real time, brings flexibility to shippers at the cost of network operators having to manage the system at short notice.

Network management at short notice may be especially difficult in cases where there is congestion. In these cases, congestion management procedures are used in order to decide which shippers will have the right to use the infrastructures and which shippers will be disrupted. Thus, the flexibility given to shippers to decide on close-to-real-time infrastructure use complicates the network operator actions to make unused contracted network capacity available to other potential users.

The wrong matching between nomination and real use of network implies different approaches to defining punishments. Higher punishments for mismatching mean higher enforceability of the nomination rules. There are heterogeneous approaches, rules and penalties to enforce shippers' correct nominations, nevertheless, they are largely set through national regulations, so the real incentives to match nomination and network use depend on national determination to enforce the rules and penalties. Nomination timing impacts shippers' flexibility. In fact, shippers face costs when the real use of the network is different from the nominated flows. Countries with severe rules incentivize shippers to nominate the capacity as closely as possible to real use. Strict nomination rules and penalties decrease nomination flexibility,[23] but it tends to decrease the possibility of capacity contractual foreclosure. Countries with soft rules tend to allow higher flexibility to shippers, but they may have problems making the unused capacity available.

1.1.5   Congestion Management: Transport Rights in Overbooked Situations

There is a distinction between contractual and physical congestion. On the one hand, contractual congestion refers to the situation in which the entire capacity has been contracted but the network capacity is not completely used (ERGEG, 2008). Contractual congestion may even take place before pipeline construction. On the other hand, physical congestion refers to a situation where pipelines are actually being used at their maximum transportation capacity within safety parameters.[24]

Most GFPPs operate as middle and peak load generation, so daily and intra-day volatility should be expected, as they will be frequently called into operation at short notice. In the coming years, the significant increase in intermittent electricity generation in Europe is expected to be balanced by GFPP technologies, and thus it will lead to new patterns of congestion (Glachant and Finon, 2010).

GFPPs demanding transport flexibility, highly concentrated in the short term, may cause contractual congestions if there is an inefficient allocation of short-term transport capacity. But they may also provoke physical congestion and some supply disruption or some decrease of the volume supplied. An increased level of congestion creates uncertainty regarding the level of access available to all generators, as congestion can often result in constraining some generators. Congestion risk may become a barrier to investment, as developers, investors and bankers begin to factor this into their investment decisions. The main consequence of physical congestion is the cost of the supply disruption. On the other hand, contractual congestion costs appear as an entry barrier to new gas shippers, and/or as increases in capacity prices (and so as capacity costs for final consumers). ERGEG (2009) has pointed at the lack of effective congestion management as one of the key issues to explain the small amount and even the absence of short-term capacity.[25]

Contractual congestion
In the case of contractual congestion, the nomination, in principle, should allow the unused capacity to go back to the market. The problem is that, in the short term, there is a trade-off between the increase in flexibility associated with short-notice nominations, and the corresponding decrease of the available capacity. In order to guarantee that unused capacity will be brought back to the market, the EU regulation recommends the utilization of the 'use-it-or-lose-it' (UIOLI) principle (ERGEG, 2009). Under this principle, any unused but reserved capacity needs to be released to the market: 'The capacity holder or the system operator need offer this capacity to other interested parties in an objective, transparent, non-discriminatory and effective way'.[26] The UIOLI mechanism aims at maximizing the usability of pipelines and also to reveal the willingness of shippers to hoard capacity. In order to avoid contractual congestion ERGEG (2009) has underlined the importance of release programmes. This recommendation focuses on the countries where the gas market is strongly dominated by incumbents, and where they have also contracted in the long term a significant part of transmission capacity.

Physical congestion

Physical congestion happens when network operators actually sell more capacity than the infrastructure may make available, and the shippers, who have the right to ask for the service, cannot use the service contracted. In the case of physical congestion,[27] the network operator needs to take some measures in order to guarantee the security of the network.[28] In this case, some nominated gas flows will be transported and some will not. In the physical congestion context, the choice of which nominations will be respected may be regulated or decided on through trades in the capacity market. Under the EU regulatory framework, there are two sets of short-term tools[29] aiming to deal with physical congestion: first, the regulated tools that reallocate resources under a defined set of rules; and second, the secondary market that allows shippers to trade transport capacity in order to allocate resources. Although the EU guidelines have strongly commended the market tools, they have actually created stronger congestion management rules. Physical congestion management may actually be a strong source of uncertainty, as the shipper contracting capacity may not be able to use the service.

Regulated tools

In the case of physical congestion, three different mechanisms are applied in EU countries in order to decide which shippers will be served, and it depends on the regulated capacity contract. It may be decided according to pro rata, first-come-first-served or capacity auction methods. Moreover, Lapuerta and Moselle (2002) believe that the choice of capacity type may also depend on the level of physical congestion: '[I]n a highly congested system the value of additional capacity may be so high as to justify the use of relatively inflexible capacity definition, while maximum flexibility would be appropriate for a slack of system'.[30] The regulated tools to manage congestion are actually defined by the regulated capacity contract, which gives different priority rights to shippers according to different criteria.

Secondary market

The secondary market of transport capacity may be a tool to manage congestion, through which the transport capacity could be reallocated more efficiently. The mechanisms of UIOLI and release programmes have been seen as regulated mechanisms to simulate secondary markets, in order to avoid gas foreclosure, which may be caused by contractual congestion. The impact of regulated measures may obstruct the development of secondary markets, as it may drive down capacity prices.

Article 5 of EC 715/2009 (EC, 2009b) specifies that contractual congestion management should be made through market-based methods. The TSO should offer unused capacity on the primary market at least on a day-ahead basis through interruptible capacity, and shippers who have capacity contracts and wish to resell or sublet their unused contracted capacity on the secondary market should be entitled to do so.

The EU Commission has underlined the importance of developing a secondary market in Article 8, which states that TSOs must take reasonable steps to allow capacity rights to be freely tradable and to facilitate such trade. In order to achieve this objective, the EU TSO directives (in particular the Second and Third Directives) explain the need for harmonization and procedures for trade in TSOs' transportation contracts.[31]

1.2 COMPATIBILITY OF GAS TRANSPORT SERVICES AND ELECTRICITY GAS DEMAND SHORT-TERM VOLATILITY

Capacity contracts timing can be quite different in practice and in theory, but in Europe most of the capacity is sold on a yearly basis. Shorter-term contracts exist in most of the countries but they are usually more expensive.[32] Moreover, monthly and daily capacity prices often present components that include seasonal variations, so that prices are frequently higher for winter periods. The mechanisms to do so may be the addition of a premium for capacities reserved in winter or discounts to the capacity in summer. These seasonal criteria are quite effective in dealing with the dynamics of household gas demand; however, the dynamics of GFPP gas demand is much closer to the dynamics of electricity demand. In electricity demand, one may observe a seasonal component, but its amplitude is lower than the household heating demand. Moreover, the electricity demand has larger weekly and daily volatility than heating demand.

The availability of gas transport is a necessary condition to run a power plant, so there are two possibly problematic mismatches between electricity and gas industries: first, in the long run, the current mechanisms of gas transport capacity allocation may increase the uncertainty of electricity generators, which do not have the right to secure the transport capacity in the long term; second, in the short term, electricity dispatching is decided on a much shorter-term basis than gas transport nomination scheduling. Thus, there is significant potential for mismatching between decisions on gas transport use and electricity demand.

The two types of mismatching are detailed in the next subsections. First, mismatching under short-term constraints of electricity market and gas transport nomination is described. Second, long-term contracts are analysed. In this regard, it will be shown that EU anti-trust rules have restricted the possibility of some long-term gas transport contracts.

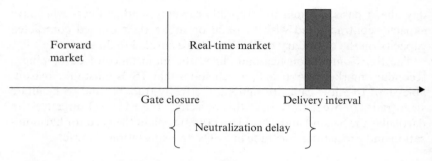

Source: Author elaboration, data from Maupas (2008).

Figure 5.2   Summary of electricity wholesale markets

1.2.1   The Time Mismatch between Gas Transport Capacity Allocation and Electricity Market Decisions

There are strong heterogeneities among the electricity markets of EU countries. Wholesale electricity markets are, in fact, a sequence of several markets. The sequence of markets serves to organize the interactions between a number of modules by either merging or separating them (Saguan, 2007; Maupas, 2008). These market modules include a future market, a day-ahead forward market, a congestion management mechanism, a reserve market and a balancing market. It is also possible to find explicit markets for transmission capacity and markets for long-term generation capacity.

Figure 5.2 synthesizes the sequence of electricity markets. Nonetheless, one of the general consequences of liberalized electricity markets is the possibility of short-term decisions regarding power plant generation and dispatching. In this context, the delay between decisions and real-time dispatches may be less than one hour.

Gas-fired power plants are generators frequently used to attend to peak demand and for back-up generation. It means that the short-term electricity market is important in the output decisions of GFPPs, and consequently in the decision to use transport capacity, to use storage and to use line-pack.[33] Thus, we can split the technologies into two groups: one group of flexible technologies, which may respond to randomness after the closing of the forward market, and another group of inflexible technologies, which cannot start up after gate closure. GFPPs, being flexible technologies, are frequently utilized to balance the intra-day electricity market. The short notice regarding when and how much a gas-fired power plant would run, brings a new difficulty to shippers' decisions, when the gas transport nominations need to be made long in advance. As transport nomination is daily, intra-day decisions may bring problems to shippers. Moreover, there is a small delay between GFPPs' decisions on gas consumption and their actual consumption, and so with regard to the use of gas transport capacity. This small delay increases the difficulty to apply rules such as UIOLI to gas transport capacity.

Another problem in gas daily capacity contracts concerns the time basis of the electricity product, which is usually hourly. This causes mismatches between what gas-fired power plants need in a transport capacity product, and what is offered.[34]

1.2.2 Observed Failures in Allocation Capacity Generated by the Interaction between Gas and Electricity Markets

As natural gas is the fuel that runs GFPPs, there is a clear interaction between gas and electricity industry contracts. The mismatching of long-term contract periods faced by many GFPPs may have two sources: first, the liberalized electricity market requires long-term contracts to sell new power generators, and second, EU anti-trust rules act against long-term contracts.

Long-term contracts, as claimed by New Institutional Economics theory, should aim to decrease transactions costs in the presence of asset specificities. Hauteclocque and Glachant (2009) show that managing asset specificities is one of the main economic reasons for long-term contracts in the electricity industry. A similar reasoning can be applied to the gas industry, as described by Crocker and Masten (1996) and Mulherin (1986). However, long-term contracts have also been identified as a tool for market foreclosure by the European Commission (Hauteclocque, 2009).[35]

Concerning gas-fired power plants, long-term contracts can be seen as an efficient coordination mechanism in different parts of the chain: buying gas supply, buying gas transport capacity and selling electricity. The power plant generator often adopts long-term contracts for selling electricity, and financial credit is frequently needed. However, if the long-term gas transport contract is forbidden, we observe a misalignment of GFPP contracts. The difference in contract periods in electricity and gas industries may increase the uncertainty about the capacity of power plants to hedge electricity long-term contracts. On the one hand, electricity producers look for contracts for 15 or 20 years to sink the high fixed costs of investments. On the other hand, gas transport contracts tend to be constrained to smaller intervals, usually around a year.

Moreover, as explained by Hauteclocque (2009), energy regulations have dissociated supply and transport capacity markets, and therefore they do not recognize long-term priority rights as an economical condition to develop the gas industry. In other words, the uncertainty concerning long-term contracts in the EU and the role of DG-COMP in the electricity sector, as discussed by Hauteclocque (2009),[36] increases in the case of gas-fired power plants. GFPPs that need to contract transport capacity of existing networks are subject to a set of constraints, aiming to guarantee Third Party Access principles. As a consequence of many network access rules, there is no guarantee that capacity will be available to gas-fired power plants, even if it was contracted. In the long term, the uncertainty of having transport capacity available comes from the constraints of capacity allocation rules. In the short term, the uncertainty is a consequence of possible congestion and the corresponding congestion management tools.

2   Competition Between the Flexibility Provided by Gas Transport Networks and Other Tools Offering Flexibility

We may observe that the gas industry has different mechanisms by which to offer flexibility. For instance, gas flexibility can be acquired from storage infrastructures, liquid spot markets, or the use of pipeline storage. Regardless of the tool utilized to provide flexibility, it is clear that the gas transport network is central to the flexibility of the gas industry. The physical properties of natural gas allow flexibility by means of pressure management, and it may provide two kinds of physical flexibility: mobility and storability. The changes in pressure compress natural gas so the pressure differences drive gas motion. The transport network is the central infrastructure to carry gas and to offer flexibility to shippers. The network has been the main mechanism to carry gas, and thus an essential part of the gas industry chain to allow commodity trade. On the other hand, the use of the transport network is also a necessary condition to provide flexibility in the gas system.

First, as discussed in the last section, network services are complementary to other flexibility tools, such as underground storage, liquefied natural gas (LNG) infrastructures and gas trade. As network services are the main mechanism to connect different sites the use of flexibility tools that are not physically connected to the demand depends on the use of the network as a complementary service.[37] Also, gas network services may directly deliver flexibility through line-pack storage. In this way network services may also be competitive to other flexibility tools. Gas transport networks actually offer two different kinds of services through the same infrastructure, and these two services are rivals. Moreover, the increase in the economic value of flexibility associated with the new players in the demand and supply sides of the gas system has increased the demand for this service.

It is worth remembering that provision for flexibility has an actual cost, as it subtracts the use of the infrastructure to the available resources to offer transport services. The use of network infrastructures by a shipper, using flexibility or transport services, decreases the available services to other users, thus the offer of flexibility or transport services by networks has an opportunity cost. The regulated framework constrains the use of infrastructures, determining the transport and the flexibility services that the network may offer (Keyaerts et al., 2011).

The network balancing system is the main set of rules defining the use of the network as storage, which is by definition a competitive service to other kinds of storage and even to spot trade itself. Network adjustments defined by balancing rules may strongly impact the gas industry, first, because this key source of flexibility impacts infrastructure allocation, and second, because it may inhibit the development of other sources of flexibility by non-regulated parts of the gas industry. In other words, if the cost of network adjustments is misallocated, it may impact not just on the network service efficiency, but also on the development of other non-regulated infrastructures and even on the gas spot market itself.

2.1   PIPELINE STORAGE AND BALANCING RULES

The balancing rules in Europe have determined the duties of TSOs regarding supply and demand temporal adjustment. TSOs may use different tools to adjust this gas volume: they may trade gas, they may use underground storage or they may use re-gasification facilities. However, the main (or the first) tool utilized by TSOs has been gas storage inside the pipelines. The physical characteristics of natural gas networks allow some flexibility about how much gas is kept inside the pipes, called line-pack flexibility. The use of line-pack flexibility by TSOs to balance gas flows is not costless and, depending on the balancing rules, this allocation may be inefficient and may affect the market for other flexibility tools.

2.1.1   Production of Line-pack Flexibility

The production of line-pack flexibility depends on the pressure that gas pipelines can manage and that compressor stations are able to input into the system. On the one hand, the natural gas is carried because of the pressure differential among points. On the other hand, the natural gas is stored inside the pipeline when this pressure differential is not too high.

Physical transport capacity is the main product offered by a pipeline. It is the result of the association of the two basic elements: ducts and compressors. However, transport capacity can change along the pipeline if the exogenous variables change. According to IEA (1994), the capacity of a uniform length of pipeline is determined by pressure differential between its ends, and its diameter. With the same pressure differential, larger diameters mean increase of transport capacity, more than proportionally. As the diameter increases, capacity rises faster than the cross-sectional area of the pipe, since gas moving in a larger pipeline suffers proportionally less frictional drag from the wall. Hence, the increase in diameter means a larger increase in the pipeline volume. If the pipeline size is constant, the maximum transport capacity is determined by the maximum differential of pressure between the extreme points. It is also limited by the pipe wall features.

Transport capacity can be seen as the capacity to transport a certain number of molecules of gas or a quantity of energy. The two concepts become equivalent if a constant and equivalent gas quality is assumed. The capacity of transport is also measured over a determined period. It is the quantity of gas or energy that can be transported in such a period. So, besides the gas volume, the velocity at which gas can be transported is another important variable in the determination of transport capacity. However, gas velocity has its own limitations. It needs to be kept below the maximum allowable velocity in order to prevent pipe erosion, noise or other variation problems. In most pipelines, the recommended value for gas velocity in the transmission pipelines is 40 to 50 per cent of the erosion velocity.[38]

It should be remembered that the maximum transport capacity of a pipeline is not the same as the maximum efficient transport capacity of a pipeline, because there is a cost of energy lost from friction.[39] Therefore, what is called 'gas transport congestion' can be seen either as an inefficient transportation zone or as the actual incapability of transporting.

According to Shaw (1994), pipeline system optimization has two physical constraints and one economic constraint. The physical constraints can be explicit or implicit. Constraints are explicit when observed directly by the user, like maximum and minimum pressure, and flows at a certain point in the system.[40] Constraints are implicit when originated in the modelling of compressor and pipe control data,[41] to define the range of safe network operation. The economic constraint is associated with the cost of transporting gas, especially the cost of compression, as pressure increases can be technically possible but economically inefficient.

Under any of these constraints, when the pipeline does not work properly to minimize gas transportation cost that constraint is said to generate a congestion problem. The first and simpler kind of gas transport congestion is a demand for gas transport larger than the gas transport capacity. It occurs when an increase of gas flow in the system conflicts with safety conditions because the maximum possible pressure has already been reached. It happens if an increase in gas injection into the pipeline decreases the pressure differential (upstream vis-à-vis downstream) to a lower level, being lower than the frictional factor. It comes from the fact that it is not enough to inject gas to make it flow in the pipe given the resulting pressure differential. It happens when it is no longer possible to further increase that pressure at the injection point. However, transport congestion can also occur when the decrease of pressure differential does not lead to stopping the gas flow, but to decreasing the delivery flow or increasing the delivery pressure. Congestion can also be caused by the economic inefficiency of increasing pressures. This is the case when one can technically increase the gas flow but at a non-optimal cost (larger than the increase of benefits), as explained by Menon:

> There is a limit to the number of compression stations that can be installed in a given pipeline system, since the horsepower required continues to increase with flow rate and, hence, the capital cost and operating costs as well. At some point, the costs increase at a very high rate compared to the increase inflow rate. Each pipe size has a particular volume that can be economically transported based upon cost.[42]

The decrease in pressure ratio at inlet and outlet points can be undesirable as negative congestion effects. It may carry inefficiencies or even block the transport system. However, decreased pressure ratio in a pipeline can also be desirable as storage: the 'line-packing service': storing gas inside the pipeline network by boosting the line pressure, employing the flexibility allowed by the range of possibilities to use the same network (Menon, 2005).

Moreover, a pipeline company can use interconnected pipeline segments to store gas. These new segments of pipes are called loops.[43] The line-pack is a storage tool characterized by a fast process of injections and withdrawals, and it is often used to balance the system in the short term. However, it has a limited capacity and is a costly type of long-term storage resource, as line-pack capacity is constrained by the pipeline diameters and the limits of pipeline pressure.

Thus, we can observe that, while transport capacity depends on the pressure differential between inlet and outlet points, line-pack storage actually increases when this differential of pressure decreases, by increasing the pressure in the entire system. Consequently, there is a trade-off in the use of the same infrastructure. Loosely, assuming the same infrastructure features, the higher the pressure differential, the larger the transport capacity; and the lower the pressure differential, the greater the gas stored inside the pipeline.

2.2   MANAGING PIPELINE OPERATION: BALANCING CASE STUDIES

Line-pack is the main tool used for daily balancing services, but it is not the only one. Storage, gas imports, re-gasification and spot markets are also utilized by TSOs. The preference for one or another depends on the market structure, on the pre-existent infrastructure and, especially, on the balancing rules. As we will see in our three case studies, balancing rules are strongly interrelated with infrastructures. The UK has balancing rules based on spot markets; Spain has rules based on LNG charges; and Italy has rules based on shippers' storage portfolios. The choice of preferred flexibility for TSO balancing services is strongly correlated, and even reinforces, the countries' choice of the preferred flexibility tools.

Within the balancing period, the flexibility necessary to balance the network is used at the expense of the TSO, and it enters the transport tariff as a cost to be socialized to all shippers:

> 'Balancing period' means the period within which the off-take of an amount of natural gas, expressed in units of energy, must be offset by every network user by means of the injection of the same amount of natural gas into the transmission network in accordance with the transportation contract or the network code.[44]

In other words, the network must ensure for each shipper who buys transport capacity that the network will be balanced for free, if they have equal injections and withdrawals during the day. The European Commission also recommends a daily balancing:[45]

> The network code on gas balancing shall provide that the balancing period for a transmission system is a standardized daily interval, at the end of which network users are financially settled for any deviations, as accumulated over the course of the preceding 24 hours, between their inputs into and off-takes from the balancing zone.[46]

In the three case studies, the balancing period is the day. In this context, we see that within the balancing period the cost of adjustment is subsidized through TSOs' cost allocation. There is, thus, a clear incentive to shippers to allow the balancing to be made by the TSO, at least within the balancing period. This in turn decreases the trade of other adjustment tools within the balancing period. Consequently, the TSO who is responsible for the system balancing becomes the main (or only) demander of adjustment tools within the balancing period. As we will see in the UK, Spain and Italy, they first use line-pack storage, and after that they may demand other tools (typically, the tool that the regulatory framework defines as the most favoured).[47]

The case studies will show that the cost of balancing may be just the line-pack, but also it may include underground and LNG storage costs, or even short-term trade transaction costs. In addition, in Italy and Spain, the mechanism of cost socialization through the TSO's balancing services may be also observed through the margins of tolerance. Margins of tolerance are extra services bundled in transport services (which imply that shippers buy flexibility implicit in transport services). When balancing services cross the limit of free bundled services, they are paid for by balancing charges (the cost of balancing should be covered by the balancing charges). In this regard, the mechanisms to charge inter-day balancing are different in each of the studied countries.

2.2.1 The UK: Balancing Services Based on Supply Swing

The UK gas system operates a daily balancing regime in one single zone. Any residual intra-day imbalances are contractually cleared by the action of the TSO to balance the system. The UK TSO may use different tools to balance the network system: 'The tools available to National Grid Gas to allow it to balance the system include line-pack, the (On the Day Commodity Market) OCM, storage injections and withdrawals, interruptible capacity buyback and firm capacity buyback'.[48] However, the regulated tools dedicated to the TSO balancing are line-pack and LNG peak-shaving,[49] the first one being the usual tool, and the second one applied only in extreme conditions. There is a strong use of line-pack as a tool to manage balancing (KEMA, 2009). However, the use of line-pack by the TSO is also regulated. It has a free allowance of line-pack change of 2.4 mcm (million cubic metres) per day, which can be used to manage system imbalances.[50] These two kinds of storage are the quickest available tools, and they are mainly restricted to within-day use.

Figure 5.3 plots the maximum range in any day in each month between the highest and lowest hourly NTS (national transmission system) line-pack.[51] We can observe that the range can achieve more than 25 mcm/day, which is almost 50 per cent of a total LNG peak unit and almost 30 per

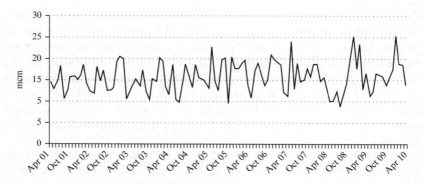

Note: The line-pack can be defined as follows: $Line\text{-}pack_t = Line\text{-}pack_{t+1} + Injection - Withdrawal.$

Source: Author elaboration, data from National Grid (2010b).

Figure 5.3 UK/maximum daily range of within-day line-pack changes

cent of the total daily UK storage withdrawal capacity (National Grid, 2010b).[52]

Moreover, we may underline the supply swing as the second daily source of flexibility. The supply swing may be observed by the change in the beach supply (North Sea gas production arriving from offshore pipelines to the network system) or by the utilization of the intra-day market. Supply swings are mainly provided by national fields (UK Continental Shelf – UKCS), whose daily swings can be up to 18 per cent, and the Norway fields, whose daily swings achieve 15 per cent.

The UK underground storage capacity has high daily withdrawal rate/working capacity. Moreover, the UK has, after Spain, the highest daily LNG re-gasification injection capacity. Besides the underground storage and the LNG re-gasification capacity, the national gas system also includes three LNG peak-shaving facilities. Part of their services is offered at regulated tariffs, and is dedicated to balance the network:

National Grid Liquefied Natural Gas Storage (NG LNG) own three LNG storage sites; these are at Avonmouth, Glenmavis and Partington. Historically, these sites have competed commercially in the storage of gas, and have also derived part of their revenues from the provision of price regulated services to National Grid Gas (NGG) and Scotia Gas Networks (SGN).

All three sites have supplied operating margins (OM) services to NGG. In addition, Glenmavis supplies LNG by tanker to SGN to serve the needs of the Scottish Independent Undertakings (SIUs); and Avonmouth, has in the past provided Constrained LNG. All of these services are provided at prices regulated by Special Licence Condition C3 (these prices are referred to as the 'C3 prices') of the gas transporter's licence.[53]

2.2.2 Italy: Balancing Service High Priority in the Use of Storage Withdrawal Capacity

In Italy, physical balancing as well as commercial balancing is based on storage, namely line-pack storage and underground storage. Imbalance charges are differentiated for shippers with storage portfolio and without it. As in the UK, shippers are charged for imbalances on a daily basis, but only if they break a limit.

The TSO uses a fixed price as a basis for imbalance settlements, and there is no difference between imbalances caused by over-injection or over-withdrawal.[54] Physically, the TSO has the priority to use an important part of the storage, as well as the withdrawal and injections rates. Within the day, the first tool applied by the TSO is the line-pack, and underground storage is used only if line-pack is not enough to balance the system.

2.2.3 Spain: Balancing Based on Bundled Line-pack Capacity and Priority for Re-gasification

In Spain, as well as the two other countries, there is just one balancing zone. Energy is traded in a virtual point, as in the UK. In this context, shippers may trade gas at the Spanish balancing point within the day to adjust their balance.

As there is not much available storage capacity, the main balancing tools are line-pack and LNG storage. As we underlined before, it is important to note that the transport capacity that the shippers pay for includes the line-pack costs. In addition, the system operator organizes a daily auction to restore any deviation to an acceptable level.

As in Italy, the Spanish balancing system has tolerances, allowing shippers to use the line-pack implicit in the transport service. It means that the shipper can store up to 50 per cent of its daily capacity in order to use it the following day. The Spanish balancing equation, elaborated by the author using data from the Spanish National Energy Commission (CNE, 2008), is as follows:

$$B_d = B_{d-1} + I_d - W_d - A_d \pm M_d$$

where:
B_d is the amount of gas in the line-pack at the end of the day d;
B_{d-1} is the amount of gas kept in the line-pack from the day before;

I_d is the volume injected during the day d;
W_d is the volume withdrawn during the day d;
A_d is the gas auto-consumed by the network during the day d;
M_d is the gas bought or sold after it was injected into the network during the day d.

We observe that in order to avoid paying any penalty, the B_d of each shipper needs to be greater than 0 and lower than 0.5 of its capacity. The difference between $B_d = 0$ and $B_d = 0.5 *$ *Capacity* is the degree of 'tolerance' that the shipper has in the balancing mechanisms. In addition, shippers have up to five days of contracted capacity in LNG facilities. It is thus clear that the balancing approach is largely based on LNG re-gasification capacity.

The Spanish case includes different fees: if there is over- or under-use of capacity, and if the shipper in the gas portfolio has LNG storage. In this view, it is similar to the Italian scheme, where the balancing principles are based on the storage portfolio of the shippers. In Spain, as one of the main sources of flexibility is LNG storage in the tanks, it is seen as a valuable back-up to the deficit of gas in the network. Excess and deficit of LNG storage are also penalized: the former is regulated; the latter is negotiated and depends on the LNG terminal (CNE, 2008).

3   Conclusions

This chapter has shown how the regulated use of infrastructures may provide more or less flexibility to shippers. Network flexibility is actually a choice of infrastructure usage. That infrastructure can provide more or less gas mobility or gas storage. Different levels of mobility and storage allow flexibility to be delivered to shippers. Players may then wait and see before making consumption decisions. It allows shippers to change their market strategies, by changing gas injections and withdrawals, and gas localization and timing.

The approach utilized to bid for storage and mobility services may also bring more or less flexibility. Mechanisms to offer network services that favour long-term decisions are less flexible than mechanisms that allow short-term modifications. Thus, the flexibility services that may be offered by network infrastructures depend on the mobility and storability services offered, as summarized in Figure 5.4.

The flexibility provided to shippers may involve the timing of gas withdrawal, as the network may offer storage services. It may involve the choice of geographical location to inject or withdraw gas. It may also involve the time lag between the notification of an infrastructure use and

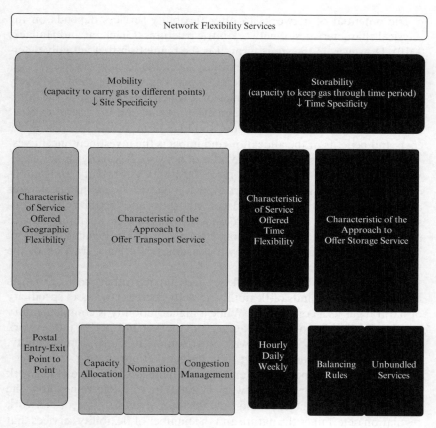

Source: Author elaboration.

Figure 5.4   Flexibility services that may be provided by a gas network

real use. All these flexibility services are tools allowing shippers to wait and see before the actual withdrawal of gas.

The networks may provide more or less flexible services, storage or geographical flexibility. In addition, the mechanism to offer the services may also provide more or less flexibility in the access to these services.[55] As a result, the flexibility offered by the network to shippers comes from a combination of the network service features and from the definition of access to these services. In Europe, the characteristics of the services that a network may offer, as well as the practical access to these services, are constrained by national network regulations and the EU regulatory framework.

The potential of networks to offer flexibility services depends on the physical characteristics of network infrastructures (Glachant and Hallack, 2010). However, in the short term, it is the regulation that actually determines the level and the type of flexibility available to shippers.

In Europe, the offer of the different forms of network flexibility is largely constrained by the regulatory framework, which determines how the infrastructures can be utilized. This regulation impacts on the use of existent infrastructures in the short, medium and long term. It also touches on the costs and benefits of the allocation and impacts the investment incentives.

This chapter has shown that the offer of network flexibility entails costs. Within the same infrastructure, more flexibility (storability and mobility) means less available transport capacity. Networks are infrastructures offering at least two kinds of services: transport and flexibility. The consumption by one consumer of a unit of transport or flexibility service prevents consumption by other consumers: it acts as a rival consumption. The units of service consumed by a consumer subtract a fraction of the total available resources.

Moreover, the offer of network services impacts other parts of the gas industry. The two kinds of flexibility actually decrease the asset specificity of natural gas as a commodity. While a higher mobility is complementary to other flexibility tools (e.g., storage, spot market and LNG), the network line-pack is mainly competing with other sources of short-term flexibility. These two kinds of services have different market positioning.

The increasing appetite for flexible flows increases the value of network flexible services. However, network regulation still determines how the infrastructures may be used and how flexibility may be offered. Network regulation determines the nature and the number of flexibility services that networks, in fact, may deliver to shippers. Regulation influences the decisions that shippers can make vis-à-vis network investment. From a long-term perspective, the rules framing the short-term usage of infrastructures strongly impact the development of the network and of the gas system.

NOTES

1. At the EU level, the set of rules that define the use of gas networks are outlined by Article 6 of Regulation (EC) No. 715/2009 on conditions for access to the natural gas transmission networks. Before that, European regulation (EC No. 1775/2005) had left the establishment of network rules to each country.
2. The application of the still ongoing Third Energy Package has changed these nationally based rules, and the EC, through ACER (Agency for the Cooperation of Energy Regulators) guidelines, has tried to make the rules more EU oriented (e.g., ACER, 2011a, 2011b).
3. At least during the period between World War II and the 1990s the EU gas industry

was characterized by vertical integration of publically owned monopolies (European Parliament, 2009).

4. There is a comprehensive literature regarding the economic concept of flexibility and economic value of flexibility (e.g., Saleh et al., 2009). Here flexibility is understood by its general meaning in order to take into account all the services enabling players to wait to define their final position.

5. Site specificity is defined as 'where successive stations are located in a cheek-by-jowl relation to each other so as to economize on inventory and transportation expenses' (Williamson, 1991, p. 281). Where there is high site specificity, there is a high cost to dislocating a good between demand and offer sites.

6. Temporal asset specificity is concerned with the extent to which timely performance by a supplier is critical to the value (Artz and Brush, 2000). It means the value of a good strongly changes according to delivery timing. However, as explained by Joskow (1988), temporal asset specificity can be seen as a different specificity or as a form of site specificity, because as Williamson (1979) underlined site specificity can be seen as a 'presentation' specificity where presentation has reference to efforts to make or render present in place or time.

7. Within-day services offering line-pack to TSOs (Transmission System Operators) can be seen in the Netherlands, for example.

8. National Network Codes are the rules that oblige TSOs to offer the same service to different customers under equal contractual terms and conditions. This may be done by means of harmonized transportation contracts or a common Network Code approved by competent national authorities (Talus, 2010).

9. EC (2009b), Article 14.

10. In other words, given a network, the capacity that can be offered by the operator depends on the features of the capacity (Lapuerta and Moselle, 2002; Keyaerts et al., 2011).

11. They also distinguish tariff type and capacity type. The first concerns the way that the tariff is calculated, the second means the rights acquired by the shipper when a capacity contract is signed.

12. Postal transport capacity can be also called postal stamp or postage stamp.

13. Lapuerta and Moselle (2002, p. 56).

14. It is interesting to note that an advantage of point-to-point methodology is the simplicity and so the higher possibility to verify if there are any discriminatory actions, as explained by Lyon (2000).

15. Site specificity, according to Williamson's (1989) classification, increases transaction costs and so the costs to use market coordination.

16. Lapuerta and Moselle (2002, p. 60). The relative merit of different systems will depend both on network topology and on the extent and nature of congestions.

17. There is a substantial difference between explicit and implicit auctions. Implicit auctions bundle natural gas as commodity and network services. In the EU context, implicit auctions have been considered only for short-term periods (such as the National Balancing Point [NBP] example in the UK, a virtual trading location for the sale and purchase and exchange of UK natural gas) (Neveling, 2011). The characteristics of auctions linking capacity and gas (implicit auctions) have been discussed in the context of balancing services, especially in the NBP case (Heather, 2010; Vazquez et al., 2012).

18. As with pro rata, open subscription periods do not prioritize long-term capacity allocation over short-term capacity allocation.

19. The difference between pro rata and open subscription periods is in regard to the timing of capacity reservation. If the timing to reserve capacity is tight, the flexibility provided is low.

20. ERGEG (2009, p. 6).

21. One example of short-notice nomination has been observed in the UK Interconnector Pipeline, which has created two classes of nomination: firm as the highest priority and reasonable endeavours as the lower priority. A third priority was later (2000) created

as interruptible capacity. This enables shippers to utilize capacity above their limits if system conditions result in a total available capacity higher than the original firm capacity (Futyan, 2006).

22. 'Re-nomination' means the subsequent reporting of a corrected nomination. 'Re-nomination is a flexibility tool that permits a shipper to adjust day-ahead their estimate/ nomination by an intra-day (re-) nomination' (EC, 2006, Second Phase, para. 854, p. 258).

23. Decreased nomination flexibility may be also understood as increased mismatching costs between nomination and real flows.

24. The different concepts of congestion depend on the transport capacity definition and on the specificities of capacity localization rules and balancing rules (which are detailed in the next section). For further details concerning transport capacity, see Lapuerta and Moselle (2002); for a discussion on the impact of UK balancing rules, see Lapuerta (2003).

25. In the USA there are intra-day pipeline markets; even they are more volatile and less liquid than day-ahead markets; they are in major use by GFPP shippers.

26. Talus (2010, p. 105).

27. Physical congestion in natural gas may mean different things, from changes in variable costs to completely stopping gas flows. Physical congestion depends on the pressure differential. Thus, in Europe, network operators need to guarantee flows, final pressure standards and flows under security margins.

28. It is interesting to note that the overbooking of transport capacity has been proposed as a tool (and used by the UK) to deal with contractual congestion, as underlined Moselle and White (2011).

29. In the long term, investment is the main instrument recommended by ERGEG (2008).

30. Lapuerta and Moselle (2002, p. 61).

31. No public analysis by the EU Commission was found on secondary market development specifically addressing the need for definition and firm control of property rights.

32. There are some exceptions when the short-term prices are lower than long-term ones. It happens when the short-term expected demand for transport service is lower than long-term demand. For instance, it was observed in some countries in 2008 and in 2009, as a consequence of the worldwide economic crisis, which drove some short-term capacity prices down.

33. Just as an example, Italy's GFPPs represent between 35 and 54 per cent of the marginal power plants (IEA, 2007).

34. The mismatching between transport nomination and gas-fired power plant demand have been frequently compensated by networks through the offer of daily balancing, as we discuss in depth in the next section.

35. This trade-off is also discussed by institutional economists with regard to the importance of long-term contracts reducing the risk of ex post hold-up in the presence of specificity (i.e., reduction of transaction costs) versus decrease in flexibility and ability to react to changes. This discussion relating to the natural gas industry can be seen in Crocker and Masten (1988) and Glachant and Hallack (2009).

36. The legal status of long-term priority access rights still remains unclear and creates a risk of long-standing legal disputes (Hauteclocque, 2009).

37. GFPPs may be physically linked with a storage facility and/or LNG re-gasification without any relation to the transmission network, so that the flexibility may be provided directly by these infrastructures. However, this implies high transaction costs, and the infrastructures need to have vertical (or quasi-vertical) integration. Furthermore, it is a mechanism outside the gas market, and not the usual mechanism.

38. As a rule of thumb, pipe erosion begins to occur when the velocity of flow exceeds the value given by the equation: $V_e = C/\rho G0.5$, where: V_e is the flow velocity; C is an empirical constant; ρG is the mixture (gas) density (Salama, 2000).

39. As explained by André (2010), the pipeline diameter, pressure and topology combination may lead to different outputs. The optimization of a pipeline depends on diameter,

number and characteristics of entry and exit points as well as the topology and compressor stations' power and location.

40. Examples are maximum supply pressure or minimum contracted delivery flow.
41. Examples are wall thickness and maximum compression, maximum and minimum compressor flow, maximum and minimum compression ratio and so on.
42. Menon (2005, p. 180).
43. 'The purpose of a pipe loop that is installed in a segment of a pipeline is to essentially reduce the amount of pressure drop in that section of the pipe. By doing so, the overall pressure drop in the pipeline will be reduced. This in turn, will result in an increased pipeline flow rate at the same inlet pressure. Alternatively if the flow rate is kept constant, reduction in total pressure required will cause reduction in pumping horsepower' (Menon, 2005, p. 177).
44. ERGEG (2006, p. 11).
45. After consultation with stakeholders, the Agency for the Cooperation of Energy Regulators (ACER) proposes, even if in an unclear way, the possibility of TSOs establishing some within-day balancing rules. However, 'this shall only occur where, in order to ensure system integrity and to minimize the need for the TSO to take balancing actions, it is necessary to incentivize network users to take appropriate balancing actions during the day' (ACER, 2011b, p. 12).
46. ACER (2011b, p. 12).
47. For more detail on this issue, see Hallack (2011, Chapters 5 and 6).
48. Heather (2010, p. 9).
49. Peak-shaving is shifting demand from 'peak times' (e.g., noon) to times with lower demand (e.g., night) and thus 'shaving' the peak.
50. In the UK, if the transport operator uses more than the 'free' allowance, they 'will incur an incentive charge (daily capped to –£30 000 for using more). This has changed since 1 April 2009 – up to 1.5 mcm National Grid Gas receives the max payment, at 2.8 it starts to incur a charge' (KEMA, 2009, p. 49).
51. For example, if the highest hourly line-pack recorded was 330 mcm and the lowest was 315 mcm in the same day, and that constituted the largest daily range in that particular month, 15 mcm would be plotted on the graph for that month.
52. The daily withdrawal capacity in the UK is 89.96 mcm (GIE, 2009c).
53. Ofgem (2011).
54. A new balancing price setting system was implemented in December 2011. However, the pricing will be still connected to a 'storage market'.
55. This could be called contractual flexibility, or agreement or service delivery flexibility. Capacity allocation and nomination and congestion management rules are actually providing an opportunity to shippers to buy network services in a flexible way. It is not the service itself that is necessarily flexible, as is the case with storability or geographical flexibility, but the mechanism to acquire the network service that may provide more or less flexibility.

PART III

EU regulation in the context of the EU target model

6.   Introduction to Part III

Michelle Hallack, Miguel Vazquez and Jean-Michel Glachant

In order to bring coherence to the various forthcoming Framework Guidelines and Network Codes, European regulators have launched a consultation process to define a gas market target model. It is a non-binding architecture aiming to provide a unified vision of the future layout of the EU gas market in 2015–20.

A gas target model should define the key characteristics of gas transactions and their institutional framework. However, in reality, it strongly interacts with how transmission capacity should be allocated in the medium and short terms, and how it should be built into the long term. There are, at the beginning of 2012, five target model reports published and currently discussed (Boltz, 2011). However, our book will only present details two of them, those having been conceived from within our ranks.

The 'MECO-S' was the first gas target model published by the Florence School of Regulation, in June 2011. The model aims to be a 'Market Enabling, Connecting and Securing (MECO-S) Model' (see 'A vision for the EU gas target model: the MECO-S model', Glachant, 2011 and Chapter 7 this volume). It was the first complete set of rules and market architecture propositions to build an EU gas target model. It has been very influential in the European energy regulation community.

Following that, another gas target model was conceived in Florence: the 'European American Model' (EURAM). The EURAM aims to improve the debate through the understanding of American gas market architecture. It also suggests how these lessons could be turned into a European model and how it would impact the European regulatory framework (especially Network Codes development) (see 'An American model for the EU gas market?', Ascari, 2011, and Chapter 8 this volume).

The three other contributions to the debate are the following. The first, *Market Design for Natural Gas: The Target Model for the Internal Market*, was published in March 2011 and produced by consulting group LECG for the Office of Gas and Electricity Markets (Ofgem). It presents different possibilities and trade-offs between gas model rules (Moselle and White,

2011). It supports the idea that the new interconnection rules should interfere as little as possible with the existing national markets. Those should be linked across EU countries through rules avoiding contractual congestion at the national borders (UIOLI/UIOUI and over-selling mechanisms are recommended).

Another report, *Target Model for the European Natural Gas Market*, was developed by Frontier Economics for GDF Suez. It first considers the objective of an EU gas target model in itself. It then provides a new vision of an efficient target model that mainly requires an industry initiative instead of a regulatory intervention. Third, it expresses concerns regarding the impact of other target models on the gas industry (Frontier Economics, 2011).

The fifth model named 'Ample, Secure and Competitive Supply' (ASCOS) was launched at the Netherlands Institute for International Affairs by CIEP (Clingendael International Energy Programme) and Jacques de Jong (the former Dutch regulator). It underlines that an EU target model should by no means offer a detailed market design (as MECO-S does), but just a broad set of principles allowing market forces to give dynamics to the process (see *CIEP Vision on the Gas Target Model*, CIEP, 2011).

As we observe, these five 'target models' were built with different objectives, and they also support quite different purposes for the EU gas target model itself. Regarding the natural gas supply side, the MECO-S model mainly supports the importance of gas price alignment among EU gas prices, where Frontier Economics, on the other hand, is concerned about the decrease of gas prices to final consumers. Security of supply has been a necessary achievement of the EU gas target model for all models. Along the same lines, new investment in pipelines has been seen as key condition for the European gas market. Long-term contracts have been underlined by the five gas target models as mechanisms to coordinate players on a long-run basis, as well as the use of several market tools (like different kinds of open season) before the investment decision.

However, there is no general agreement on the importance of long-term contracts regarding network investment and capacity allocation. EURAM, Frontier Economics and ASCOS underline long-term contracts as the main tool for investing in new capacity and for guaranteeing the required infrastructure investment. It is worth noting that EURAM proposes a centralized mechanism for long-term contracts ('Open Subscription Procedures'), in which tariffs are kept regulated to avoid any monopolistic abuse by pipelines, and where 'public interest' authorities would be able to buy capacity like any other shipper. Regarding the changes in existing long-term contracts, the LECG report mainly recommends attention to the legal and incentive impacts that a gas target model would have on current contracts. The MECO-S model does not disregard the importance of long-term contracts and open season mechanisms to reveal information, but it gives a say to public authorities in the definition of infrastructure development required at a local or European level.

Another key divergence among the models is to what extent the existing EU gas markets should be merged or coupled. Two issues arise here: the relevant size of the entry/exit regions and how to trade the cross-border capacity. Should the border capacity be implicitly or explicitly allocated? Should the 'commercial' network reflect or simplify the key physical network features in the allocation of cross-border capacity? Most of the models do not enter into details when tackling these fundamental questions. LECG, MECO-S and EURAM do so a little. LECG actually draws up a set of possibilities for network use regulation and shows their trade-offs. MECO-S proposes pushing the use of implicit auctions to solve cross-border contractual congestion, and advocates a higher network simplification, aiming to have a more unified gas pricing. EURAM underlines the risks and costs of building virtual hubs for all EU gas markets, and proposes a hybrid solution allowing market evolution to say whether and when the hubs should take place.

Thus, MECO-S and EURAM have tackled most of the questions pertinent to building a framework for the future European gas market architecture. These two proposals have both convergent and divergent points. As Chapters 7 and 8 show, the main divergence involves the degree of regulatory interference, especially in the organization of the marketplaces and the development of new infrastructures.

7. A vision for the EU gas target model: MECO-S

Jean-Michel Glachant

1   Introduction*

The discussion on a target model for European gas network access has been going on for sometime, officially starting with the conclusion of the 18th European Gas Regulatory Forum in September 2010, which invited 'The Commission and the regulators to explore, in close cooperation with system operators and other stakeholders, the interaction and interdependence of all relevant areas for Network Codes and to initiate a process establishing a gas market target model'. Based on this conclusion the Council of European Energy Regulators (CEER) started – by the end of 2010 – the process of developing a gas target model for Europe. The desired target model will provide a unifying vision on the future layout of the European gas market architecture. That vision will assist all stakeholders in quickly and efficiently implementing the Third Energy Package on the internal gas market in a consistent way.

This chapter describes a proposal for the European gas target model with a special focus on market architectures and investment. The proposed gas target model is termed MECO-S model. The MECO-S model is a 'Market Enabling, Connecting and Securing' model describing an end-state of the gas market to be achieved over time.

The MECO-S model rests on three pillars (see Figure 7.1) that share a common foundation: making sure that economical[1] investments in pipelines are realized:

- *Pillar 1:* Structuring network access[2] to the European gas grid in a way that enables functioning wholesale markets so that every European final customer is easily accessible from such a market.
- *Pillar 2:* Fostering short- and mid-term price alignment between the functioning wholesale markets by tightly connecting the markets through facilitating cross-market supply and trading and potentially

Figure 7.1 MECO-S model pillars

implementing market coupling as far as the (at any time) given infrastructure allows.
- *Pillar 3:* Enabling the establishment[3] of secure supply patterns to the functioning wholesale markets.

The MECO-S model aims at the creation of a number of functioning wholesale markets within the EU (together enabling easy access to all European final customers of gas), at connecting these markets tightly in order to maximize short- and mid-term price alignment between those markets, at enabling secure supply patterns to those markets and at making sure that all economic investments in gas transmission capacity are made.

Pillar 1 will realize the goal of enabling functioning wholesale markets. Such markets are an essential feature of the internal market since they contribute to efficiency in managing gas and gas-related assets such as supply contracts, storage and gas-fired power stations. Additionally and no less important, such markets are an essential basis for retail competition. Finally, functioning wholesale markets are a basis for market-based balancing and market coupling. Without functioning markets, both of these concepts could not be harnessed.

Pillar 1 is realized by structuring Europe into markets that are sufficiently large[4] and well connected to sources of gas[5] so that the emergence of a competitively traded wholesale market is likely. Where necessary, with a view to that goal, Member States have to create cross-border markets in order to increase market size and connectivity. Two models are presented to realize these markets, both based on the entry/exit regime: (1) market areas that implement integrated balancing zones reaching down to the final customers; and (2) trading regions that implement integrated wholesale markets that are tightly connected to national end-user zones. Both models may be used in parallel in Europe, whereby the market area model appears attractive for larger Member States and the trading region model has specific merits for smaller Member States that need to cooperate cross-border in order to gain sufficient market size and connectivity.

Pillar 2 aims at maximizing the efficiency of managing gas and gas-related assets on a European scale by making sure that the existing interconnecting infrastructure is put to the best use. The resulting tight connection of markets will lead to price alignment[6] between European markets as far as the – at any time existing– infrastructure allows. Price alignment virtually unifies all European markets by enabling cross-portfolio optimization via those markets on a European scale. Measures are foreseen so that TSOs do not suffer any loss from price alignment.[7]

Pillar 2 is first realized by implementing hub-to-hub transport products and a number of harmonization measures that make inter-market supply and trading significantly easier. The allocation of hub-to-hub transport products will be by auction for the mid- and short-term markets and by first-come-first-served for the intra-day market.

Second, it is proposed to implement pilot projects for day-ahead market coupling to explore if the theoretical benefits of market coupling can be realized in practice for gas. If so, day-ahead market coupling would become an integral part of the MECO-S model.

Pillar 3 aims at enabling secure supply patterns to the European markets. Specifically, Pillar 3 creates the preconditions for underpinning long-term supply contracts with appropriate transport products, taking into consideration that currently about 30 per cent of all gas consumed in Europe crosses more than one border point. Additionally, Pillar 3 aims at providing a market-based solution for realizing transport security of supply where collaboration with adjoining markets is required.

Pillar 3 is realized by foreseeing the execution (if demanded by shippers) of new long-term transport contracts. These contracts can be requested periodically in an open-season-style process for the full term of interest to the shipper, for example, 15 years. If in the process the demand for long-term capacity proves higher than the availability of such capacities, then capacities will be expanded by investment if economical. In order to allow for such investment, the lead time for allocating long-term capacity shall always be at least as long as the time required for expanding capacity. Since in this structure capacity can always be expanded, long-term capacity is not a scarce good any more and auctioning of that capacity can be avoided.[8] Allocation questions at the fringe[9] of the allocation problem can be solved by an optimization procedure. In order to deal with shippers interested in long-distance transport (for example, from a European border point to the next but one market) link chain products are introduced. Link chain products are packages of (hub-to-hub) transport products at several border points on a continuous route that may be requested by the shipper as a whole and are allocated at the same level of capacity on all requested border points.

After allocation they may be used as separate hub-to-hub capacities.[10] In the area of transport security of supply the instrument of the fallback capacity contract is introduced. It provides a means for Member States to secure that sufficient capacity in a neighbouring market is made and kept available in order to cater to the security needs of said Member States. Under a fallback capacity contract a Transmission System Operator (TSO) (A) of the Member State in need of redundant transport capacity (as defined by a competent authority) books the required capacity long term with a neighbouring TSO (B). TSO B charges to TSO A only that part of the capacity that is not booked by shippers directly with TSO B (hence the name 'fallback contract'). TSO A allocates the cost for this security measure to final customers in his market.

The common foundation of the MECO-S model is economic investment. Investment aims at supporting the other pillars in realizing their respective goals, for example, in contributing to the creation of functioning markets (by new interconnection to these markets) or in contributing to improved price alignment between markets (by new/expanded interconnection between these markets). Several issues are discussed in the study regarding investment, including the structuring of investment appraisal processes, the evaluation of investment in interconnection and intraconnection[11] pipelines and the financing of investment.

The key results on investment are the following:

- Investment appraisal and the allocation of long-term capacity should always (even on existing systems) be an integrated process in the style of an open season (see also above under Pillar 3).
- The quantity of capacity that shall be reserved for the mid- and short-term market shall be created (and hence invested) on top of any investment required to satisfy (economic) long-term capacity requests.[12]
- The economic appraisal of investment shall take into account the return from long-term contracts as well as the value[13] expected to be generated by price alignment due to the capacity reserved for the mid- and short-term markets. The cost for mid- and short-term capacities that are not directly recovered by tariffs shall be allocated to the beneficiaries.
- In the case that TSOs declare that they can/will not invest in an otherwise economic investment project, the project shall be tendered to the market. The scope of the tender would be to build and finance

the pipeline (or other asset) against a yearly fee paid long term. After construction, the realized project would be integrated into the operational responsibility of the respective TSO.

2 Analysis of Problems and Operationalization of Goals

The goal of this chapter is not to nicely sum up the good and the bad, the pros and the cons of the many possible angles when addressing a controversial and disputed issue such as a gas target model for the EU. Various theories, analytical frameworks, combinations of interests or pure visions are possible and legitimate. The MECO-S target model aims to give the author's view of the current debate. In addition, the Agency for the Cooperation of Energy Regulators (ACER) is expected to coordinate the Gas Regional Initiatives (GRIs), giving them top-down guidance, as expressed in the EU Commission's Communication on the 'Future Role of the Regional Initiatives' (EC, 2010).

A gas target model (GTM) will be a non-binding, top-down framework of principles and characteristics that are as broad as possible, providing a description of how the market is expected to develop, let's say until 2020. This would serve as a tool for guiding and assessing the ongoing process of developing Framework Guidelines and guidelines that are the foundations of the broader Network Codes under the Third Energy Package. In addition, its objective will also be to guide and assess the ongoing process of the GRIs. A GTM will furthermore have to take due account of the wider energy policy objectives with regard to sustainability and supply security.

The Third Energy Package brought into force in 2010 defines a number of structural elements towards realizing an architecture for the internal market for gas, the most notable among these elements being the mandatory entry/exit organization of TSO network access and the processes that will lead to a harmonized system of European TSO Network Codes. Now, many different stakeholders at European and national level are working on the implementation of the Third Energy Package. These include:

- lawmakers in the 25 Member States with natural gas;
- regulators in the 25 Member States with natural gas;
- ACER;
- ENTSOG (European Network of Transmission System Operators);
- the EU Commission;
- members of comitology committees;
- TSOs, DSOs (Distribution System Operators) and their associations;
- suppliers, wholesalers, retailers and traders and their associations.

A challenge for these implementation efforts is that the Third Energy Package does not include a comprehensive vision of the organization of network access across the European Union. For instance, the Third Energy Package does not outline:

- if every single TSO will set up its own entry/exit system or if the number of entry/exit networks will be smaller than the number of TSOs;
- if the TSO balancing system will include distribution networks or not;
- if entry/exit network access will extend from transmission systems down to distribution networks or not, and so on.

Depending on the answers to these questions certain issues need to be addressed whether on a European level or not. For instance, if the TSO balancing system includes distribution systems, the European balancing harmonization has a much wider scope (and requires much more detail) than otherwise; also, national action would be required obligating DSOs to blend into that system. Or, if the entry/exit systems include distribution systems, then action on a national level will be required to deal with the corollary cost (and tariff) issues for DSOs (which may receive a cost allocation from TSOs in such a system).

Now the risk is that – within a very limited timescale – many of the policy-makers and other stakeholders, while doing their best to implement the Third Energy Package, interpret and implement the package in a different way or work on different strands of implementation, which after having been elaborated on in great detail, contradict each other. This problem is aggravated by the fact that – inter alia due to resource limitations – not all European Network Codes envisaged at the moment (e.g., for capacity allocation management, balancing, interoperability, tariffs, etc.) can be developed at the same time. It is in this potential problem area where a gas target model can play a beneficial role by helping to make visions about the future of the internal gas market transparent and by enabling discussions about unifying those visions.

A gas target model is not foreseen in any existing European legislation. Therefore, it will be non-binding. This does not mean, however, that it is not required or cannot play a vital role in developing the internal gas market. The role foreseen for the gas target model in the time being is that of a communication tool. It will assist stakeholders in discussing the future of the internal gas market, in relating their work to that future and overall in streamlining the implementation work of the Third

Energy Package. Unlocking the value of that tool requires the goodwill of all stakeholders. The rewards will be easier and there will be better alignment of implementation work and overall a more successful (i.e., consistent, cost-efficient and quick) implementation of the Third Energy Package.

2.1 PROBLEMS OF EUROPEAN MARKET INTEGRATION

The development of the European gas market under the first and second liberalization packages has been kept under tight monitoring by National Regulatory Authorities (NRAs) and by the European Commission, also through the three Gas Regional Initiative regions. In particular, the 2006 Energy Sector Inquiry and several studies have analysed in depth the successes and difficulties of gas market liberalization. Overall, this monitoring effort has been mostly national in focus and driven by the national scope of NRA competences and by the institutional role of the EC to address lacking or ineffective implementation of European legislation by Member States. Even the important actions undertaken by DG Competition have usually addressed specific problems, although often with a far-reaching impact as in the case of lifting destination clauses of gas supply contracts. In turn, the assessment resulting from the GRIs tends to list more problems than successes, and the latter are often limited to pilot experiences, although of some relevance. In other words, the benchmarking of national cases has prevailed so far and the European dimension of the market remains largely to be addressed. Most problems that were identified had been at the root of the Third Energy Package itself, yet the Package does not always solve them as such. It is those problems that will be addressed by the gas target model as well.

Of course, not all of these problems exist everywhere, but most Member States' gas markets suffer at least from several of them. These problems of gas market integration include the following:

- Ineffective congestion management procedures, also limiting access by new players and reducing the utilization factors of some facilities.
- Diverging capacity allocation criteria among the markets, often not market based but privileging access by incumbents' long-term contracts, and sometimes foreclosing access to markets.
- Lack of coordinated procedures for access to adjacent infrastructure, except for traditional suppliers and infrastructure owners,

hampering the provision of new cross-border supplies, notably from far origins.

- Reduced transparency of access tariff-setting criteria, notably as regards tariff design, with a certain risk that tariff systems may overweight on transit flows with respect to domestic destinations.
- Lack of coordination of operational procedures, despite progress achieved through the EASEE (European Association for the Streamlining of Energy Exchange) gas process, starting from the setting of the gas day and its main sessions and deadlines.
- Diverging balancing regimes, in terms of periods, tools, scope and relationships with markets, sometimes creating an uneven playing field among national markets.
- In spite of some important achievements, connection practices at borders between Member States and transmission networks still require harmonization, and the lack of interconnection point and operational balancing agreements in a few locations still hinders cross-border trade and causes balancing problems for shippers.
- Whereas open seasons have become a generalized way of providing the necessary commitments for infrastructure investments, their regulation is still uneven and their planning suffers from lack of coordination, thereby jeopardizing some supply procurement efforts.
- Whereas gas hubs and exchanges have fast developed in Europe, their legal and regulatory status as well as the criteria and transparency of price formation have been uneven, which has been one important (if not the main) reason for competitive markets developing at very different speeds.
- Limited interconnection infrastructure has also led to substantial isolation of, for example, the Iberian Peninsula, whereas the Baltic Republics and Finland are still not connected with the rest of Europe and totally dependent on Russian supplies.

Even though several issues have been solved or eased in some parts of Europe, a recent Commission non-paper[14] noticed that several of them are still fully applicable. In particular, a few quotes from the non-paper are relevant for wholesale markets:

- 'Interconnection capacity remains insufficient notably as regards the Baltics and the Iberian Peninsula'.
- 'Although Western Europe profited from the availability of cheap LNG, Central and Eastern Europe only received small amounts of that additional supply as gas systems remain relatively isolated from the rest of the continent. As a result, the difference of average

prices between Central and Eastern Europe on one side and Western Europe on the other has increased from €0.55/MWh in 2008 to €4.86/MWh in 2009'.

- Further, 'even if interconnections exist, the absence of harmonization of market rules in the different Member States leads to market segmentation and higher transaction costs, which constitutes a barrier in particular for smaller players. This can even lead to the inefficient situation where gas and electricity flow from high-price areas to low-price areas. Furthermore, too many hindrances remain to trade across borders: in gas integrated cross-border transmission services are not yet available, booked but un-used capacity is not offered to other market parties and trading and balancing rules create obstacles to market integration; in electricity the implementation of market coupling is still at an early stage and trading in longer-term products can be difficult'.

As a consequence the non-paper stresses the need to implement the Third Energy Package, and most thoroughly concludes:

- 'In gas, the allocation of transmission capacities should become more efficient and market based. It should also facilitate trade across the border, rather than maintaining the common system applied today, where gas is traded at the border between Member States. At the same time harmonized mechanisms should be put in place to resolve congestion to the benefit of all network users and consumers. For example, cross-border transport capacities today are rarely ever fully used, even though price differences between adjacent markets should provide sufficient incentives to do so. Congestion management mechanisms will aim at resolving such contradictions and bring unused capacity back to the market. Artificially splitting up of markets by means of illicit instruments such as destination clauses in supply contracts or by applying specific conditions for transit of gas flows should no longer be tolerated'.

- Moreover, 'More interconnection capacity is needed to trade gas and electricity freely from Lisbon to Helsinki and from Bucharest to Dublin . . . For gas, progress has been made since the January 2009 supply crisis which revealed dramatically the cost caused by the missing links, but overall the situation remains largely insufficient both from a security of supply perspective and from an internal market perspective'.

2.2 A FEW CRITERIA TO ASSESS THE LEVEL OF INTERNAL GAS MARKET INTEGRATION TOWARDS 2014

Before a GTM is outlined, it would be useful to explore possible criteria for assessing the different options available and, especially, for later monitoring progress achieved on the way towards connecting the various markets into, finally, a single EU gas market. These criteria will have to be:

- clear and objective so that their achievement can be monitored by observable measurable indicators;
- not too general in order to maintain their effectiveness and recognizing regional differences;
- independent of the measures adopted to foster their achievement, which will be discussed in the following sections.

The MECO-S model basically suggests three groups of criteria, that is, relating to supply security, to price alignment and market integration, and to infrastructure and investments. It should be underlined as well that in order to implement the assessment mechanism, an adequate monitoring procedure is required together with a clear allocation of tasks. Some of the key features of the three groups and the monitoring system will be briefly discussed.

2.2.1 Ample and Secure Supplies

Ample and secure supplies across the EU market are to be considered as a primary criterion for assessing the effectiveness and efficiency of the market. A distinction could, briefly speaking, be made at three levels: operational, technical and strategic. The first two are already covered in the Gas Supply Security Regulation with the '1-in-20' and 'n−1'[15] requirements for the operational and technical aspects. The more long-term-oriented strategic level is not covered. This could be done via a periodical (forward) review of the EU gas supply structure, distinguishing, for instance, between both the commodity supply contracts reflecting market parties' evaluation of market conditions, risks and their own positions (LT [long-term], over-the-counter [OTC], spot), and on the other hand the underpinning transmission, treatment and storage arrangements. Such a review could then be used as a tool to analyse the working of a GTM. The kind of indicators that are useful at this level may incorporate the market shares of main suppliers to the EU, specified by regions if needed, the roles of the main importing wholesale companies, together with the extent to which they are able to renew and replace their supply contracts and the conditions under which they are able to do so.

2.2.2   Price Alignment and Market Integration

Using *price indicators* as a critical success factor for market integration is politically speaking a very easy and welcome tool. But it is also a very risky one, as underlying definitions and market structures are determinant factors for price formation and comparisons. A variety of price information is available, rating from spot prices in day-ahead markets and hub prices for shorter-term transactions via commodity only or transmission-including prices to end users, all being regulated or not, with or without tax.

Price levels per se could be seen as one indicator of a successful and competitive GTM. Assessment, however, is not easy when the increasing globalization of gas markets with its unexpected or underestimated developments is taken into account, together with the uncertain relationships with related markets such as oil, coal, carbon and electricity. Public policies and investment cycles and the related expectations are playing major roles as well. Price levels per se are therefore a less reliable indicator.

Price comparisons, alignments and convergence are maybe more useful criteria for assessment, but always need an in-depth understanding of the underlying factors that are determining them. Having said this, a number of considerations have to be taken into account when using price data:

- As gas transactions are largely based on long- and medium-term contracts, changing supply/demand conditions will not emerge immediately and lead to price changes. Only renegotiation of contracts will do, depending on the degree of competition. Moreover, in many EU markets end-use price regulation still exists. More immediate changes in prices can be expected in the traded markets.

- In theory, a hub-to-hub market can be regarded as properly working if prices in the hubs do not differ; this is called the absolute 'Law of One Price' (LOP).[16] If prices differ, it is often concluded that markets are not properly integrated. Yet, it may be that area spot prices vary in a systematic manner, reflecting structural differences between the markets; then the relative LOP holds. Differences may include transportation costs and levels of taxation. Prices in these markets may also only converge after some time, reflecting differences in arbitrage opportunities. Market integration could then be measured as the degree to which prices have converged after some days, or the degree of convergence after one day.

- Prices and the cost of transmission: marginal transmission costs are generally rather small as markets can often be driven to equilibrium with limited net variations in transmission patterns, provided interconnections are not congested. If prices differ more than justified by marginal transmission costs, congested interconnections could play a role, lagging further market integration. This could then require a further discussion on solving congestion or expanding interconnection capacity.

- Prices and liquidity: sources of market liquidity may be manifold as market parties are always trying to balance their own supply/demand conditions, using, for example, secondary markets, swaps, redirecting liquefied natural gas (LNG) (or transferring title to inventories, using flexibility of local production, involving self-trading large consumers etc.). In addition, in the liberalizing market, suppliers will diversify their portfolios to be able to react to and exploit market opportunities. Most of these trades are based on OTC. For spot markets, depending on the number of (potential) sellers and buyers, the liquidity of the market would be a meaningful indicator in order to assess the potential for more immediate changes in prices. Liquidity could be measured by the bid–ask spread, the number of transactions being executed in the spot market, the number of market players and by churn factors (expressing the ratio of physical transport versus traded volumes). Liquidity indicators should not be seen as an objective, but merely as an indicator to assess, for instance, the relevance of market outcomes, that is, prices.

All these arguments suggest that absolute spot price convergence between areas, hubs or exchanges could be a far too stringent criterion to monitor real progress in market integration. Given the factors above, however, it could be argued that a relative LOP is much more likely to hold and that partial or lagged price convergence is definitely an acceptable second-best outcome. Nevertheless, less than full price convergence of spot prices, taking into account actual transport costs, may point to the existence of solvable impediments to intra-hub trade, between existing hubs as well as for the new hubs that are expected to emerge in the Iberian Peninsula as well as in Central and Eastern Europe.

As for *market integration*, one could imagine that national and/or regional markets would integrate in the larger space of the EU. Balancing supply and demand over a larger number of such markets would extend the number of (potential) buyers and sellers and give rise to an even more efficient allocation and pricing of gas. Trading volumes of gas crossing borders can be undertaken via inter-area OTC contracts, which would reflect the preferred conditions of the buyers and sellers. The elimination of destination clauses and the recent tendency towards an increased flexibility of take-or-pay clauses are, however, reducing this effect, and an important contribution to market liquidity actually comes from usage of such flexibility. A more efficient solution would be to organize inter-area trade via gas hubs, where each would reflect the area's supply/demand balance in national/regional spot prices.[17] By facilitating trade between the hubs these market outcomes can be rebalanced over a much larger area; this is called hub-to-hub trading. Such a system of hub-to-hub trading will function more or less effectively, depending on a variety of conditions.

Useful indicators might be the *market shares* of the main wholesale companies, the amounts of gas they supply under the different medium- and shorter-term contracts, their control over essential facilities in markets, like gas storage, LNG re-gasification terminals and access to exempted transmission pipelines. Regional wholesale gas prices (in comparison with others) are an indicator and a point of departure for raising questions on issues such as the accessibility of these markets via transport routes and their interconnection with adjacent markets; the regional structure of demand; the prevailing contract structures, and, lastly, the potential for abuses of market power. Interpretation of these indicators, however, is more an issue for competition policy, where the potential for market abuse might be assessed in relation to guaranteeing ample and secure supplies. Incumbents' market shares could be expected to fall as integrated markets become more competitive, but it is also to be noted that incumbents have seen market share reductions in one market and growth in other markets. Most economists agree that in the EU with its limited resource base and needs to import, further industry fragmentation is neither likely nor desirable. Therefore, any simplified use of this indicator is risky. The same could be said of simple market structure indicators like the Herfindahl–Hirschman Index.

2.2.3   Infrastructure and Investments

It is quite clear that effectively using existing interconnections and other infrastructures is a preferred route for markets to develop. However, market forces, including expanding demand and changing supply structures, will push for increasing (cross-border) transactions and resulting flows and hence might lead to various needs to expand these infrastructures and therefore new investments. There are a number of indicators suggested and it may be appropriate to assess these needs and assess the case for new investments as well. In a GTM context the following two indicators should be considered to play a role: (1) *Using capacity load factors*:

it could be expected that the opening up of trade and capacity leads to an increase in capacity use, at least as regards the capacity of interconnections between systems or national markets. However, US experience has shown a reduced capacity use as a consequence of liberalization, and a successful integration might well be related to renewed investment efforts. Further, capacity use should primarily follow demand, and if capacity is released to new market players, usage by incumbent capacity holders may well be reduced as a consequence. Further, the increasing role of LNG and arbitrage and swaps conducted by means of its diversion may also indirectly affect pipeline load factors. Using capacity load factors, therefore, is not a very reliable indicator. (2) Assessing the options for a more *effective use of existing capacity*, a trade-off may emerge between the improvement of market liquidity and the need to ensure the availability of long-term capacity, which is likely to be necessary to foster adequate investment. This potential conflict has already been noted in the power sector. For example, reservation of some capacity for long-term allocation even if allocated by explicit auction could be liable to capacity hoarding or market power abuse, and poses the problem of a regulatory ex ante decision about capacity shares by duration. There are several ways out of this conflict on the basis of solutions proposed in the electricity sector.[18]

Assessing the needs for new infrastructure capacity should be based on market needs and players should be in a position to take part in a procedure aimed at assessing market demand for capacity increase. The new Ten-Year Network Development Plan (10YNDP) from ENTSOG is an appropriate framework for this, but it should go hand in hand with more specific open season procedures for different transmission corridors. The number of such open season procedures on an annual basis could be seen as a useful indicator when market parties are committing to book such capacity. The achievement of this criterion would help to overcome the often highlighted vicious circle, through which hubs are not developed or are not liquid due to limited supply, due to lack of available capacity; but such capacity (including the necessary upstream investment) is hardly developed by market forces if no liquid market is working to reassure investors about the revenues that would arise from their investments. An additional indicator might be to assess the time period between the successful conclusion of an open season and the final investment decision by the TSOs involved. If this time frame is more than a certain period (i.e., two to three years), then regulatory uncertainty might be a relevant feature. This could either be a too lengthy permitting process or a regulatory framework that is not able to accommodate shippers and TSOs to go forward. This uncertainty might also be due to cross-border characteristics and bordering NRA inabilities.

2.2.4 Monitoring and Implementation

Considering indicators and criteria for assessing developments towards an efficient and competitive EU gas market is one thing; applying these tools in a reliable and effective way is the next step. It could be argued that defining and collecting the necessary data to do so is a task for ACER. This complies with other tasks of the new agency, including the ones on monitoring market transparency and integrity in the expanding derivative markets. Analysing the data and arriving at recommendations for policy-makers could also be seen as ACER's responsibility. It might, however, be advisable to base these annual reports on independent expert overview and assessment, as ACER conclusions can only come from its Board of Regulators. The BoR may achieve more stature and trust when an independent expert Market Monitoring Committee is established and used as a 'first line of action' for applying the indicators and criteria in a coherent and meaningful way.

The desired target model will provide a unifying vision on the future layout of the European gas market architecture. That vision will assist all stakeholders in quickly and efficiently implementing the Third Energy Package on the internal gas market in a consistent way. The following section describes a proposal for the European gas target model with a special focus on market architectures and investment.

3   The MECO-S Model: An Architecture for the Gas Target Model

3.1   OPERATIONALIZATION OF OBJECTIVES FOR THE MECO-S MODEL

The MECO-S model is a target model for the 'big picture' architecture of the gas market. As a target model it describes a future state of the gas market. The goal of the MECO-S model is to specify a European vision of an internal gas market that can serve as a common beacon for further implementation work.

When talking about market architecture in this chapter, I focus especially on issues that are relevant for implementation in the ACER Framework Guidelines ('FWG') and subsequently in the ENTSOG Network Codes for gas transmission systems ('Network Codes'). In addition to that, the MECO-S model addresses some issues that go beyond the planned scope of the FWG, for example, in the area of new infrastructure. Where required some hints are provided that even surpass the realm of the regulation of network access (e.g., when it comes to describing preconditions of market coupling).[19] The term 'market architecture' was chosen to differentiate my view from the broader topic of market organization that would include, for example, the issue of unbundling or aspects of retail market organization.

The development of the MECO-S model starts out with an operationalization of the political goals. Those operationalized objectives (which in my opinion are essential for a well-functioning internal gas market) are the following:

- Every European final customer shall be easily accessible from a functioning wholesale gas market.
- The alignment of short- and mid-term wholesale gas prices between those functioning wholesale markets shall be fostered as much as the (at any time) existing transport infrastructure allows.
- The establishment of secure supply patterns from gas sources to every functioning wholesale market shall be enabled.
- The effectiveness of Pillars 1 to 3 shall be improved continuously by realizing every investment into pipeline capacity (new and extension) that is economic.

The following subsections will elaborate on each of these objectives. Means to realize the ends will be discussed later.

3.1.1 Functioning Wholesale Markets

Objective 1: Every European final customer shall be easily accessible from a functioning wholesale gas market.

I assume that a functioning wholesale gas market is an essential prerequisite of a functioning retail gas market. The rationale for this assumption will be provided later in this section.

Due to the scope chosen for the MECO-S model (mainly FWG, Network Codes), it focuses on the wholesale side of gas markets, that is, the MECO-S model does not go deeper into the issue of competitive retail gas markets other than supporting their emergence through fostering functioning wholesale gas markets.

This focus is also in line with the wording in bold text of Article 1: 'Subject Matter and Scope' of Regulation EC 715/2009 (i.e., the so-called Gas Transmission Regulation), where it says in paragraph 1 that this (EC 715/2009) regulation aims at 'facilitating the emergence of a well-functioning and transparent wholesale market. . .'. Here the 'functioning wholesale gas market' (for brevity also termed 'market' in the rest of this chapter) is defined as a single price zone that is accessible to incumbents and new entrants on equal (i.e., non-discriminatory) terms[20] and where trading is liquid (i.e., vivid and resilient at the same time), so that it creates reliable price signals in the forward and spot markets, which are not distorted even if substantial volumes are bought or sold in this market (in other words: no single transaction shall distort the market price).

As can be seen from the definition above, a functioning wholesale gas market involves the criterion of liquidity but goes beyond that. I therefore prefer to use the term 'functioning' instead of the narrower term 'liquid' to denote the desired market properties. A functioning wholesale gas market requires the following success criteria:

- a sufficient presence of wholesalers active in the market that 'inject' gas into that market from national production and outside sources (e.g., from other markets within the EU or from outside the EU) and that engage in liquid trading among each other and with other market participants, optimally entailing an HHI[21] below 2000;
- the combined portfolios of those wholesalers comprising gas from at least three different producers[22] (directly or indirectly);
- a multitude of final gas customers in that market.

Of course, regulation of gas networks cannot oblige wholesalers to enter a market or to shape their portfolios in a certain way, but it can create structural conditions regarding network access that make it more likely that they will do so.

I assume that implementing the following set of structural conditions would fertilize the later emergence – driven by market forces – of functioning gas wholesale markets:

- organizing the market as an entry/exit network with a virtual point, the virtual point being the single place of trading-induced change of ownership within that market (this pools trading activities and thus adds to liquidity and the relevance of the price signals generated);
- making sure that the market caters to final customers with a combined annual consumption normally[23] not below 20 bcm (this should ensure that the market is sufficiently attractive for a large number of wholesalers);
- making sure that the market is linked to at least three entry points[24] originating from substantial and different EU or non-EU[25] gas sources or other functioning markets (or any combination of those)

(this ensures that the required diversity of gas sources is available so that gas to gas competition is spurred on).

The MECO-S model suggests (see below) two optional models to realize the structural criteria listed above. It is important to note that all of these criteria focus on the development of a functioning *wholesale* market. I assume (and there is also evidence for that in the market) that a functioning – and therefore competitive – wholesale market that is easily accessible for incumbents and new competitors alike also drives competition in retail markets. This will, at least to a certain extent, be facilitated by new entrants into the retail market using the wholesale market on the virtual point as a point of price reference (for pricing of offers), as a point of piecemeal procurement (i.e., synchronized with sales activities), as a source/sink for physical portfolio balancing and for risk measurement and risk management purposes. In that regard, a functioning wholesale market may be considered as fertilizing retail competition.

An additional advantage of a functioning wholesale market deserves recognition. Every wholesaler draws on a portfolio of supply contracts and optimizes the use of these contracts according to cost within certain constraints. A functioning wholesale market provides wholesalers with the opportunity to not only optimize their supply contracts (and other assets) within their own portfolios, but also against the portfolios of others – mediated by the market. This yields economic efficiencies that in a competitive market will eventually trickle down to final customers as well.

The question may arise, why does the MECO-S model suggest structuring Europe into more than one functioning market? The answer is quite simple. Entry/exit networks are not a physical reality, but a commercial overlay over those physical realities (the physical reality being gas pipelines, not market zones [aka 'gas lakes']). Depending on the degree of interconnection of the existing pipelines, maintaining this commercial overlay causes costs[26] (e.g., for constructing improved interconnection and for procuring flow commitments or system energy).[27] The larger an entry/exit network becomes, the higher this cost usually becomes.[28] On the other hand, the creation of entry/exit zones is a precondition for the creation of functioning markets in the EU. I think that this dilemma is solved best by designing entry/exit zones as large as is required in order to enable a functioning market[29] but to avoid the extra cost attached to going beyond that size (unless there is a specific reason to do so – for example, a small market that is not yet a functioning market may, in order to become part of a functioning market, merge with an adjoining market that already qualifies as functioning before that merger).

Two more interesting questions in the context of creating functioning wholesale markets will be briefly discussed: (1) Could a number of smaller markets that are tightly connected by bookable cross-market capacity also qualify as a functioning wholesale market? (2) Could a smaller market become functioning by simply 'attaching' it via bookable cross-market capacity to a functioning wholesale market? In my view the correct answer to both questions is 'no'.

In case (1), wholesale trading is split between various markets that are only connected by time-consuming and costly booking (or bidding) processes with uncertain outcomes, which will in the future[30] only be available during given booking windows (e.g., once a year for yearly capacity). This neither enables the liquid trading patterns required to qualify as a functioning market nor does it create the sort of environment that really drives retail competition.[31] It would also prevent the implementation of market coupling since the most fundamental precondition for market coupling is a functioning market in *all* of the coupled markets. Therefore, – even if it was physically possible – full price alignment is less likely in such a set up. Just about the same is true for market-based balancing, because this concept is also based on a functioning wholesale (spot) market in *every* market where it will be applied (and not only in the neighbouring market).

In case (2), the situation is better insofar as a functioning market exists in the larger market, but the problems for retail competitors in the smaller market (and in a similar way for all other market participants in the smaller market that are interested in structured procurement or trading, for example, the operator of a gas-fired power plant) remain the same. In fact, in this case the smaller market would not properly work as such, but all trading would occur in the larger one, to which the smaller one would be attached as if it was some sort of distribution zone that is segregated by bookable capacity. Also, the comments made above on market coupling and market-based balancing apply to case (2) in the same way.

3.1.2 Price Alignment

Objective 2: Alignment of short- and mid-term wholesale gas prices between those functioning wholesale markets shall be fostered as much as the (at any time) existing transport infrastructure allows.

The price alignment here is defined as the conformity of traded[32] gas prices prevalent in the wholesale markets that Europe is structured into under the MECO-S model. Full (also termed 'absolute') price alignment would be achieved, if traded gas prices[33] (spot and forward, that is, the full so-called 'price forward curve' aka 'contract curve') would be identical across all markets at all times. For the avoidance of doubt this does not mean that the curve will be flat, but merely that prices would be equal for every delivery date. This means that full price alignment is more than just a high correlation of prices[34] in neighbouring markets.

It is important to note that conformity of European gas wholesale prices would not mean that retail prices become identical all over Europe. These may still differ[35] due to, for example, different local tax regimes and network cost.

Since we have been focused on the traded wholesale market here, price alignment will by and large be limited to the time horizon that is (actively) traded, that is, the short- and the closer portion[36] of the mid-term markets. It is expected that this suffices in order to achieve the economic benefits outlined below.

The limits to wholesale price alignment are transmission capacities and to a certain extent also transmission tariffs. If prices are higher in market 'A' and lower in an adjoining market 'B', then the degree to which price alignment can be achieved is on the one hand determined by the available (i.e., yet unused) transmission capacity. The higher the available unused transmission capacity for flows from market 'B' to market 'A' is, the higher the chances for full price alignment. On the other hand, it appears that the applicable transmission tariff sets a technical limit to price convergence that can be achieved by cross-market arbitrage. In practice this is only partly true. Consider, for example, the case of a shipper that has booked capacity for a medium term, say a year. Such a shipper could be inclined to use the capacity (as far as it is not required for other purposes) for cross-market arbitrage deals in the spot markets as long as there is a price spread a little[37] above zero.[38]

The benefit of price alignment is an increase in allocative efficiency. Consider that the gas transport business is to a very large extent a fixed cost business. In such a world, the 'connection' of wholesalers' portfolios via the market and their efficient use (brought forth by cross-portfolio optimization via the market) will be best if the market prices (along the forward price curve) are equal for all markets within the EU. As is well known, this also leads to an increase in total welfare (measured as grand total of consumer and producer rent over all connected markets).

The efficiency of the European wholesale market would be maximized if gas wholesale prices within the EU were identical at all times for all traded products. This condition is apparently not[39] fulfilled at present, despite the (in some places) availability of unused cross-market capacity that could be utilized to this end. Therefore, the MECO-S model foresees measures that enable the best use of the (at any time) existing infrastructure in order to maximize price alignment between markets.

The expansion of pipeline capacity in order to improve price alignment even more than the existing capacity allows is dealt with in the section on new investment.

3.1.3   Secure Supply Patterns

Objective 3:   The establishment of secure supply patterns from gas sources[40] to every functioning wholesale market shall be enabled.

In recent years there has been an intensive debate about the necessity and benefit of long-term supply contracts in the gas industry. In such a contract a gas wholesaler would buy a substantial volume of gas for a long term (e.g., ten to 20 years) usually directly from a producer.[41] Now, it is generally agreed that in the gas industry long-term supply contracts will maintain an important role. Important reasons for this are the following:

- Due to decreasing indigenous production, Europe will likely[42] have to import an increasing quantity of gas in the future. In many cases this increase in import quantity will have to be procured from new production sources. Developing these production sources (and the sometimes required new pipelines) involves enormous investment. Consequently, producers (and in some cases their banks) insist on risk allocation between producers and their customers to risk investing in new production sources and the pipelines required to transport the gas from the well-head to a European border point (their argument goes: 'no long-term contracts → no investment → no supply').
- Some producers are increasingly faced with alternative options to sell their gas outside Europe; long-term supply contracts bind them to Europe, which in turn secures supplies.
- Some suppliers are selling gas to certain final customers (e.g., gas-fired power plants, the chemical industry) on the basis of long-term supply contracts (with tenure of, e.g., five or more years).

When analysing the issue of long-term supply contracts in the context of network access in a gas target model, the question arises, what does a shipper need from the transport sector in order to underpin his long-term supply contract? The answer is straightforward. If long-term supply contracts are enabled, long-term transport contracts must be enabled too.

A corollary question is whether these long-term transport contracts need to be enabled only at EU import points or also at cross-market points within the EU. It appears unrealistic that wholesalers will settle for the opportunity to enter the first EU market 'behind' the EU import point, hoping that they will find sufficient buyers in that market or hoping to be able to transport the gas into other markets by means of short- or mid-term capacity (which they would need to secure in the future at acceptable prices). Therefore, I do assume that long-term transport contracts also have to be permitted at intra-EU cross-market points. One has to be careful though not to foreclose short- and mid-term market entry by allowing all of the available capacity to be contracted long term.

Unfortunately, allowing long-term transport contracts on all EU border points and intra-EU cross-market points is not enough. For several Member States at least part of the gas that they consume has to be transported through other Member States beforehand, leading to approximately 30 per cent of European gas consumption crossing at least two Member States' borders before it reaches the place of final consumption. This creates a serious challenge for structuring network access.

Take the example of a supplier buying pipeline gas from an Eastern source for a Member State in Central or Western Europe. This supplier will have to cross a number of market border points in order to deliver the gas to the market where he intends to sell it. For this supplier only a 'chain' of entry/exit transport products will provide the security he needs to underpin his long-term supply contract. At first glance this issue seems to be at odds with the principle of entry/exit networks. On the other hand, if Europe is not structured into a single entry/exit network (which is not foreseen by the Third Energy Package, or by the MECO-S model or by any other source I am aware of) one has to deal with the issue of cross-market transports while of course avoiding any 'captive transports' as they were practised in many countries in the past (and to a certain extent even nowadays).

The MECO-S model therefore foresees measures to deal with long-term, long-distance transportation into and within Europe. Regarding long-distance products, these measures will ensure that shippers interested in long-distance transport have occasion to simultaneously book (or bid for) whole packages[43] of cross-market capacities[44] at different border points on their intended transport route while still making sure that every cross-border point may be used separately and gas may be dropped[45] and picked up[46] on all virtual points en route.[47]

A completely different issue regarding secure supply patterns is the issue of redundant transport routes to a market. Some principles for this (especially the 'n−1' criterion) were laid out in Regulation (EU) No. 994/2010. The MECO-S model devotes a brief section to this issue, presenting some further thoughts on the practical realization of international network redundancy.

3.1.4   Improve by Investing in Pipeline Capacity

A foundation common to all pillars of the MECO-S model is that every investment in pipeline capacity (new and extensions) that is economic shall be realized. There are various economic reasons for investing in transmission pipeline capacity, the most important being:

- to connect a non-European gas source with a European market ('upstream connection');
- to connect gas markets with each other ('*inter*connection');
- to overcome congestion within a gas market ('*intra*connection');
- to create new capacity for delivering gas to additional final customers ('downstream connection').

As can be easily deduced, all of these investments are not isolated in the sense of being objectives of their own, but they serve other objectives. That is why I consider investment a common foundation of the MECO-S model.

For instance, upstream connections, inter- and intraconnections can serve the emergence of a functioning wholesale market, interconnection can help to reduce price spreads between markets and downstream connections cater to the needs of physically supplying more end users. Downstream connection is insofar a special case, as it may also require investment in one or more of the other categories.

In theory one would expect widespread approval for the idea of realizing any pipeline investment that is economical in order to create markets that function better, or to align prices better, and so on. In practice widespread disagreement is repeatedly observed on the actual implementation of investment appraisals and decisions. Therefore, the MECO-S model (while not trying to completely solve the investment conundrum) provides some hints on structuring and evaluating investment decisions in the areas of interconnection and intraconnection, both of which are of special importance to the creation of functioning markets and price alignment and some additional thoughts on financing investment in pipelines.

This section concludes with some brief notes on the relation between 'security of supply' type of investments and 'economic investments' in gas transmission capacity. At first glance, these investments appear to serve different purposes.[48] This is true only to a certain extent. Since 'security of supply'-driven investment creates extra capacity, it will in most cases have an impact on the market and therefore contribute to, for example, creating functioning markets or reducing price spreads between them. In other words, security of supply investment creates redundancy and redundancy increases competition.

3.2 OUTLINE OF THE MECO-S MODEL

The MECO-S model rests on three pillars that share a common foundation. It aims at the creation of a number of functioning wholesale markets within the EU (together enabling easy access to all European final customers of gas), at connecting these markets tightly in order to maximize short- and mid-term price alignment between those markets, at enabling secure supply patterns to those markets and at making sure that all economic gas transmission investments are made.

The following is devoted to describing the instruments used by the MECO-S model in order to achieve its objectives. Unless explicitly stated, these measures are not a tool box to be chosen from but essential elements of the MECO-S model that only in combination realize the model's stated objectives.

It is worth reiterating that this chapter describes the MECO-S model as a desirable end state of the gas market architecture. The following sequence of representations of the MECO-S model's pillars and foundation does not imply that this is necessarily a sequence of implementation. On the other hand, permanently omitting one pillar would lead to a different model with different properties. If, for instance, the pillar of 'functioning wholesale markets' were skipped, large groups of final customers would be excluded from the benefits of functioning wholesale markets and the adoption of market coupling (which could be the capstone of price alignment as will be presented later in this section) would also be prevented for several Member States.

3.2.1 The Creation of Functioning Wholesale Markets

There are two ways of organizing the entry/exit zones that are (see above) an essential element of functioning gas wholesale markets: (1) entry/exit zones that comprise a number of transmission and distribution systems in a single balancing zone (termed 'market areas' in the rest of this document); entry/exit zones that comprise a number of transmission systems in a single balancing zone, which in turn is closely linked to one or several end-user zones with their own balancing systems (this model will be termed 'trading region model' in the rest of this chapter). Both of these models feature a virtual point (or 'hub') where changes of ownership can be effected. Both of these models fit perfectly well into an overall picture of hub-to-hub trading based on large hubs, as has been discussed for a while now in the regulatory community.

The MECO-S model incorporates these two models as options that may co-exist in Europe. They may be chosen at will in the course of implementation with some need for regional consistency. European consistency is not required though. Markets that implement the market area model can be connected perfectly well with other markets that are organized according to the trading region model.

The market area model

In the market area model transmission and distribution networks that are situated in the same geographical area and that are well interconnected are forged into a single entry/exit system.[49]

From a structural perspective this entry/exit system (i.e., the market area):

- stretches from the entry points into the combined systems to the end-user exit points on those systems;
- integrates distribution systems into the joint entry/exit area (likely involving some cost allocation from TSOs to DSOs and requiring DSOs to send allocation data to the market area balancing entity so that balancing accounts can be settled);
- features a single virtual point being a fictitious point in the market area where all gas that has entered the market area and that leaves the market area is accounted for and changes of ownership can be effected;
- does not support any place other than the single virtual point of the market area for wholesale-related changes of ownership (i.e., no flange trading – trading gas before acquiring an entry capacity in the network) with the exception of flange trading at EU import points;
- features a single balancing system[50] with a single balancing entity and a single set of balancing rules for the whole market area (i.e., regarding: balancing period, prices for balancing energy, tolerances, rights and obligations of shippers regarding the management of their balancing accounts, etc.);
- is based on a single set of rules for the measuring of (a) final customer consumption and (b) the exchange of gas with other markets and storage;
- is based on a single set of rules estimating small final customer consumption during the year (i.e., standardized load profiles) and the treatment of related estimation errors;
- the virtual point of the market area would be the focal point of the wholesale gas market.

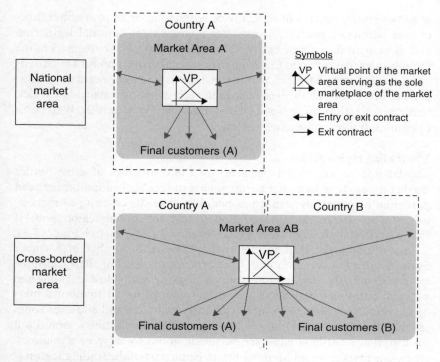

Source: Author elaboration.

Figure 7.2   Scheme of national market area versus cross-border market area

The market area model can be implemented within a Member State or cross-border. Figure 7.2 visualizes one scenario where a Member State implements a (one) national market area and a second scenario where two adjoining Member States implement a cross-border market area.

The structural description above underlines that market areas can be realized better within a single jurisdiction (i.e., Member State), and that creating cross-border market areas that span more than one Member State requires substantial legal alignment between the participating countries. Therefore, the market area model might be considered the model of choice for larger Member States, especially where the gas consumption is large enough to allow the emergence of functioning wholesale markets within their own borders.

This does not mean that Member States with smaller gas consumption may not implement the market area model. They only have to be aware that the following cross-border merger of their market area with other

Member States, which will normally be required in order to enable a functioning wholesale market, necessitates alignment of national legislation and agreement on a single entity[51] for balancing all final customers in the cross-border market area. Ensuring proper legal protection for the citizens of all participating Member States and establishing clear regulatory competence are special challenges regarding such common balancing entities. Summarizing, the creation of a cross-border market area is likely to be an onerous and time-consuming process.

The trading region model
The trading region model picks up on the difficulties of cross-border market areas. It reduces the requirements of legal coordination between participating countries as much as possible while still creating a functioning gas wholesale market. In the following text, the trading region model is thus described in the context of a cross-border application (see Figure 7.3).

In a cross-border trading region the TSOs of a number of Member States establish a common entry/exit zone on the level of their transmission systems (the eponymous trading region) with closely connected national end-user balancing zones (each comprising all final customers of the respective Member State), with entry/exit zone and end-user zones sharing the same virtual point.[52] In other words, the trading region is put on top of the national end-user balancing zones to serve as a common wholesale market for all Member States being part of the trading region.[53]

From a structural perspective the cross-border trading region model:

- creates a trading region as an integrated entry/exit system that stretches from the entry points into the participating transmission systems (crossing several countries) to virtual exit points[54] to each national end-user zone;
- integrates distribution systems into the respective national end-user (exit) zone (possibly but not necessarily involving some cost allocation from TSOs to DSOs[55] and requiring DSOs to send allocation data to the national end-user zone balancing entity so that balancing accounts can be settled);
- features a single virtual point that is shared by the trading region and all attached national balancing systems and where changes of ownership and the accounting of gas flows in the trading region as well as to the national end-user zones are effected;
- does not support any place other than the single virtual point of the trading region for wholesale-related changes of ownership (e.g., flanges or further virtual points in the end-user zones) with the exception of flange trading at EU import points;

- structures the trading region as a fully nominated[56] system involving a trading account kept per shipper to (ex ante) ensure an even balance of their nominations in the trading region;
- assigns *all* national final customers to national end-user balancing zones ('end-user zones') that may be operated by a national balancing entity according to national balancing, SLP (standard load profiles) and metrology regulations;[57]
- allows the shifting of gas from the trading region to an end-user zone via a single (i.e., bundled) nomination at the common virtual point.[58]

In the trading region model the virtual point of the trading region would be the focal point of the wholesale gas market. Since the trading region model is an innovation in the ongoing discussion, some additional remarks are in order:

- The trading region model does not withstand the harmonization of national balancing regulations or the mandating of common cross-border end-user balancing entities. But – as opposed to cross-border market areas – it does not depend on this.
- There are various ways to structure trading regions in detail (see an example below). The most important principle in creating a trading region is to merge the wholesale market horizontally across several markets with separate national end-user balancing zones that are closely connected (via a virtual exit) to the trading region.
- There are two ways to organize roles in the trading region itself. In one model, the involved TSOs establish a central balancing operator for the trading region. As in the cross-border market area model, such cross-border entities raise some (but fewer) questions of legal alignment among the involved Member States. In the second approach all (interested) TSOs offer to keep an account (the 'trading account') for the shipper in the trading region and effect the necessary exchange of information in the background based on cooperation contracts. The second model appears feasible because the trading region is a fully nominated (aka allocated as nominated) system; balancing of shippers' imbalances involving the use of system energy is therefore not required. Problems due to the interruption of capacity in or out of the trading region can be sorted out between the TSO who interrupted the capacity and his customer, the shipper, or alternatively by the TSO chosen by the shipper for 'balancing' his transports in the trading region.
- The choice of the national end-user balancing entity involves a

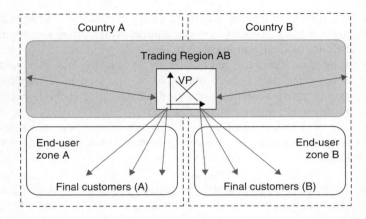

Legend and Symbols

End-user zone = National balancing zone for national final customers, no matter the
      system (distribution or transmission) they are connected to

Trading Region AB = Cross-border entry/exit system including all nominated points on the
      transmission systems of countries A and B

⟷   Entry or exit contract

⟶   Exit contract

VP   Virtual point of the trading region serving as the sole marketplace of the trading
      region and all attached end-user zones. Shifting of gas between trading region
      and end-user zone is done by nominating a virtual exit on the VP.

Source: Author elaboration.

Figure 7.3   *Scheme of the trading region model in cross-border application*

degree of freedom for implementation. It would be expected that
Member States task TSOs at least with the physical balancing of
the national end-user zones. The keeping and settling of the balancing accounts for a national end-user zone may be tasked to another
entity. If another entity is mandated with that task, it will require
close cooperation with the national TSO(s) in order to account for
the use of system energy for purposes of the national end-user zone.
● The trading region model foresees that all final customers in a
Member State – including those connected to transmission systems –
are balanced in the national end-user zone. This raises the legal question whether every final customer that is attached to a TSO system
must also be balanced by that TSO. In that regard Regulation (EC)
715/2009 stipulates in Article 1 (4): 'The Member States may establish an entity or body set up in compliance with Directive 2009/73/
EC for the purpose of carrying out one or more functions typically

attributed to the transmission system operator, which shall be subject to the requirements of this Regulation'. Therefore, I see no legal obstacle to mandating a special entity for the balancing of all national final customers even if they are connected to transmission systems. NB: from a physical perspective the inclusion of final customers attached to the TSO's system into the balancing mechanism of the end-user zone is fairly trivial. It simply means that the exits to those final customers are integrated into the virtual exit to the end-user zone and thereby into the competence of the end-user zone balancing entity and its usual balancing activities. The rest is mainly an issue of proper bookkeeping of gas in the trading region.[59]

Since the capacity on the exit points from the trading region to the end-user zones is allocated in the course of the change of supplier process, the switch from the trading region to an end-user zone poses no market entry barrier for retail competitors; instead it is a simple technicality in the nomination management processes. Therefore, one can expect the impact of the trading region model on retail competition[60] to be on the same level as with the market area model.

As can be seen from the structural description above, the trading region model entails lower realization hurdles than the market area model, if – in order to achieve a functioning wholesale market – the wholesale markets of a number of Member States have to be consolidated. Therefore, the trading region model might be considered the model of choice for Member States with smaller gas consumption, not big enough to host functioning wholesale markets within their own borders. This does not mean that larger Member States may not implement the trading region model. The rationale for this would require scrutiny though.

Of course, nothing in the trading region models prevents a group of Member States that went for a trading region model in the first place (in order to speed up the development of a functioning wholesale market) to evolve their model into a full merger based on the market area model in a second step. Nevertheless, before this step is actually taken, the additional cost and benefits should be evaluated carefully.

National/regional policy options for the creation of functioning markets
How can Member States that do not host a functioning wholesale market still utilize the two models for the creation of functioning wholesale markets? They can either:

- wherever this is possible create market areas that fulfil the criteria for functioning wholesale markets within the borders of their own

country (this may require investment in order to improve interconnection with other European or non-European markets); or
- act jointly with adjoining Member States in creating trading regions that fulfil the criteria for functioning wholesale markets; or
- act jointly with adjoining Member States in creating merged market areas that fulfil the criteria for functioning wholesale markets; or
- accede (based on mutual consent) to the market area of a neighbouring country that has already succeeded in creating a functioning wholesale market within its own borders.

Two parallel concepts for the creation of functioning markets in Europe?
The question may be raised whether the co-existence of the market area and the trading region model in Europe is an obstacle to market integration rather than an asset. The trading region model is a clear asset for the following reasons:

- It has the potential of substantially speeding up the development of functioning wholesale markets.
- It can be evolved into fully merged market areas in a second step after all problems (especially legal alignment and legal protection) regarding this matter have been solved.
- It makes no difference in the methods (see next section) that may be used for market connection. Every single one of the methods described in the respective sections of this chapter that work between two market areas also work between a market area and a trading region or between two trading regions.
- It does not require much differentiation in Framework Guidelines and the ENTSOG Network Codes (e.g., all provisions regarding cross-border capacity, gas quality, network connection, interoperability, etc. will be identical for both models).
- It does not obstruct the harmonization of balancing systems.

3.2.2   The Connection of Markets

In order to achieve the maximum degree of short- and mid-term price alignment possible, markets have to be connected as tightly as the given transportation capacity between markets allows. The connection of markets takes place between the transmission systems of adjoining markets using the (at any time) existing interconnection capacities. The methods used for connecting (and the results achieved for price alignment) are the same, no matter if the markets to be connected are organized according to the market area or the trading region model (or mixed).

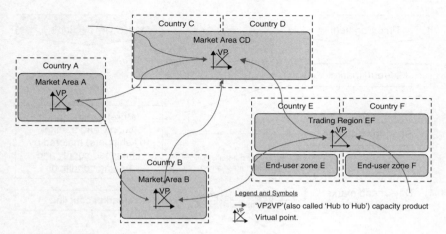

Source: Author elaboration.

Figure 7.4 Scheme of connections between adjoining markets

This is due to the fact that the connection always takes place between the two (or more, if more markets are involved) virtual points using the existing physical interconnection capacities. Now, since the virtual points are the 'location' of the markets,[61] market connection is achieved in both cases.

Figure 7.4 shows connections (based on hub-to-hub capacity products; see details on connection methods below) between adjoining markets that are organized according to different principles. It has to be reiterated that this picture would only display a proper application of the MECO-S model, if each of the connected markets qualified as a functioning wholesale market.

When it comes to connecting markets, one has to consider that the gas market is not one but several markets that exist simultaneously along the time axis. For simplicity I split the gas markets into the following time segments:

1. long-term market (i.e., more than four years ahead);
2. mid-term market (from more than one year to maximum four years ahead);
3. short-term market (from two days ahead to maximum one year ahead);
4. day-ahead (spot) market;
5. intra-day (spot) market.

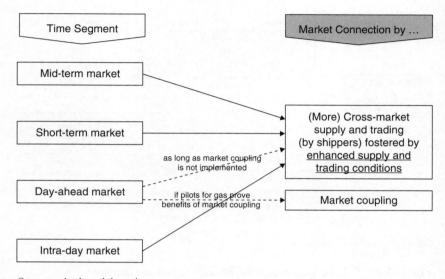

Source: Author elaboration.

Figure 7.5   Scheme of MECO-S model market connection

For price alignment I focus especially on the time segments 2 through 5. As was already discussed in this chapter, the issue of long-term (and long-distance) transport poses special challenges and is discussed in a separate section (see below).

Regarding the means to achieve price alignment there are two essentially different ways to connect markets that may be applied differently on different time segments: (1) cross-market supply and trading by shippers; and (2) market coupling. In the following section these will be defined and described.

Figure 7.5 shows the market connection method foreseen in the MECO-S model per time segment of the gas market (excluding the long-term market for reasons given above).

Cross-market supply and trading by shippers

The theory behind connecting markets by cross-market supply and trading effected by shippers is that suppliers and traders will always be inclined to do a cross-market deal if the deal is economical, and they are given the opportunity to (more or less) safely do so. The more of these deals done, the more the price differences between the affected markets will vanish.

I explicitly include supply activities here, because price alignment will be furthered by any activity of buying gas in a lower price market, shipping it to the higher price market and selling it there, even if the gas is directly sold to final customers in the higher price market.

Of course (as was the case with functioning markets above) suppliers and traders cannot (and shall not) be forced to do cross-market deals. But again, structural conditions can be put in place that make it safer and easier for suppliers and traders to do such deals. I term these structural conditions 'enhanced supply and trading conditions' or 'ESTC'. A lot of the issues regarding the establishment of ESTC are already being addressed by the currently ongoing Framework Guideline process and the CMP (congestion management procedures) Annex to Regulation (EC) 715/2009 undergoing comitology at the time of writing this chapter. Among those, the most important principles regarding ESTC in the context of the MECO-S model are:

- the implementation of hub-to-hub capacity products between the virtual points of the market areas and trading regions;
- the implementation of efficient capacity allocation mechanisms including auctioning of certain (but not all) types of capacities;
- the harmonization of essential elements of the balancing and nomination management system[62] (e.g., the gas day used for balancing and capacity products).

Details on individual elements of ESTC will be given in the section of this chapter devoted to the implementation of the MECO-S model.

Market coupling

When it comes to market coupling, the connection of markets is effected by an administrative process that, acting as a principal arbitrageur between markets, is vested with special powers (usually monopoly access to some or all interconnection capacity of a time segment) in order to effect an 'as much as is possible' connection of markets and thereby price alignment for the respective time segment of the market.

There are various ways of organizing this administrative process (price or volume coupling, etc.) including in relation to the allocation of roles between the participating TSOs and gas market operators. An in-depth discussion of this goes beyond the scope of this chapter. Figure 7.6 provides a brief introduction to day-ahead market coupling.

The implementation of market coupling has a number of prerequisites, the most notable being the existence of viable and resilient (i.e., liquid) wholesale spot markets usually operated by gas exchanges in both markets. These exchanges must operate on the same schedule and deploy largely harmonized contract specifications, which in turn requires some of

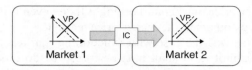

- Adjoining day-ahead spot markets (organized as exchanges operating on the respective virtual points) are connected by an administrative process in the course of which gas is bought in the cheaper market and sold in the pricier market with the goal of price alignment and within the capacity limits of the interconnection capacity available to the market coupling process.
- Market coupling may involve more than two Member States at once (multilateral market coupling).
- Market coupling may be organized on the basis of auctioned spot markets or continuously traded spot markets.
- NB: Market coupling is not synonymous with the limitation of renomination rights. The first is a process of capacity allocation, the latter is a process aiming at increasing the availability of day-ahead capacity. If available day-ahead capacity is not allocated by way of market coupling, it is auctioned off (explicit auction).

<u>Legend and Symbols</u>
IC   Interconnection capacity between markets

⬚ Virtual point of the market

Source: Author elaboration.

Figure 7.6   Scheme of the day-ahead market coupling

the balancing rules in the connected markets to be harmonized (especially the gas day, its time basis and the use of daylight saving time).

The potential application of market coupling in the MECO-S model is another reason why functioning wholesale markets are an essential element of the model. Without a functioning wholesale market, market coupling with its substantial price alignment merits would not be an option.

For a number of reasons I conclude that market coupling is only an option for the short-term (i.e., spot) end of the market. The most important of these reasons being the apparent negative selection[63] by market players of exchange organized futures markets at least in some markets, leading to far lower liquidity on these markets than on spot markets.[64] Without much liquidity in these markets, market coupling is not even an option for time segments with delivery further away than the day ahead. Therefore, the MECO-S model foresees market coupling only for spot markets.

An interesting question is whether market coupling should be implemented for the day-ahead market only or also for a potential within-day market. The answer to this is quite straightforward. If there is a liquid within-day market (e.g., organized as a 'balance of day' market) and market coupling is implemented for the day-ahead market (see conditions below) then within-day market coupling has a high potential of progressing price alignment even more. Since achieving liquid within-day markets can be quite hard though[65] I do not elaborate further on this question.

Another interesting question regarding market coupling is how much (if any) capacity shall be reserved for the coupling process? A detailed analysis of this goes beyond the scope of this chapter. One thing in that regard is already clear though: if market coupling is applied for coupling the day-ahead spot markets, then all capacity that is technically available and not required by shippers should be used for market coupling in order to maximize the price alignment effect. The legitimate interest of shippers being party to a longer-term transportation contract to not fully lose their re-nomination rights[66] should be considered when implementing this policy.

Two further merits of market coupling deserve mentioning. For one thing, as can easily be shown by arbitrage arguments, price alignment in spot markets also drives price alignment in forward markets. Therefore, market coupling need not be implemented for all time segments in order to foster price alignment on the whole price forward curve, for the MECO-S model assumes that price alignment between spot markets suffices to create satisfactory price alignment in the forward markets as well.

For another thing, market coupling most effectively inhibits any conceivable scheme by market participants to influence market price differentials by not using cross-market capacity they purchased by first-come-first-served (FCFS) or by auction. If the market coupling process is endowed with (basically) all unused capacity, the process will always use it as long as more price alignment can be achieved. A prior restraint by market participants on the use of capacity would therefore be rendered ineffective.

Concluding, market coupling has a number of prerequisites that will take time to realize, especially when it comes to the prerequisite of functioning spot markets for all Member States (or groups thereof, forming, for example, a joint trading region). From then on it can contribute significantly to price alignment between markets, and even (where there is sufficient capacity) achieve full price alignment.

Although the theoretical benefits of market coupling are evident there is currently a lot of uncertainty about the optimal design and the resulting cost/benefit ratio of market coupling for gas. Therefore, before market coupling is considered an official element of the gas target model, pilot studies on market coupling should be conducted. In such studies alternative designs of market coupling (e.g., based on auctioned spot markets or on continuously traded spot markets) should be tried out. Also, the issue of full reimbursement of TSOs for capacity they provide to the market coupling process (for which they would only receive a congestion charge,[67] which may be lower than the regulated tariff) needs to be addressed.

If the pilots prove that the theoretical benefits of market coupling can also be realized in practice, market coupling should be made an integral part of the gas target model. Until then, explicit auctioning of day-ahead capacity should be implemented, and the capacity that would otherwise be used for market coupling should be auctioned off. If the pilots prove that market coupling does not deliver its theoretical benefits, explicit auctioning should be maintained for allocating day-ahead capacity.

3.2.3   The Enablement of Secure Supply Patterns

Long-term/long-distance transports
As pointed out and justified in the section on secure supply patterns, it is required to offer to shippers for booking: (1) long-term contracts at EU border points and at cross-market points inside the EU; and (2) long-distance transport (e.g., from an EU border point to the next but one market). In the following subsections, some hints and caveats on structuring these capacity products will be given.

Long-term capacity contracts
In this subsection I will deal with the question of long-term capacity bookings on a single border point (e.g., EU import point or market border point). I start with a set of requirements regarding long-term contracts under the MECO-S model:

- Long-term capacity shall be offered for contract tenors of more than four years up to a maximum tenure (to be defined).
- Existing long-term capacity shall be sold with a lead time (sell-ahead period) matching the time required to expand that specific capacity if this should prove necessary and economic. In order to achieve this linkage of long-term capacity allocation with potential investment, existing long-term capacity shall only be allocated in open-season-style processes to be performed periodically.[68]
- New long-term capacity (which may be incremental capacity on existing systems) shall also be sold in open-season-style processes.
- The amount of capacity sold as long-term capacity shall be limited (e.g., to 65 per cent as in Germany or less as required by the market) but, this shall primarily be achieved by constructing enough capacity so that all economic[69] long-term capacity requests can be fulfilled and building the required[70] short- and mid-term capacity on top of

that[71] (accompanied by a mechanism ensuring that TSOs do not have to assume undue investment risk for the part of capacity that is built but not sold long term[72]).

- Shippers shall be enabled to request long-term capacity in a single request (from start date to end date) and that single request shall be subject to allocation as a whole. (This is opposed to merely offering shippers the opportunity to bid for yearly capacity contracts for a long period into the future. For practical purposes, e.g., to ease secondary capacity marketing, TSOs may decide to contract long-term capacity – after their allocation as a package – in a series of, for example, yearly contracts.)
- Long-term capacity shall be sold as flat capacity (i.e., not structured).
- Long-term capacity shall be allocated as requested wherever this can be achieved by realizing economic investments. Where this is not possible, acceptance shall be limited to – and related investments shall be realized – the portfolio of capacity requests (including the capacities to be reserved for the short- and mid-term markets) that maximize(s) capacity expansion while still achieving the set criteria for economic investment in gas transmission capacity.

Some rationale and clues on how to deal with the requirements stated above are given below, structured by the following questions:

1. For which contract tenors shall long-term capacity on EU import points or market border points be sold?
2. How long should the lead time be between the selling of such capacities and the first day of transport (i.e., the 'sell-ahead period')?
3. How much capacity shall be sold long term?
4. In what increments shall long-term capacity be sold (e.g., in yearly increments or in longer increments)?
5. Shall long-term capacity be sold as flat capacity only or also (if demanded by a shipper) as structured capacity (i.e., with contracted capacities varying over time)?
6. By which allocation mechanism shall long-term capacity be sold?

1   For which contract tenors shall long-term capacity on EU import points or market border points be sold?
Long-term capacity shall serve to underpin long-term supply contracts. Such contracts are regularly concluded for tenors derived from production profiles of specific gas fields and can easily have a duration of 15 to 20 years. Therefore, in order to not unnecessarily limit (or increase the risk for) supply arrangements by network access rules, long-term bookings

should be allowed with contract tenors up to 15 (better 20) years. This does not preclude that for secondary marketing (parts of) this capacity, it is split up into shorter time slices if the shipper so wishes at a later point of time.

2   How long should the lead time be between the selling of such capacities and the first day of transport?

Regularly, long-term supply arrangements are concluded well ahead of the first day of the actual delivery of gas. This is often triggered by the fact that substantive implementation efforts are required for, for example, preparing the supply field for production, building new pipelines to Europe or strengthening existing ones, and so on. Therefore, I assume that it should normally be possible to sign the required transport contracts with substantial lead time. This is good insofar as it makes a lot of sense to foresee a substantial lead time, because if the demand for long-term capacity was higher than the current availability, the TSOs would be in a position to add additional capacity (if economic) as opposed to rationing (by whatever means) the existing capacity on the requests filed. Against this backdrop a lead time between the execution of long-term capacity contracts and the first day of transport amounting to the expected investment cycle of the capacity in question would be reasonable.

Introducing such a (large) sell-ahead period would have a number of effects:

- There would be enough lead time for capacity increase if there is sufficient long-term demand to justify such investment.
- At any point of time any capacity that was not booked long term in the past is – and fully remains – available for the short- and mid-term markets (e.g., four years ahead according to the respective definition in this chapter).
- If on an existing system more than the limit foreseen for long-term capacity contracts is booked long term, this is not a problem because investment can be triggered[73] to build additional capacity for the mid- and short-term market.[74]

3   How much capacity shall be sold long-term?

On general principles a substantial amount of capacity will be held free of long-term capacity contracts. This is required in order to provide the medium- and short-term capacity backbone for the desired emergence of a traded market in these time segments.

The discussion on how much of the capacity shall be offered long term is still ongoing and the range of opinions is wide. As a point of reference for the discussion I refer to the German example, where in 2010 a limit on long-term capacity contracts of 65 per cent of technical capacity was decreed.[75] This may appear too much to some and too little to others. In fact, if the sell-ahead period is sufficiently long, and the investment processes are working, it does not matter from the perspective of capacity management. Any desired limit can be realized by simply adding as much capacity as is required to achieve the targeted limit for long-term capacity.[76]

4   In what time increments shall the long-term capacity be sold?

Let us assume for the discussion in this section that a wholesaler signs a long-term supply contract (say 15 years) with a flat delivery profile (the question of structured profiles will be discussed below). Now this whole-saler (assuming the role of shipper) looks for long-term capacity to under-pin their supply contract. What type of capacity offer would this shipper be interested in? Would they be interested in the opportunity to bid for 15 single yearly capacity contracts with the risk of receiving an uneven capacity profile over the years? Or would they be interested in the opportunity to request (and get allocated) an equal amount of capacity of the desired size in every one of those 15 years? The answer appears obvious. Having the opportunity to request and get allocated an equal amount of capacity for the full contract term (without any limitation in secondary capacity marketing of slices out of that contract) is more attractive for the shipper. So, from the buyer's side the solution is clear, but how does it look from the seller's perspective? The TSOs selling the capacity are potentially challenged by a situation that is best explained by an example in Table 7.1.[77]

Consider the structure of the long-term requests. Now let's assume that the existing capacity does not suffice to fulfil all these requests and that the criteria for economic investment[78] are not sufficiently fulfilled so that meeting all capacity requests by capacity extension is not possible.[79]

In such a situation it is tempting to fall back on a solution where capacity is offered in yearly tranches, accepting that the allocation percentage of a shipper's request may vary over the years, and let the market sort out the

Table 7.1   Structure of long-term requests

Start Date	End Date	(→ Tenure)
2015	2025	10
2017	2028	11
2015	2030	15

Source: Author elaboration.

rest (e.g., by secondary capacity trading). This solution would be associated with considerable risk for the long-term buyer of gas.

Another solution – and this is the one that would better fit the idea of underpinning long-term supply contracts – would be solve the allocation problem by optimization. In this solution an optimization model would be set up with the capacity requests and estimated capital expenditure per capacity step-up as inputs, with the criteria for economic investment (e.g., including an internal rate of return) as conditions to be met, with the constructed capacity as target function to be maximized,[80] and with the acceptance rate[81] per request as variables. The outcome of the optimization would be a set of acceptance rates[82] (one per request) that cannot be increased without violating at least one of the criteria for economic investment.[83] Of course, in such a model, requests for a longer term have a higher likelihood of being accepted than requests for shorter terms. This may sound discriminating at first glance, but it is not. Because discrimination means that shippers are discriminated against because of who they are. Differentiating between shippers' requests based on hard facts (e.g., the tenure of a specific request) is not discrimination, it only handles different things differently. And after all, all of this is done to enable long-term contracts, and shippers interested in shorter contract periods still have the opportunity to go for capacity in the mid-term market (which reaches four years into the future and capacity for that market is assuredly made available at a certain percentage of total capacity).

5 *Shall long-term capacity be sold as flat capacity only or also (if demanded by a shipper) as structured capacity (i.e., with contracted capacities varying over time)?*

Consider a shipper contemplating to sign a long-term supply contract with an upward delivery slope, a plateau phase and a downward slope. Such a shipper may be interested in signing a capacity contract that explicitly matches the supply profile to be transported. On the other hand, for TSOs, offering such structured capacity is a challenge. It would lead to higher tariffs (if TSOs increased the tariff as much as was required in order to meet the criteria for economic investment) or to a higher risk of under-utilization for the TSO (or the final customers to whom such risk is allocated). I think that this issue is best solved by only offering flat capacity profiles under long-term capacity contracts. The arguments in favour of this view are as follows:

● Capacity allocation (if one follows the approach of selling capacity packages spanning several years) is easier and the results of allocation (e.g., by optimization as introduced above) are more comprehensible.

- Shippers can mitigate their risk of under-utilizing the booked capacity on the upward and downward slope of their supply contracts by turning to the secondary capacity markets.
- Shippers are not in a (much[84]) worse position than if they (under an exemption) were to build the capacity themselves (or in a joint venture with other interested shippers). In such a scenario shippers would also have to build (and pay) for the full capacity themselves.

6   By which allocation mechanism shall long-term capacity be sold?

The answers to this question have already been given above. The following paragraphs sum up the results and provide the rationale on an alternative that was not chosen.

First, if all capacity requests (including the required percentage of capacity to be set aside for the short- and mid-term markets) can be met by investment that meets the criteria for economic investment, all requests for long-term capacity shall be accepted without need for rationing. Remember that the sell-ahead period for long-term capacity shall be long enough to realize such investment. Therefore, it is required to integrate the processes of long-term capacity allocation and investment appraisal even for existing capacity on existing systems into periodic open-season-style processes.[85, 86]

Second, if rationing is still required, for example, due to the step-wise nature of investment in gas transmission systems, *and* long-term capacity shall be sold as flat profiles over a long-term (i.e., not in yearly increments), there are two alternatives available to achieve this: (1) the 'optimization' approach introduced under question 4 above, and (2) auctioning.

For reasons given above, the proposed approach to allocating (meaning: rationing) long-term capacity is optimization. In that regard it has to be noted that this optimization would frequently have to be performed by two adjoining TSOs in cooperation, because the market-connecting capacities foreseen in the MECO-S model are hub-to-hub capacities including exit capacity from one TSO and entry capacity from the adjoining TSO.

Why is auctioning not considered for allocating long-term capacity? Well, in the standard auction designs one can only offer the *same* product and then determine the price that bidders are prepared to pay for a given quantity (or the other way round). So given the notion that long-term capacity requests shall be allocated for the full requested term at the same level of capacity, auctioning would entail a preceding definition of the one unified tenure of long-term capacity products (e.g., a tenure of 15 years) that shippers can bid for. This would unnecessarily limit the choice of shippers. Another option would be to 'stripe' the capacity (e.g., into a 20-year tranche that is auctioned first and a 15-year tranche that is auctioned second and so on). This 'striping' has some arbitrariness to it, and it is even more difficult to do, if the capacity of the system in question can be expanded by investment.[87] The optimization approach avoids all these problems.

Long-distance transport

In this subsection I will discuss the question of long-distance transport over several bookable points. Figure 7.7 visualizes and describes the problem that will be solved with long-distance transport products.

Now, how can one address this challenge without introducing captive transport through the back door? First let us narrow down the problem. It appears reasonable that the most severe long-distance transport problems (as displayed in the figure) arise in the context of long-term capacities. I will therefore focus on long-term, long-distance transport in this subsection. This does not preclude that TSOs offer long-distance transport products for mid-term markets or shorter terms according to the principles presented in what follows, if beneficial to the market.

So the problem to be discussed here is: how can shippers realize long-distance transport patterns that are contractually secured for a long term? A proposal frequently put forward to resolve the issue is to time-wise coordinate auctions of single-point capacities. There are two problems associated with this approach. First, as outlined in the subsection on long-term

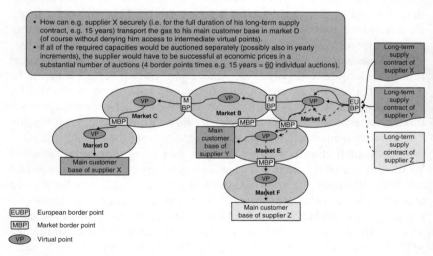

Source: Author elaboration.

Figure 7.7   Scheme of long-distance transport

capacity contracts above, auctioning is probably not the best approach to allocate long-term capacity. Second, if the capacity on different points was allocated by separate procedures (e.g., by separate auctions), the results of these allocation procedures could vary widely leaving the shipper with an unwanted long-term 'capacity profile' (due to differing success in the various allocation procedures) that does not match their needs and that they may not be able to rectify via the secondary capacity market. If the capacity was auctioned individually on every point, the shipper may, of course, bid such high prices that they receive an allocation amounting to the desired amount of capacity on all required border points; but in the end the price may be so high that the underlying supply deal is not economic any more. This in turn will lead the shipper to the conclusion that it is risky to sign the supply contract before they know how much the capacity will cost them and on the other hand they will only know how much the capacity on the whole transport distance will cost them after the last auction was finished (and this will likely not be at the same point of time, leaving them with capacity booked at least on some points). This is a substantial chicken and egg problem when it comes to the execution of new long-term supply contracts for securing supply to European gas consumers.

So it appears that a mere time-wise coordination of single-point capacity allocations does not solve the problem. Before I come to the solution to this issue proposed by the MECO-S model, I will discuss two facts that reduce the gravity of the problem.

First, the problem is decreased by investing. If capacity is increased wherever this is economic, situations where capacities need to be rationed should occur less frequently. But, as was discussed in the subsection on long-term capacity contracts, in certain cases it may not be possible to avoid rationing completely.

Second, the problem is made smaller by the 'functioning markets' feature of the MECO-S model. If stakeholders cooperate to create cross-border trading regions or cross-border market areas this potentially (depending on the markets in question) reduces the number of bookable points between non-neighbouring markets and therefore reduces the complexity of the problem.

In order to solve the problem of long-distance transport, the MECO-S model foresees the offering of 'link chain capacity products' to interested shippers. Link chain products feature the following properties:

- Link chain products are packages (i.e., strings) of bundled (i.e., hub-to-hub) capacities at different market border points.
- Link chain products may be requested for any combination of

market border points (as long as they are on a specific route) and also for more than one year.
- Capacity under a link chain request is either awarded at the same level of capacity at all requested points and for all requested years, or not at all.
- The capacities awarded under a link chain capacity product may be used separately, that is, gas may be dropped and picked up on all virtual points en route.

Let us look at those properties of link chain products in more detail on the basis of an example. A shipper interested in transporting from the EU border point in market A to market D (see Figure 7.7) could specify a request for the desired quantity of capacity for the desired number of years for the full transport from the EU border point in market A through markets B and C to market D. For instance, the shipper might specify a capacity of 100 for 15 years (e.g., from 2015 to 2030). Together with his request he would be entitled to specify a minimum rate of allocation (e.g., 80 per cent) that would be acceptable to him; below that he would retract his request. It is important to note that the shipper may only specify requests for capacities on a continuous (i.e., uninterrupted) route.

In the following allocation process (see notes on the logic of that process below) the shipper would either be allocated:

- his full capacity request (i.e., 100) for the full requested duration on all requested points; or
- a quantity of capacity between his (if specified) minimum acceptance rate (e.g., 80 per cent) and his full request on all requested points; or
- no capacity at all on any point (e.g., because the allocation mechanism would (otherwise) allocate to the shipper a capacity below his minimum acceptance rate).

Of course, as was already discussed in the subsection on long-term contracts, all efforts would be made to allocate to the shipper his full request and to expand capacity wherever this was necessary to do so and economic at the same time.

The capacity allocated to the shipper would be structured as several individual capacities (e.g., in the above example a market entry capacity at the EU border point in market A, a hub-to-hub capacity from market A to market B, etc.) of the same size for the same number of years. These individual capacities put the shipper in the position to transport gas from the EU border point to market D (as desired) while at the same time the capacities may be nominated at different values, enabling the shipper to drop and pick up gas on every virtual point en route.

The difficulty with long-term, long-distance transport is the structure and logic of the allocation process. So far,[88] an allocation mechanism was described for simultaneously allocating long-term capacity on single points with different contract tenures. Additionally, in the case of hub-to-hub capacities, the allocation involved two TSOs.

Now, adding link chain products, the allocation problem becomes more complicated because capacity on more points has to be allocated simultaneously. Two solution strategies exist to deal with this problem: (1) Extending the optimization procedure described in the subsection on long-term capacity contacts so that it includes long-distance contracts. In this case the optimization would involve all affected TSOs and the target function would have to be adapted to simultaneously allow for capacities at different points considering that different transport routes compete for long-term capacity at specific points only. (2) Reverting to a strategy of 'predetermining' transport routes (e.g., based on a market survey) and performing separate allocation procedures for each chosen transport route and also for individual points. Again this 'predetermination' has some arbitrariness to it.

Security of supply investments

The second issue (in addition to long-term and long-distance transport) regarding the enablement of secure supply patterns is security of supply ('SoS') according to Regulation (EU) 994/2010. While not trying to comprehensively address that complicated issue I will present a few thoughts on related network access issues that appear to be relevant for a gas target model.

Specifically I address the issue of how the cost for keeping SoS capacity available (or creating it) in a market different from the market having security requirements can be covered so that the TSO(s) in whose networks that capacity is located suffer no disadvantage from contributing to security of supply in other markets and also cross-subsidies between end users of different markets are avoided. The instrument for solving this problem I will put forward in what follows is termed the 'capacity fallback contract'. I will develop the concept based on a stylized example for the two markets displayed in Figure 7.8.

Let us consider that markets A (with TSO A) and B (with TSO B) are in different Member States and that market A in order to fulfil the 'n−1' standard for transport infrastructure according to Regulation (EU) 994/2010 requires capacity on the market border point ('MBP') from market B. The current capacity on MBP shall be 100 and the SoS demands for that capacity shall be:

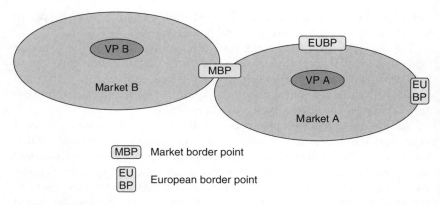

MBP Market border point

EU
BP European border point

Source: Author elaboration.

Figure 7.8   Scheme of market border point

Case (a)   90 (i.e., less than the current capacity); or
Case (b)   120 (i.e., more than the current capacity).

These SoS requirements exist irrespective of the actual bookings of shippers. Therefore, TSO B in market B would need to keep available (or even increase) capacity on MBP, even if he does not foresee a market for it. TSO B also should not (make and) keep the SoS capacity available based on cost allocation to final customers in his home market B, because it is not the SoS demands of market B that shall be catered to here, but those of market A.

Now, since there is bookable capacity between market A and market B, a contractual solution, that is, the fallback capacity contract, to this problem exists that fits nicely into the general network access regime. Under the concept of the fallback capacity contract the following procedures would be implemented:

- The competent authority in market A defines how much SoS capacity on MBP is required from the virtual point (VP) in market B to market A to serve as a fallback supply route in case not enough gas can be delivered through the EUBPs leading to market A.
- TSO A from market A books (based on a fallback contract) with TSO B long-term firm exit capacity from the virtual point in market B ('VP B') amounting to the requested SoS capacity.
- The fallback contract would oblige TSO B to (create and/or) maintain the booked capacity from the VP in his market to the exit point to market A whether it is booked by shippers or not.

- TSO A pays TSO B, on the basis of the regulated tariff of TSO B, for the capacity booked under the fallback contract minus the capacity on the same route that is booked by shippers. That is, TSO A would only pay for the 'redundant' part of that capacity.
- The extra cost TSO A takes on is considered in the cost recognition of TSO A in market A so that TSO A suffers no negative impact from booking the fallback capacity (he may, e.g., be allowed to allocate these costs down to final customers in market A).

The solution presented above has a number of interesting features:

- The relation between the TSOs of different markets (and in the example even of different Member States) is purely contractual.
- TSO B is not forced to do anything that is not economical for him in the interest of another market.
- Market A can determine on its own how high the demand for SoS capacity for its market is and then long-term commission that capacity from the neighbouring TSOs.
- It does not matter if the capacity from market B to market A is main flow or physical reverse flow capacity, the concept works in both cases.

The concept of the fallback contract can be extended to cater to the needs of Member States that require capacity not only (as in the example) to the virtual point of a neighbouring market but to (e.g.) the virtual point of the next but one market or even specific entry points (e.g., EUBPs) to other markets. More TSOs would be involved in that case – but again it would be on a purely contractual basis.

3.2.4 The Implementation of Economic Investments

When it comes to realizing economic investment in gas transmission capacity, a substantial number of questions arise. In the context of this chapter and the MECO-S model the following questions will be addressed:

- How shall projects for investing in interconnection capacity (i.e., between markets) be offered to the market and how shall the economic viability of these projects be determined?
- How shall investment into intraconnection capacity (i.e., investment to overcome congestion within markets) be evaluated?
- How can sufficient finance for investment into gas transmission capacity be secured?

Investment into interconnection capacity

Investment into interconnection capacity can be realized under the regulated regime or under the regime of exemptions.[89] This subsection mainly addresses the process for investment in interconnection capacity under the regulated regime.

The background for investment into new or expanded regulated capacity is formed by the various network development plans foreseen in European legislation. Against this backdrop a process of investment appraisal has to discover if the market (i.e., the shippers) is really prepared to pay for the envisaged (additional) capacity. I believe that appraising an investment project and allocating the capacity on that project should be integrated as tightly as possible. This ensures as much as possible that the market really needs the envisaged capacity because it is prepared to pay for it. The consequence would be that investment projects into interconnection capacity are appraised on the basis of actual long-term capacity requests for that capacity (as filed by shippers).

The limit to this approach is the requirement to reserve some capacity for the mid- and short-term market in order to support the emergence of traded markets. The economic viability for this type of capacity cannot be appraised on the basis of actual long-term capacity requests. Other benchmarks (described below) are needed to evaluate investment into such capacity.

The best procedure known to me for dealing with the inherent uncertainties on the parts of all stakeholders with regard to investing in new capacity is the open season process, the details of which I assume are known.[90] In order to fully integrate investment appraisal and capacity allocation, such open-season-style processes would have to be the only processes under which long-term interconnection capacity is allocated. This would have to be done not only for new projects but also for existing capacity – because if the demand is high enough the allocation of existing capacity should immediately evolve into an investment appraisal. Therefore, these open-season-style processes would have to be performed periodically for all existing interconnection capacity and on demand, if new interconnection projects are envisaged.

During the process shippers would be invited to file their requests for long-term capacity on the particular interconnection point.[91] For new and existing interconnection capacity alike the lead time[92] for the capacity sale would be long enough so that the system can be constructed (in the case of new systems) or expanded (in the case of existing ones) if economic. Requests for main as well as (physical) reverse flow capacities should be invited and treated equally in the process. Regarding the nature of acceptable requests and the allocation logic I refer to the discussion earlier in this section.

If in the case of an existing system not more capacity than already exists is requested and the set percentage of capacity to be reserved for the short- and mid-term market is available on top of that, the process ends with a 100 per cent allocation of all requests for long-term capacity. The phase of investment appraisal (i.e., analysing the economic viability of the investment project by putting revenues and investment/cost in relation to each other in various scenarios) is only entered if: (1) the capacity on an existing system does not suffice to fulfil all requests; and (2) in the case of new projects. When it comes to preparing the investment appraisal of the project it has to be considered (as already mentioned above) that long-term contracts are not the only source of income from the project, but that the capacity reserved for the short- and medium-term market represents an additional element of value. Therefore, the 'revenue' appraisal of an investment into interconnection capacity has to consider two sources: (1) the 'guaranteed' return from long-term contracts signed with shippers in the course of the open season process; and (2) the expected return from mid- and short-term contracts to be signed in the future (this may include a 'congestion' rent accruing to TSOs from coupling day-ahead markets). These two sources of income have to be determined by different means. The revenue from long-term contracts is easily derived from the long-term capacity requests (provided at an estimated tariff) filed by shippers and the respective allocation per investment scenario appraised.

The revenue from future mid- and short-term contracts has to be estimated. One way of estimating the economic value of these contracts would be to study the impact this mid- and short-term capacity would have on the price differential between the two connected markets (taking into account that the new long-term capacity will also have an impact on said differential). The avoided price differential that comes about with the creation of capacity for the mid- and short-term markets would be an indicator of the value of that capacity. Of course, it would have to be made sure that the investor into the (long-term) creation of capacity for the mid- and short-term market receives an adequate return. As a variant, regulators may offer, and TSOs may accept that TSOs bear a share of the utilization risk associated with constructing capacity for short- and mid-term markets in exchange for a higher rate of return on that part of the investment.

A brief digest is due on the question of who shall finally pay for investing in capacities that shall only be sold mid- and short-term. The answer is twofold. First, those who contract that capacity shall (and will) pay for it. But what happens if the capacities are not fully contracted or the revenues achieved from auctioning them are smaller than the regulated tariff so that the investor in those capacities is left with uncovered cost? In this case the market that benefits from those capacities shall pay the bill.

If both markets benefit from the investment, then uncovered cost should be allocated to both markets (in an appropriate ratio). In order to avoid discussions when the problem (uncovered cost) has already arisen, investment of the latter type should be protected by fallback capacity contracts as discussed before in this chapter.

Now, after the (potential) revenues have been determined, how does one appraise whether the expected revenues justify the cost of constructing and operating the new (or expanded) system? Well, once cost (including cost of debt) and revenue (or value) streams (both over time) of an investment are known, the most important[93] missing component to evaluate the investment is a required return on equity. Based on this return figure, a net present value can be calculated (which would have to be at least zero) or the internal rate of return of the investment can be compared to that rate (which would have to be at least as high as the required return on equity). The details of both approaches would go beyond the scope of this discussion.

A final interesting question when it comes to 'open-seasoning' long-term capacity is whether the tariff offered during the open season (that is the basis for the long-term requests by shippers) shall be adapted over time if actual cost rises or drops. This is a difficult question also going beyond the scope of this chapter. I shall restrain myself to presenting the assumed views of shippers and TSOs to that question.

From a shipper's perspective it is quite likely valuable to have a fixed tariff (maybe indexed with general inflation) over the full contract period that – if it is changed at all during the contract period – would only be lowered (e.g., in order to let the shipper participate in efficiency gains of the TSO). From a TSO's perspective all costs pertaining to constructing, financing and operating the system must be covered – and these costs are not completely clear at the time of the open season because the new system (or expansion of an existing system) is yet to be built. So if a TSO would be forced to keep the tariff fixed over the full contract period they would be incentivized to set a tariff for the open season that is high enough to securely cover all future costs and cost increases.

Summarizing, under the MECO-S model the process of investment appraisal is fully integrated with the allocation of long-term capacity in an open-season-style process. No long-term capacity is awarded outside of such processes, not even capacity on existing systems. This makes sense because long-term requests will lead to capacity expansion if economic and open seasons are a good way of dealing in a step-wise manner with the uncertainties of all affected stakeholders when it comes to investing until an economic solution is found. This type of long-term capacity allocation is made possible by choosing a sell-ahead period for long-term capacity (see Section 3.2.3) that is as long as the (estimated) time requirement for expanding (or creating for the first time) capacity. This structuring avoids numerous problems of long-term capacity allocation that arise otherwise. A specific effect of this is also that long-term capacities are not (need not be) auctioned in traditional ways because auctioning is a way of allocating a scarce resource, but if investing is always an option, long-term capacity should not be scarce.[94] Instead it may be 'auctioned' by a system similar to the price-step/volume-step system used in the United Kingdom for identifying efficient investment projects. Additionally the amount of capacity to be reserved for the short- and mid-term market is also planned in the course of the open-season-style process and the economic viability of that capacity is determined based on the expected reduction of price differentials between the connected markets.

Investment into intraconnection capacity
Intraconnection capacity within a market serves a completely different purpose than interconnection capacity between markets. While interconnection capacity helps to connect markets better and thereby improve price alignment, intraconnection capacity fulfils its tasks within a market (i.e., within an entry/exit area). Intraconnection capacity can either serve increased demand in a market or can help to 'de-bottleneck' an entry/exit area. In what follows, I focus on de-bottlenecking investment.

What is the goal of a de-bottlenecking investment in the context of an entry/exit network? In order to answer this question I have to digress into the challenges of calculating capacities in an entry/exit network. The problem with this type of network is that capacity has to be calculated for every individual entry or exit point and the calculated entry capacity will entitle shippers to enter gas at that point up to the designated capacity and to take it off again at any exit point of the same network. Since shippers do not have to designate their 'transport path' beforehand, a lot of potential transport patterns ('scenarios') between the various entries and exits on the network have to be allowed for. When calculating the resulting entry and exit capacities under the various scenarios, it may (in most cases: will) occur that the capacities that can be offered in a network modelled according to the entry/exit logic are smaller than the point-to-point capacities formerly offered (or even contracted) on the same physical network. In order to avoid these results a number of actions may be taken, some of them associated with costs. Among the more popular of the measures with costs (apart from investing; see below) are the purchase of flow commitments by the TSO from shippers and the use of localized system energy (aka 'control energy') by the TSO in case a bottleneck should arise within the network. Usually the use of localized system energy entails cost for the

TSO (e.g., for paying shippers to permanently keep the required system energy available for the TSO to call up or at least in the form of the price differential that the TSO loses, if they buy system energy on one side of the bottleneck and sell it on the other; another way [also with costs] to use localized system energy would be by the TSO using storage).

Having said that – where do intraconnection capacities come into play? Well, such capacities are a means of avoiding the purchase of flow commitments or of spending money on the use of localized system energy. And this also points to how these investments should be evaluated – by estimating how much cost for alternative measures, for example, for flow commitments and localized system energy, are avoided by investing in the intraconnection capacity in question. This avoided cost is the economic 'return' of the new intraconnection capacity. The rest is standard investment appraisal. Of course, since shippers can not book (and therefore TSOs can not sell) intraconnection capacity, it has to be made sure that the cost (including capital cost) associated with that investment is properly recognized in favour of the TSO. The Ten-Year Network Development Plans should be the framework within which the appraisals above are made and where the investment is finally approved of by regulators.

Financing investment into gas transmission capacity
One of the toughest problems when it comes to investing in gas transmission capacity is financing. At first glance it appears reasonable that companies taking over the role of TSO for a specific area will also invest in new systems or capacity expansions wherever this is economic.

The problem with this approach is that there are numerous reasons why an investment that is economic from an economist's view may not be economical (or even feasible) for the specific TSO affected. For instance, the capital structure of that TSO may be such that they can not take on the additional debt required to finance the investment, or the regulated rate of return may be too small from the perspective of the TSO in order to take on the risk associated with the investment project and so on. There has been much discussion on these issues, especially on the rate of return, and that discussion will not be continued here. One thing is clear though. As long as TSOs are established as private companies they should not be coerced to invest if they are not ready to do it. This would be command economy style and would run the risk of scaring away the private sector from the gas transmission business.

A solution that is frequently put forward when it comes to the question of financing investment is to harness exemptions in accordance with Article 36 of Directive 2009/73/EC in order to attract private finance for gas transmission investments. Two issues have to be mentioned in that regard. First, exemptions for gas transmission systems based on Article 36 are limited to interconnection pipelines. So other capacity investment, notably investment in intraconnection capacity, is excluded from utilizing that instrument. This is a substantial disadvantage in that the bigger markets get, the importance of interconnection capacity is reduced while the importance of intraconnection capacity rises. Second, the 'typical' exempted pipeline interconnecting two Member States is a bit foreign to an integrated European gas network. This is due to the fact that exemptions for such pipelines may not only grant an exemption from regulated tariffs (which would be OK if required to attract finance) but may also grant exemption from the Third Party Access rules that would otherwise apply. The latter is what makes such exempted pipelines hard to integrate in the European network access architecture. For instance, an exempted pipeline with its own (commonly point-to-point) network regime, based on its own Network Code would not integrate into bundled capacity products between markets that are a core element of the envisaged market architecture.[95] Also, imposing other 'public service obligations' on exempted pipelines (like reserving parts of capacity for the short- and mid-term market) is difficult because it endangers the economics and bankability of such a project. Of course it would be possible to 'pay' the investors of an exempted pipeline for taking on such public service obligations, for instance by the adjoining regulated TSOs signing a fallback contract with the operator of the exempted pipeline for the capacity to be reserved for short- and medium-term markets. The latter would indeed be a reasonable course of action if an exempted pipeline is built and where it would be uneconomic to build a parallel non-exempted line.

While not at all trying to do away with exempted pipelines – since they are an instrument foreseen by European law and they can play very important roles, consider, for example, long-distance feeder lines like Nabucco that would not be built without an exemption – I suggest an additional instrument to attract private finance for pipeline investment that avoids many of the problems analysed above. That instrument is the tendering of investment projects to the market.

Tendering of investment projects is an option already foreseen in Article 22 (7) of Directive 2009/73/EC. In what follows I will present how such a mechanism could work in practice on the basis of an example:

Investment project:

- An intraconnection capacity project is analysed. The appropriate investment appraisals show that the investment is economic and therefore the decision is made that the project will be realized.

- The TSO in whose network the intraconnection capacity will be built declares (e.g., due to finance limitations) his inability to invest in the project at this point in time.
- Therefore, it is decided to tender the investment project.

Tendering:

- The investment project is worked up as much as is required to tender the project.
- The scope of the tender is procuring, building and financing the required gas transport assets (including land, rights of way, etc.) and leasing them out to the TSO for operation against the payment of an annual fee for the next xx years (e.g., matching the depreciation period).
- Companies with the necessary technical skills and financial clout are invited to bid for the project. NB: at this stage the TSO may file his own bid for the project as well.[96] If the TSO wants to participate in the tender, the tender would have to be conducted by a third party.
- The bids are made on the annual payment that the successful bidder would receive for building and financing the new assets.
- The contract is awarded to the (qualified) bidder ('the developer') that demands the lowest annual payment.

Construction and hand-over:

- The developer constructs the new assets and organizes the financing model for the lifetime of the contract that was awarded to him.
- After successful construction the new assets are handed over by way of a lease model to the TSO for operation.
- After the hand-over the TSO assumes full responsibility for operating and maintaining the new assets.
- Now that the riskiest phase of the project is over, the developer may decide to sell his shares in a project company that holds the new assets, the finance contracts and the lease contract with the TSO, for example, in order to release funds for new projects.

Operation:

- The TSO integrates the new assets into his network access model and all network-related processes as if he was their owner.
- The TSO maintains the new assets as if he was their owner.

- The lease fee for the new assets (for the full duration of the lease) and the cost for operating and maintaining the new assets are considered in the regulation of the TSO ($\rightarrow$cost recognition). NB: further discussion is required on the issue if the TSO earns a service margin on the cost incurred for operating and maintaining the new assets.

End of lease:

- At the end of the lease period the leased assets are transferred to the TSO free of charge and enter his asset base with asset cost of zero.

The model presented above has a number of interesting features:

- New sources of finance are tapped for developing gas transmission projects; finance for those projects is no longer limited to the financial clout of the TSO himself.
- The model does not (re-)introduce an exclusive leasing of assets from the vertically integrated mother or sister company because the investment project is tendered to all interested and qualified parties.
- The number of TSOs is not unnecessarily increased, even if a TSO is not able or willing to invest in a specific gas transmission project, because the operation of the new capacity is still handled by that TSO.
- The model does not implement a market for capacity (which can be problematic for reasons given above) but a market for investment that will likely attract a larger number of players and therefore produce more efficient outcomes than a market for capacity.
- The model relieves TSOs and NRAs from cumbersome (and potentially endless) discussions about regulated rates of return for new investment. That number is decided by the market, based on current market conditions at the time of each tender.

The lease part of the model presented in the example above may seem at odds with the bold wording of Article 17 (1)a of Directive 2009/73/EC. That article foresees that independent transmission system operators ('ITOs') own all assets that are 'necessary for the activity of gas transmission, including the transmission system'. But looking at the genesis of the discussion on ITOs the true intention of the said paragraph may be interpreted as being only to refrain ITOs from leasing assets exclusively from their (vertically integrated) mother or sister company and that the intention was not to refrain ITOs from leasing assets at all. If this assumption is correct (also considering the provisions of Article 22 (7) of the same directive as cited above in this chapter) and given some political will to unleash finance for gas transmission systems, that problem should be a solvable one.

3.3 ANCILLARY QUESTIONS

3.3.1 Impact on Balancing and Nomination Management

Regarding the impact of the MECO-S model on balancing and nomination management, I will discuss the minimum harmonization required in the respective fields in order to realize the various concepts of the MECO-S model. For brevity I will not discuss the issue of what could be gained by more harmonization than the required minimum. The discussion is structured by the pillars of the model.

Pillar 1: Enabling functioning wholesale markets

Two architectures were presented to enable functioning wholesale markets: market areas and trading regions. *Market areas* have the following minimum harmonization requirements per market area as regards balancing:

- Fully harmonized balancing system (i.e., one set of balancing accounts settled according to a single set of rules valid for the whole market area).
- Full harmonization of the data provisioning system underlying the balancing system (i.e., the data regarding injection and withdrawal into/from the network that enters the balancing accounts should be determined based on harmonized rules. Such rules would include the threshold for the use of standardized load profiles, the rules for determining and using these profiles, certain measurement provisions, etc.).

Trading regions have the following minimum harmonization requirements per trading region as regards balancing:

- Single set of trading accounts on the level of the trading region itself, implementing an ex ante 'no-imbalance' regime in the course of the nomination process.
- Implementation of allocation by declaration (aka 'allocated as nominated') at all points leading into and out of the trading region.[97]
- Harmonized gas day for the trading region (NB: implementing the same gas day for all national end-user zones would make a lot of

sense, but is not absolutely necessary in the model if the virtual exit from the trading region to the national end-user zones is nominated in hourly time units).

NB: harmonizing basic rules for keeping the trading accounts in the trading region and the balancing accounts in the national end-user zones, though not an absolute necessity, would also be reasonable (e.g., harmonizing the accounting unit, e.g., MWh).

Pillar 2: Connecting markets

The two most essential concepts of Pillar 2 impacting on balancing and nomination management are hub-to-hub transport products and (potentially) market coupling. *Hub-to-hub transport products* (that include capacities in different markets) have the following minimum harmonization requirements for the connected markets as regards nomination management:

- harmonized nomination system (nomination quantity unit, e.g., MWh);
- harmonized nomination time unit (e.g., hour);
- harmonized nomination schedule (including time basis and a harmonized decision on the use or non-use of daylight saving time) etc.

Market coupling has the following minimum harmonization requirements for the coupled markets as regards balancing and nomination management:

- harmonized gas day (including a harmonized time basis and a harmonized decision on the use or non-use of daylight saving time);
- harmonized nomination quantity unit (e.g., MWh);
- allocation by declaration (aka 'allocated as nominated') at all points subject to market coupling.

Pillar 3 (secure supply patterns) and the common foundation (investment) of the model do not require any specific harmonization in the fields of balancing or nomination management.

As a final contribution to the ongoing European discussion on the balancing Framework Guideline and respective Network Code, I provide a short frame of reference on the impact areas of a balancing system (including nomination management) that may be useful to structure discussions on the issue.

Impact areas of a balancing (and nomination management) system:

- system integrity (i.e., keeping gas pressures on the network between the defined minimum and maximum limits, so that the transmission of natural gas is guaranteed from a technical standpoint);[98]
- competitiveness (i.e., the [potentially] differing impacts of various types of balancing systems on market participants of, e.g., differing sizes or on incumbents versus newcomers);
- transaction cost (i.e., the cost for market participants of operating within the framework of a balancing system);
- balancing efficiency (i.e., the cost for maintaining the balancing system that is [by various means] allocated to market participants and final customers);
- externalities (i.e., the impact of the balancing system on other properties of the market, e.g., the liquidity on spot markets).

Formulating goals for these impact areas is not easy and is a potentially contentious task, as can be illustrated by the following examples:

- Will the balancing system ensure system integrity (including the delivery of gas to all final customers in accordance with their demand) at all times? In other words: will the balancing system make provisions for certain failures of market participants (e.g., substantially underestimating demand or not preparing for especially high demand situations) and become a supplier 'of last resort' for the market? And if yes, for how long? And if no, what will happen (to be effected by whom) after the 'responsibility' of the balancing system has ended?
- Will the balancing system only be 'competition neutral' or will it actively support competition by new market entrants (e.g., by defining flat [daily] standardized load profiles, which may even [although temperature-sensitive] be determined one day in advance as is the case in Germany)?
- Will the balancing system only have no negative externalities or will it create positive externalities (e.g., by requiring hourly balancing from shippers in combination with little or no tolerances that could spur the emergence of a within-day market)?

I suggest that in the ongoing discussions on balancing and nomination management the impacts of the various implementation proposals are analysed by a framework similar to the one presented above.

3.3.2 Role of Within-day Markets

There is a discussion ongoing in Europe on the role of within-day markets. In this subsection I will briefly discuss the role of within-day markets in the context of the MECO-S model. Let us start with a definition of the term 'within-day gas market': a within-day gas market is a market (either OTC or exchange-operated) where gas can be bought and sold for delivery on the current (or immediately forthcoming) gas day. A within-day gas market may either be structured as a 'balance of day' market where gas is bought and sold with a flat delivery profile for the remaining (with some lead time) hours of the gas day or as an hourly market where the traded product is the delivery/takeover of gas in a specific future hour.

When analysing the necessity of a within-day market, one has to look at the close interrelations between within-day markets and the balancing system of a market. This interrelation is illustrated by two (hypothetic) examples in Box 7.1

It is certain though that the concepts presented by the MECO-S model do not depend on the existence of a within-day market, but also nothing in the MECO-S model withstands the introduction of such a market. It may also be expected that the implementation of the MECO-S model (since it generally supports the emergence of functioning wholesale markets) will also support the emergence of functioning within-day markets.

3.3.3 Role of Physical Gas Hubs

'Physical gas hub' is a term not legally defined. Our working definition of physical gas hub involves a geographical point on one major pipeline or a crossing of several major pipelines where changes in ownership of gas can be effected. Usually ancillary services like back-up/down would be offered. In some cases gas exchanges have selected physical hubs as their delivery point. Examples of European physical hubs would be Zeebrugge Hub, Belgium or CEGH, Austria.

The trading procedures (and their effects on the market) on physical hubs are in general quite similar to those at virtual trading hubs[99] (examples of the latter would be NBP, TTF, NCG, Gaspool Hub, PEG Nord or Sud). However, the trades that make it into delivery on the physical hubs are limited to such gas volumes as are physically passing through the respective hub.[100]

The question to be discussed here is, what will be the role of physical hubs in the MECO-S model (or any other hub-to-hub-model)? For analysis I differentiate the following types of physical hubs:

BOX 7.1   INTERRELATION BETWEEN WITHIN-DAY MARKETS AND THE BALANCING SYSTEM

Example 1

The balancing system foresees an hourly cash-out period with little (or no) tolerance: in this case, market players will either have to buy access to a source of hourly flexibility (e.g., storage or a flexible delivery contract) or turn to the within-day market to manage their hourly flexibility needs.

Potentially (as always with markets) the within-day market can raise efficiency in bringing together market players with hourly flexibility requirements and those able to supply such flexibilities.

Other interesting features of a within-day market (in the situation of Example 1) are that market players with opposing flexibility needs (e.g., one player being [i.e., expecting to be] long, the other short for a future hour) may effectively cancel their positions via the market (which would be a very efficient action) and also that such markets are a way of efficiently integrating demand management measures into the balancing logic of a market.

Example 2

The balancing system foresees a daily cash-out period with no hourly limits and substantial tolerances for imbalances to be rolled over to the following day. In this scenario (which may be efficient for markets with substantial line-pack[101] potential), market players may find out that they do not have a need for within-day trading activities and that a day-ahead spot market sufficiently satisfies their short-term flexibility requirements.

Since the MECO-S model does not present its own proposal for the balancing system no specific conclusions regarding a within-day market need to be drawn.

- physical hubs located outside European territory (i.e., before upstream pipelines enter European territory) ('extra-hubs');
- physical hubs located at the border between two or more Member States ('inter-hubs');
- physical hubs located within the borders of one Member State ('intra-hubs').

Extra-hubs are completely unaffected by the MECO-S model, since the MECO-S model only deals with issues taking place on European territory. They may continue to play their role of being a marketplace where gas can be traded before it enters the first European market, helping market participants in avoiding unnecessary transports in and out of a market.[102]

Inter-hubs are not required any more, after the full implementation of hub-to-hub-trading[103] based on hub-to-hub capacity products. In such a hub-to-hub scenario there would be no more gas at border flanges that could be traded via the hub. Maintaining inter-hubs as a stopover between the virtual points of the adjoining markets does not seem to be efficient, because it shatters market liquidity and offers no service that could not also be offered on either (or all) of the affected virtual points. Instead it appears likely that operators of inter-hubs will relocate some of their service offerings to one (or all) of the virtual points of the markets whose borders they were formerly operating on.

Intra-hubs are affected in a way quite similar to inter-hubs. After the creation of market areas and trading regions with virtual points, they vanish into the network making up the physical background of the market area or trading region (where their physical services, e.g., wheeling [making gas flow by increasing pressure differential], may still be required in order to physically operate the market area or trading region). One would also expect that intra-hub operators would try to relocate some of their service offerings to the virtual points of the markets they are situated in.

3.3.4 Impact on Tariffs

Regarding the role of tariffs in the context of the MECO-S model I will discuss how the various concepts of the MECO-S model impact on tariff issues and what corollary measures may be required in the tariff sector (see Box 7.2). The discussion is structured by the pillars of the model.

Pillar 1: Enabling functioning wholesale markets
Pillar 1 foresees among other things that markets are organized as entry/exit networks of a certain size, possibly including several Member States. This gives rise to a number of issues. First, more and more points that have been bookable points before will become points internal to the entry/exit zone ('internal points'). The TSOs on whose network these internal points are located will lose a source of revenue. In order to deal with such a potential loss of revenue a simple solution exists, called the 'internal booking approach'. According to the internal booking approach, at every internal point the respective downstream TSO[104] books the required capacity from the upstream TSO (i.e., the exit capacity from the upstream TSO is

---

**BOX 7.2   COMMON FOUNDATION: REALIZING
         ECONOMIC INVESTMENT**

The open-season-style selling of long-term capacity and the – at
the same time – appraisal of new investment presented in the
section on economic investment does not require any corollary action in the tariff sector apart from the recognition of cost
incurred by TSOs creating and reserving capacities for the mid-
and short-term markets.

   The instrument of tendering investment projects to the market
does require reflection in the area of tariffs insofar as the lease
fee charged by the developer of the investment project needs
to be fully recognized in the cost basis of the TSO paying the
lease fee.

---

booked) and integrates this cost into their own exit tariffs. If – between
the affected networks – the gas flows interchangeably in both directions,
then both TSOs book capacity on the respective other TSO's network. By
this mechanism the cost of transmission 'flows with the gas' to the final
customers, which appears to be an equitable approach. One property of
this approach – which may be deemed problematic by some – is that an
increasing share of total network cost is collected at exits (because cost is
always allocated downstream). If this becomes an issue another potential
solution involves (partly) shifting the cost of internal points (partly) up to
the entries of the (every) affected TSO. The actual solution for a specific
market should be chosen with great care in order to avoid contortions in
the commodity markets.

   Second, the larger an entry/exit system becomes, the higher the risk that
the entry/exit tariffs will blur the actual (i.e., 'economic') cost of delivering
gas to a specific exit point. This risk is especially high if an undifferenti-
ated 'postage stamp' approach to exit tariffs is implemented, whereby the
exit of gas costs the same at every exit point no matter where this point
is located. At the second glance the issue becomes less complicated – it
even disappears – if every TSO determines the exit fees for their network
separately taking into account their own cost plus the cost for 'internal
bookings' (see above paragraph). In that case, final customers supplied
by TSOs close to market entry points would enjoy lower exit costs (which
would also be in line with the economic fact that it costs less to transport
the gas to them) and those further away from sources would have higher
exit cost.

Third, it is frequently put forward that the principles for calculating regulated network cost and/or regulated tariffs need to be harmonized among all TSOs participating in an integrated market. While not contending that this could not make some sense, I think it is not an absolute necessity for such markets to work well. Specifically I do not think that such harmonization is a prerequisite of creating cross-border markets; it may just as well be done later. The functioning of a market (market area or trading region) does not depend on all participating TSOs employing the same principles for asset valuation, the same depreciation periods or the same rate of return on equity, and so on.

Pillar 2: Connecting markets

Remember that the connection of markets for the medium and short(er) time segments is based on allocation of capacity by auctions. In most cases these will be explicit auctions, while under certain conditions an implicit auction by way of market coupling may be implemented for the day-ahead time segment.

Now auctions (implicit and explicit) depend on the demand for a certain capacity and the amount of capacity available. Therefore, auction revenues will in most situations deviate from the fixed (regulated) tariffs that would be charged otherwise. Hence auctions can result in: (1) over-recovery (i.e., the auction revenue being higher than the fixed tariff); or (2) under-recovery (i.e., the auction revenue being lower than the fixed tariff. NB: this situation can only occur if auction minimum prices ('reserve prices') are set lower than the fixed tariff.

Measures for dealing with over-recovery are well known. They include setting the over-recovery aside for the relief or removal of congestion or the lowering of tariffs on other appropriate parts of the same network (or another network within the same market; this would necessitate intra-market inter-TSO compensation).

If the implementation of the gas target model should allow situations where under-recovery can occur (i.e., by setting low or zero reserve prices for certain capacity products), measures have to be implemented so that network operators do not suffer from this market design decision.

Measures for dealing with under-recovery include raising tariffs on appropriate parts of the same network (or another network within the same market, again necessitating intra-market inter-TSO compensation) or allocating cost to adjoining network operators of the adjoining market that benefits from the transport (i.e., inter-market inter-TSO compensation). In the latter case the TSO receiving the cost allocation must be entitled to allocate this cost within their market.

The mechanism presented above can deal with any deviation of auction revenues from fixed tariffs that would be charged otherwise (i.e., if there was no auction).

Pillar 3: Enabling secure supply patterns

Under the header of secure supply patterns the issues of long-term and long-term, long-distance transport were first discussed. As was presented in the respective section I do not foresee the auctioning of long-term capacity. Therefore, issues as presented above regarding auctions do not arise when it comes to long-term capacity. I also do not see any other tariffing issues arising from the instruments presented in that context.

Second, the concept of the fallback capacity contract was introduced.[105] As was already discussed in that section it is necessary that TSOs obligated by their competent national authority to perform fallback capacity bookings for transport security of supply purposes are entitled to a full recognition of the cost arising from such action.

3.3.5   Role of Gas Exchanges

What is the role of gas exchanges within the MECO-S model? First, gas exchanges are a valuable element of a functioning wholesale market. They provide an anonymous and counterparty risk-protected marketplace with transparent price formation rules. Additionally they are a valuable source of price information for all kinds of market participants and purposes. So, even if functioning wholesale markets are not dependant on gas exchanges, since a lot can be and is done on the OTC market, they are a welcome and valuable element of any target market architecture.

There is one element of the MECO-S model though that actually depends on an exchange organized market and that is day-ahead market coupling. As described in the respective section,[106] market coupling is a process that includes actions on the two (or more in the case of multilateral market coupling) coupled gas exchanges.

In order to realize the market coupling process with existing gas exchanges the collaboration of the affected gas exchanges is required especially with respect to the timing of the market coupling process, the required information flows, the harmonization of price formation rules and certain essential spot contract specifications (to make the coupling process more or less riskless) and so on. Other than that, the MECO-S model does not foresee any specific role for gas exchanges in the market architecture.

The MECO-S model will have an indirect impact on gas exchanges though. Since, according to the pillar of functioning markets, smaller markets are integrated to (form) larger markets, the number of virtual points for exchanges to operate on will be reduced, potentially leading to (where they already exist) fewer, but more liquid and thereby relevant gas exchanges.

3.4 IMPLEMENTATION OF THE MECO-S MODEL

The following subsection provides clues on what would have to be done in order to realize the MECO-S model. Of course – since the whole model is not prescriptive – these clues cannot and are not at all prescriptive but merely recommendations for stakeholders in charge of realizing gas network access.

3.4.1 General

Implementing the MECO-S model can be separated into two questions: (1) In which sequence shall the elements of the model be implemented? (2) How shall the model be implemented? The first question can be dealt with rather briefly. The logical interrelations between the individual elements of the MECO-S model (where they exist at all) are in most cases only beneficial[107] but do not enforce a specific order of implementation. This is only true with one substantial exemption though. Market coupling can only be implemented once functioning spot markets exist.[108] Other than that I would not see any mandatory order of implementation.

The second question on how the model shall be implemented bears much more of a challenge. It decomposes into a number of sub-questions, the most important being: Which legal instruments shall/may be used in order to implement the model? Who would have to do what in order to implement the model? When analysing the issue of the legal instruments, one quickly realizes that the 'European processes' foreseen in the Third Energy Package, namely the Framework Guideline/Network Codes process, is not sufficient to comprehensively implement the model. This is due to the fact that the gas target model requires cooperation on the side of market participants not within the scope of the Network Codes or any other European[109] instrument made available by the Third Energy Package. These market participants are distribution system operators and operators of gas exchanges.

The cooperation of distribution system operators is required in order to implement market areas and (but to a far lesser extent) trading regions. For example, in a market area, distribution system operators get allocated transport costs from transmission system operators and have to provide timely allocation data to TSOs so that TSOs can provide balancing information to shippers. It appears highly unlikely that distribution system operators will accept those tasks without regulation[110] obliging them to do so or at least making sure they are permitted to recover the extra cost (e.g., from their own shippers). This type of regulation does (with a lot of variation) exist in a number of Member States, but not on a European level. Enacting this regulation in a comprehensive and uniform way will either require another act of European legislation or (well coordinated) regulation[111] in several Member States.

The cooperation of gas exchanges is required especially in order to get market coupling off the ground. Also, gas exchanges cannot be obligated by the mentioned European processes, but I deem this a lesser problem because on the one hand exchanges should have a natural interest in participating in market coupling because it can further their business and on the other hand, exchanges are (although subject to network economics) not natural monopolies. So if the dominant exchange for a market does not want to cooperate on a voluntary basis, maybe another one will or even TSOs might take over that task.

The following subsection deals with the first issue of supporting and not preventing the model in the Framework Guidelines. It lists – per Framework Guideline – issues that are important for the model without regard to the fact that some of these issues may already be covered in current drafts of Framework Guidelines. Additionally, in the next but one subsection, further issues are listed that in most cases will require additional, mostly legislative action, but for which the Network Codes are not the appropriate legal instrument.

3.4.2   Implementation in the Framework Guideline Process

This subsection lists issues that may be implemented in the ACER Framework Guidelines and later on in the ENTSOG Network Codes. The list focuses on issues that are of particular importance for implementing the MECO-S model no matter if they are already reflected in existing drafts of Framework Guidelines.

Framework Guideline on capacity allocation management
Regarding the structure of TSOs' commercial network model:

- TSOs shall generally structure their networks as entry/exit zones (aka 'entry/exit networks') where capacities at entries are not assigned to specific capacities at exits and may be bought separately.
- TSOs shall structure their entry/exit capacities in a way so that

shippers may request redelivery of gas at any exit point of the entry/
exit zone no matter on which entry point of the same entry/exit zone
the gas was injected or if it was taken into possession at the virtual
point of said zone.

- Cross-border entry/exit zones shall be permitted.
- TSOs implementing the market area model shall – in cooperation
  with the adjoining TSOs and DSOs in the market – create an (i.e.,
  one integrated) entry/exit zone that includes transmission and distribution systems with no bookable capacity between them.
- TSOs implementing the trading region model shall – in cooperation with the adjoining TSOs in the market – create an (i.e., one
  integrated) entry/exit zone that includes all nominated points on
  their networks and features a virtual exit to the connected end-user
  zones.
- TSOs shall implement a (i.e., one) virtual point in every entry/exit
  zone, where gas can be handed over from one shipper to another
  shipper.
- TSOs shall offer to shippers for booking only capacity at border
  points[112] of a market (i.e., market area or trading region).
- TSOs shall, where two markets are connected by more than one
  interconnection point belonging on both sides to the same TSO's
  network respectively, zone these physical interconnection points
  into one virtual interconnection point.

Regarding capacity products:

- TSOs shall define and sell all capacity products as hourly capacities
  expressed in KWh based on gross calorific value.
- TSOs shall sell capacity at cross-market interconnection points only
  by way of bundled capacity products ('hub-to-hub products') incor-
  porating the exit capacity from market A and the entry capacity of
  the adjoining market B in a single contract to be executed with either
  of the adjoining TSOs.
- TSOs shall – as an exemption to any contrary provision herein – sell
  at every market border point unbundled entry or exit capacity to
  every holder of unbundled exit or entry capacity at the same point
  on the system of the interconnecting TSO with a tenure no longer
  than the tenure of the existing capacity contract at the same market
  border point held by the requesting shipper.
- TSOs shall offer commercial (i.e., non-physical) back-haul capacity
  at every market border point, unless physical reverse-flow capacity
  is offered at that point.

- TSOs shall harmonize contract tenors (e.g., day, month, quarter, year), start dates and start hours for capacity products, whereby start dates for the same tenor shall have no overlap (e.g., only one start date and hour for yearly contracts and so on for the other contract terms).
- TSOs shall use reasonable endeavours to align tenors and start dates for transport contracts with commodity contracts traded on gas exchanges as far as these feature the virtual point of their 'home' market as the delivery point.
- TSOs shall split the available technical capacity at every market border point to contract tenors (e.g., long-term, mid-term, short-term) in a harmonized way foreseeing at least x per cent of technical capacity to be allocated to mid- and short-term requests whereby capacity that is not sold in a longer-term category shall be offered in the next shorter-term category.
- TSOs shall implement a harmonized interruption logic (especially triggers for and sequence/allocation of interruption of/to individual contracts) for interruptible capacity products (and equitably reflect that logic in the tariffs charged for interruptible products).
- TSOs shall cooperate to offer link chain products between non-adjoining TSOs (e.g., from country A to the non-adjoining country D). Those products shall enable shippers to request and get allocated[113] a string of bundled[114] cross-market capacities and (if requested) entry capacities at an EU border point on a continuous transport route chosen by the shipper whereby the allocated capacities shall entitle the shipper to drop gas and/or pick up gas at every intermediate virtual point.

Regarding the processes of selling capacity by TSOs (i.e., primary capacity):

- TSOs shall sell (primary) capacity at individual bookable points according to the following procedures:

   Long-term capacity:
   – Long-term capacity (existing and potential new capacity) shall only be sold in the course of periodical open seasons.
   – The lead time for the capacity sold (i.e., the time between the open season and the first transport day) shall be long enough so that capacity expansion can be realized if the demand is high enough and the investment is economic.
   – In such open seasons requests for main flow and physical reverse flow capacity shall be invited and allocated and investments for both transport directions shall be considered alike.

- In addition to long-term capacity requests the required capacity to be reserved for the short- and mid-term markets shall be considered in the investment appraisals. They shall be valued based on their estimated effect (i.e., reduction) on price differentials between the connected markets.
- TSOs shall define and apply a harmonized set of minimum criteria for the acceptance of binding bids during the open season and the ensuing investment decision that is fair, concrete and transparent.
- If not all capacity requests can be fulfilled, the investment problem shall be solved by optimizing for maximum capacity with economic parameters as constraints to be kept.

Mid- and short-term capacity: Auction.
Day-ahead capacity:
- Once market coupling is implemented: reserved for market coupling.
- As long as market coupling is not yet implemented: auction.
- Day-ahead capacity not required after the daily market coupling process: first-come-first-served.

Within-day capacity: first-come-first-served.
- TSOs shall coordinate auction dates for mid- and short-term capacities on individual market border points in such a way that those auctions are not all concluded at the same day and time.[115]
- TSOs shall devise a harmonized sales procedure for long-term link chain products[116] that is integrated with the open seasons foreseen for selling long-term capacities on individual bookable points, whereby an allocation to a link chain request would always involve the same amount of capacity at all requested points for all requested years.

Regarding secondary capacity:

- TSOs shall devise harmonized procedures for transferring the title to or the usage rights of primary capacity from one shipper to another shipper for all or part of the contracted capacity and its tenor.

Regarding short-term use/sell it or lose it:

- TSOs shall devise harmonized procedures that make sure that at least the majority of capacity unused (or unsold) by shippers for the following day is made available to the market (or the market coupling process) as firm day-ahead capacity.

Regarding short-term capacity management:

- TSOs shall cooperate every day to align as much as possible[117] for every market border point the amount of bookable day-ahead capacity at least with the expected requests for day-ahead capacity at that point in order to reduce or even avoid congestion at usually congested cross-market points.

Framework Guideline on balancing
Regarding the general nomination and balancing regime:

- TSOs shall define a harmonized energy unit to be used in all nominations for physical and virtual points (e.g., MWh based on gross calorific value with two decimal places).
- TSOs shall require nominations to be made in hourly quantities (i.e., 24 hourly quantities to be nominated per gas day).[118]
- TSOs shall define a harmonized nomination and re-nomination schedule.
- TSOs shall define a harmonized nomination message format (including uniform provisions on the use of encryption and electronic signatures) and in any case support the exchange of nomination messages by electronic mail over the internet.
- TSOs shall use their reasonable endeavours to align the nomination and re-nomination schedule with trading hours on gas spot exchanges.
- TSOs shall define a harmonized gas day including a unified time basis (e.g., UTC – Coordinated Universal Time) and a decision on the harmonized use or non-use of DST – Daylight Saving Time – for the whole nomination and balancing system.
- TSOs shall accept bundled nominations for bundled capacities sold at cross-market points (i.e., a single nomination for the included entry and the exit capacity to be submitted to the TSO with which the shipper signed the bundled capacity contract).
- TSOs shall cooperate to implement balancing zones identical to the entry/exit zones they created according to the market area or trading region model.
- TSOs shall implement the 'allocation by declaration' (aka 'allocated as nominated') principle at all intra-EU market border points (i.e., interconnection with other European TSOs).
- TSOs shall use their reasonable endeavours to implement the 'allocation by declaration' principle at all EU border points (aka 'import points') and at all interconnections with European storage and indigenous production.

- TSOs implementing the trading region model shall implement the 'allocation by declaration' principle at the virtual exit to the interconnected end-user zones.
- TSOs shall (also) use existing liquid gas spot exchanges (day-ahead and if available within-day) for procuring or selling the energy required for the physical balancing of their respective markets (aka 'external system energy').
- TSOs that require flows of gas at particular points on their networks for purposes of physical balancing shall either contract storage or contract the required flexibility as 'flow commitments' not including the transfer of title to gas from the vendor of the flow commitment to the TSO or vice versa, whatever is technically available and more economic.
- TSOs operating in markets without a liquid day-ahead and within-day gas spot market shall provide shippers with tolerances in their balancing accounts, whereby those tolerances shall utilize but not exceed the technical capabilities of their system.

Additional items in order to realize market areas or trading regions involving more than one TSO:[119, 120]

- TSOs shall devise a harmonized balancing system involving uniform provisions on the following elements:
  - shippers' rights and obligations regarding the management of its balancing account;
  - data provisioning by, and to, the shipper;
  - cash-out period of the balancing system (e.g., hour or day);
  - free of charge tolerances to be applied on the account balance before cash-out;
  - potentially additional, fee-based tolerances;[121]
  - pricing of balancing energy;
  - additional financial or non-financial incentives in the balancing system.

Additional items in order to enable trading regions:

- TSOs implementing the trading region model shall be entitled to set up trading regions as fully 'allocated as nominated' systems involving hourly settled trading accounts.[122]
- TSOs implementing the trading region model shall be obliged to settle imbalances resulting from interrupting capacity or from missing 'allocation by declaration' agreements on EU border points directly with their shippers on the basis of a market based price.

- TSOs implementing the trading region model shall either (depending on national legislation regarding the balancing of the end-user zone) physically balance their national end-user zone as a task separated from maintaining the trading region or provide the national end-user balancing entity with access to the virtual point in the trading region.[123]

Framework Guideline on interoperability

- TSOs shall – having due regard to the ongoing standardization work on a European gas quality standard – cooperate (and continue to cooperate) to harmonize gas quality specifications (including odorization) and where required the actual gas quality at all physical interconnection points as much as is economically reasonable and technically feasible without breaching national legislation on gas quality so that physical reverse flow is not prevented by gas quality issues.
- Adjoining TSOs at market border points shall align their network maintenance activities in the way required so that interruption of bundled capacity products due to maintenance is kept at the necessary minimum.

Framework Guideline on tariffs
NB: the following items are subject to the assumption that the ENTSOG Network Codes – once set into force by comitology – rank higher than national law also in the area of setting tariffs:

- TSOs shall set the harmonized start date of the yearly capacity product (see above) as the only day on which tariffs for network access may be changed.
- TSOs shall define harmonized criteria for allocating network cost to entry and exit points.
- TSOs shall define harmonized methods for pricing capacity products (no matter which method they are sold by) ('regulated tariffs').
- TSOs shall define harmonized auction[124] procedures (i.e., the auction method) for selling capacity products, including a uniform provision on the consideration of regulated tariffs as reserve prices that may be differentiated per contract term.
- TSOs shall define harmonized procedures for splitting among the involved TSOs the proceeds from auctioning off bundled capacity products.

- TSOs shall define harmonized procedures for dealing with over- or under-recovery of their regulated tariffs due to auctions (e.g., by building investment allowances or by adapting cost allocation to other network operators).
- TSOs shall define harmonized procedures for inter-TSO compensation required due to transporting gas from TSO 'A' to TSO 'B' (in the same or another market) either without receiving any proceeds from shippers[125] or against auction proceeds lower than the regulated tariffs. These procedures shall make sure that TSOs and national final customers are not put at a financial disadvantage from TSOs cooperating with other TSOs or from TSOs implementing auctions. These procedures shall not lead to TSOs rolling over their capacity risk (i.e., under-utilization) to other TSOs unless this is foreseen by national legislation and no cross-border roll over of these costs occurs outside of capacity fallback contracts concluded for reasons of transport security of supply.

3.4.3 Implementation in Other Processes

The following list contains further items that need to be ensured for the implementation of the MECO-S model.

Items regarding the realization of national market areas:

- DSOs to cooperate with TSOs in order to form market areas involving cost allocation (i.e., the TSOs' exit cost) from TSOs to DSOs.
- DSOs to integrate the final customers attached to their systems into the balancing system set up by the upstream TSO(s) in the market area.
- DSOs to deliver data required for balancing to the TSOs in accordance with the balancing system described in the ENTSOG Network Codes.

Items regarding the realization of trading regions:

- DSOs to cooperate with each other to form a national end-user zone.
- Appointment of an entity tasked with balancing the national end-user zones, which may be the national TSO.

Further harmonization required in order to realize cross-border market areas:

- Harmonization of the following elements of the 'data generating system' underlying the balancing system:
    - deployment and structure of standardized load profiles (SLP) (including the threshold above which SLPs may not be used);
    - handling of estimation errors of SLPs;
    - quality parameters for end-user consumption metering devices (especially acceptable measurement errors);
    - regulations for converting measured quantities into energy units (considering pressure, temperature, altitude, calorific value);
    - regulations for measuring (and/or calculating) the calorific value required for converting metered values into energy units; and
    - harmonization/clarification of legal protection for all stakeholders being part of or participating in a cross-border market area.

Items regarding TSO cost recognition:

- TSOs shall be entitled to regulatory cost recognition of the following activities:
    - (creating and) reserving transmission capacity for the short- and mid-term markets that is later on not (or not fully) booked by shippers or where the proceeds from auctioning these capacities do not cover the cost (including capital cost) of the TSO;
    - leasing parts/elements of transmission systems constructed and financed long-term by third parties determined by tender;
    - paying for capacities reserved under fallback-capacity contracts for purposes of realizing 'n-1' transport security of supply;
    - paying fees to other TSOs by way of inter-TSO compensation (e.g., between several TSOs within a market).

Items regarding capacity extension:

- TSOs shall be obliged to tender any investment project that is foreseen in a binding network development plan and that they are not willing or able to realize themselves to the market for development including long-term financing by the developer. TSOs shall long-term lease the resulting gas transmission assets, operate and maintain them and integrate them into their network access models as if they were owned by the TSO.

- TSOs shall develop a standardized business, process and contract model for the procedure described immediately above.

Items regarding TSO cooperation in the area of transport security of supply:

- TSOs shall develop a standardized capacity fallback contract to be used for inter-market transport security of supply.
- TSOs shall be obliged to perform fallback capacity bookings with neighbouring TSOs in other markets at the request of the competent national authority if a full recognition of the cost incurred by the TSO is guaranteed.
- TSOs shall be obliged to accept long-term fallback capacity bookings by adjoining TSOs at the level demanded by the neighbouring TSO for existing main and physical reverse flow capacity.
- TSOs shall be required to invest in – or tender for investment – the capacity extensions becoming necessary by fallback capacity requests in main and reverse flow direction – if the requested fallback capacity contract securely covers (as a fallback) all ensuing cost.
- TSOs shall cooperate in order to enable fallback capacity bookings that include more than one market border point.

Further tasks of TSOs regarding the organization of markets:

- TSOs shall – in order to foster market coupling and paying due attention to national legislation on exchanges – establish spot gas exchanges where these do not exist or operators of existing exchanges do not cooperate as required to realize market coupling.

Further harmonization required regarding trading arrangements:

- Gas exchanges shall harmonize their commodity contract specifications and their price formation algorithms (at least) for the day-ahead product.[126]
- Gas exchanges shall align their product offering and trading hours with the requirements of the TSO balancing system as defined in the Network Codes.
- Gas exchanges shall align the commercial properties of the traded products (e.g., start dates and hours, quantity parameter, size increments, etc.) with TSOs' capacity products (and vice versa).

NOTES

* The author particularly thanks Sergio Ascari (FSR gas advisor), Jacques de Jong and Leonie Meulman (Clingendael International Energy Programme), Albrecht Wagner (Wagner, Elbling and Company), Christophe Pouillon (GRT Gaz), Margot London (Eurogas) and Stephan Kamphues (ENTSOG). The author wants, however, to underline that the vision delivered in this chapter is only his opinion and does not bind or tie any of these persons. Sergio Ascari, on the one hand, Jacques de Jong and Leonie Meulman, on the other, have published their own conclusions separately. The author also warmly thanks the experts of the Austrian and German National Regulatory Agencies, notably: Michael Schmöltzer, Markus Krug and Stefanie Neveling. However, the author underlines that the vision expressed is his opinion and not theirs.

1. I am well aware of the fact that there are other than economic reasons to invest in pipeline capacity, notably security of supply. The latter is dealt with under Pillar 3.
2. That is, the 'commercial network model'.
3. By shippers.
4. That is, ≥ 20 bcm (billion cubic metres) of final customer consumption.
5. That is, at least three different sources of gas.
6. That is, the reduction of price spreads between markets.
7. This is ensured by allocating any uncovered regulated tariffs directly to the beneficiaries.
8. There are also some structural problems that would arise if long-term capacity was auctioned.
9. For example, if 250 new capacities are requested and only 220 new capacities are economical.
10. That is, link chain products are not captive transport; instead they are a means for a shipper to request (and get allocated) a meaningful and matching set of capacities to realize a long-distance transport pattern in Europe if they so wish.
11. That is, de-bottlenecking pipelines within a market.
12. As opposed to turning down some requests for long-term capacity on the grounds of reserving capacity for the mid- and short-term markets.
13. That is, social welfare.
14. DG Energy (2011), Non-paper 'The internal energy market – time to switch to a higher gear'.
15. 1-in-20 is the demand sensitivity that the level of daily demand that could be expected to be exceeded only once in 20 years (1:20). The 1:20 demand level is used to specify the capability of the network and therefore acts as the main driver of investment in the pipeline network. n-1 for gas supply security means that the gas supply must be able to withstand the loss of the major gas import route and continue to provide gas supply to domestic (or, otherwise-defined, high priority) customers.
16. Some would regard the apparent convergence of spot prices in the North West EU market as a clear example of the LOP.
17. An area can be explicitly shaped as a formal entry/exit area, but it may also emerge as a consequence of geographical borders or the implicit 'logic of the market'.
18. Solutions already proposed include inter alia the allocation of financial rather than physical transmission rights, ensuring their tradability, so that investors may be able to hedge interconnection as well as energy prices and plan on an integrated basis; and a strengthened anti-hoarding provision, where all capacity that is not nominated must be sold (UIOSI – use-it-or-sell-it) and used in the implicit auctioning process (e.g., in market coupling, splitting, etc.). In principle any capacity could be allocated long term provided that a strong UIOSI clause ensures that it is eventually used or prices are aligned.
19. Market coupling requires (among other things) a certain standardization of the contracts traded on gas spot exchanges. This is clearly not an issue for FWG or the

Network Codes, but a corollary of the application of market coupling for implicit auctioning of day-ahead capacity in the MECO-S model.

20. Such a market could also be called an 'open market'. For the avoidance of any doubt this part of the definition of functioning wholesale markets does not hint at gas release programmes.

21. HHI is the Herfindahl–Hirschman Index, which is calculated by adding the squared market shares (in percentage points) of relevant industry participants. Therefore, an HHI of 2000 could, for example, be achieved by five wholesalers with each having a market share of 20 per cent.

22. Which shall not only be different sales outlets of the same producer but also distinct (groups of) companies.

23. The 20 bcm is not a hard criterion. If the required number and quality of wholesalers is attracted by a market with lower volumes this market may also qualify as a functioning market.

24. In this regard interconnection with gas storage would not count as an entry point.

25. That is, EU import points.

26. I do not discuss the possible scenario here that upon the creation of larger markets, existing firm capacity is reduced or deteriorated in its quality, because this runs the risk of thwarting the goal of creating functioning markets.

27. These costs are sometimes termed 'de-bottlenecking' costs.

28. Additionally, the calculation of entry/exit tariffs always entails some regulatory decision about cost allocation that sometimes triggers disputes as some areas may feel discriminated against. As the zones get bigger this risk is enhanced.

29. Implicitly this means assuming that the value of a functioning market is higher than the cost of achieving it.

30. After implementation of the principles laid out in the current draft of the FWG on capacity allocation management.

31. From a retail competitor's perspective, being trapped in a non-functioning market is a serious complication of business. Consider a retailer whose risk-aware business model involves the regular purchase of small quantities of gas, in every case including products for the full duration (e.g., one year) of the sales contracts that were successfully concluded. In a functioning market this could rather easily be accomplished at the virtual point of the market. In a bundle of well-connected smaller markets the retailer would either have to settle for the smaller number of sellers in their home market or take the risk of setting up a portfolio of cross-market capacities that – if there is a booking window – they can book only once a year. So the retailer finds himself in a position where – before the booking window – they are in a risky position because they do not know if they will get sufficient capacity to fulfil their procurement contracts in adjoining markets or (if the capacity is auctioned off) at what price. Then – in the course of the booking or auctioning process – they have to decide if they book more capacity than they already need in order to leave headroom for future sales (and therefore procurement) growth (taking on risk) or waive all respective prospects for the coming year. This is not exactly an attractive position to be in.

32. I am not talking about pricing formulas in long-term supply contracts here but about prices for standardized gas products bought and sold in the traded wholesale market.

33. Net of all taxes that do not reduce the profit of the seller.

34. This correlation with an intermediate spread might be termed 'relative price alignment'.

35. Retail prices would then be subject to the 'relative law of one price'.

36. Trading activity drops quickly for delivery periods lying more than say two years in the future.

37. To make the effort worthwhile.

38. If the transmission tariff includes a variable element, the price spread per unit would have to be a little higher than the variable cost for transmission per unit.

39. Despite the remarkable tendency towards relative price alignment that has occurred in North West Europe in recent years.

40. Indigenous production, EU border points interconnecting (directly or indirectly) to extra-European production, LNG terminals.
41. In some cases also from another wholesaler.
42. Depending on the demand scenario one assumes.
43. The packages will be allocated for several years at once.
44. In this process, shippers requesting a package (aka 'link chain products') would either be allocated with capacity on all requested border points or with no capacity at all in order to avoid shippers having to put up with capacity fragments unusable for them.
45. For example, to be sold on the respective virtual point.
46. For example, following a purchase on the respective virtual point.
47. For the avoidance of doubt, this is not a reintroduction of captive transports through the back door, but a reflection of the practical problems of shippers that have to cross several market borders in order to reach the market where their customers are.
48. Since security of supply criteria as defined by Regulation 994/2010 focus on peak capacity, or cater to the needs of selected customer groups under extreme conditions. These are not necessarily the priorities of market-oriented infrastructure developers.
49. For the avoidance of doubt, the market area model (as well as the trading region model) does not prejudice any choice of unbundling model.
50. For the avoidance of doubt, in the market area model the entry/exit system reaches from entry points to all exit points including exit points to final customers on TSO and DSO networks and is therefore identical to the balancing zone.
51. For some Member States the issue of different currencies would also have to be dealt with.
52. For the avoidance of doubt, the trading region model (as well as the market area model) does not prejudice any choice of unbundling model.
53. In the straightforward case, where no final customers are directly connected to transmission systems, the trading region would simply be a joint entry/exit network including the transmission systems of the participating TSOs.
54. The capacity from the trading region to an end-user zone is automatically allocated to shippers in the course of the change of supplier process in the end-user zone (capacity backpack; i.e., no booking required).
55. An alternative to allocating the cost for the virtual exit down to DSOs would be to charge it directly to the shipper. This would be possible in the trading region model because the amount of exit capacity from the trading region to each end-user zone that is allocated to each shipper is known in this model.
56. Including the implementation of allocation according to the 'allocated as nominated' principle, also known as 'allocation by declaration'.
57. Some harmonization of the balancing regime (e.g., the gas day) is still in order, even if the trading region model is applied.
58. This nomination would designate the shipper's trading account (an instrument kept for every shipper to ensure that their nominations balance to zero in every hour) as the source and the shipper's balancing account (in the respective national end-user zone) as the sink.
59. Depending on the network structure, the measured consumption of final customers connected to a TSO network may have to be factored into the online flow control from the transmission systems into the distribution networks.
60. The national requirements for supplying end users have to be fulfilled in the different Member States.
61. Remember that 'market' is used as an abbreviation for 'wholesale market' in this chapter.
62. Note that from a perspective focusing on fostering cross-market supply and trading, the amount of harmonization to be done in the balancing system is much smaller than from the perspective of creating market areas.
63. Instead, market players seem to favour OTC deals.
64. Where such markets exist at all.

65. Which is the reason why within-day markets are not a core element of the MECO-S model; they would fit in nicely though.

66. Which they may require to react to changes in their load, for example, due to changes in weather conditions.

67. The congestion charge is basically the profit made by the arbitrage process from buying in the cheaper market and selling in the pricier market.

68. See Section 3.2.4 on that open season process.

69. See Section 3.2.4 on clues for assessing the economics of an investment.

70. This requirement stems from underpinning the mid- and short-term traded markets with sufficient capacity.

71. This method of providing capacity for short- and mid-term markets on top of the capacity requested for longer terms may (depending on the amount of long-term capacity requested) lead to a reduction in capacity utilization; put another way it may produce redundant capacity. At first glance this looks like a waste of economic resources. Actually, these resources are not wasted, but are an investment into competition. The rationale for this is that (by standard economic theory) for the emergence of competition a certain amount of redundancy is required. The difficult bit is, of course, to determine the efficient amount of redundancy.

72. See also Section 3.3.4.

73. Of course, regulatory processes have to foresee that the investor is remunerated for that additional investment, if they are not allowed to sell the resulting capacity on a long-term basis.

74. Example: if on an existing pipeline there are long-term requests for 100 per cent of the capacity and there would be a threshold of, for example, 30 per cent of capacity that shall be kept available for the short- and mid-term markets, then the requested 100 per cent can be awarded to long-term capacity requestors and the then 'missing' 30 per cent of free capacity for the mid- and short-term market can be built (by increasing capacity by 42.8 per cent).

75. See §14 (1) of the German GasNZV.

76. See the example in footnote 73.

77. For brevity omit the issue of extra capacity for the short- and mid-term markets in the example.

78. How they look in detail is not relevant for the point to be made here.

79. This may easily happen due to the step-wise nature of capacity investment. For instance, if shippers' requests amount to 150 and the feasible capacity steps are 100 (which would be economical) and 200 (which would not be economical any more) then 100 would be built and allocated to the requests. NB: a simple pro rata allocation would not work in this case, because the requested contract tenors differ.

80. By the structure of the model, the maximization would be constrained by the given capacity requests and the criteria for economic investment.

81. Shippers would be asked to file with their requests a minimum acceptance rate (e.g., 80 per cent) of their requested capacity they would be prepared to accept as a minimum allocation (and below which they would retract their request).

82. Either between the minimum acceptance rate specified by the shipper and 100 per cent or (if it would otherwise fall below the minimum acceptance rate of the shipper) zero.

83. Special (but solvable) problems can occur if more than one optimal set of acceptance rates exists.

84. Of course, on the upward slope of the supply contract, shippers building their own pipeline would have the opportunity to time, for example, the installation of compressors to optimize the availability of capacity (and some of the related cost) against the need for this capacity. But although the investment timing effect (pay-out structure) of this may be interesting for the sponsors of such a project, the cost effect of this optimization is in most cases small compared to the overall cost of the project.

85. For brevity, I do not go into detail on the structure of the shippers' requests for capacity. It may make sense to adopt a scheme here, where shippers are provided with a

range of potential future tariffs ('price steps') and the overall capacity (including new capacity) that can be made available at that price step. TSOs would determine these steps on the basis of estimated expenditure for capacity extension in various scenarios. Shippers would be asked to request capacity for every one of those price steps. This information would be used in the investment appraisal leading to an investment decision that is even more market based than providing only one estimated future tariff to shippers.

86. See Section 3.2.4 for details.
87. The problem here is to determine the capacity to be offered per stripe since the total capacity is yet unknown.
88. See Section 3.2.3.
89. In accordance with Article 36 of Directive 2009/73/EC.
90. I refer to the ERGEG *Guidelines for Good Practice on Open Season Procedures* (GGPOS) dated 21 May 2007 for an introduction.
91. Which may be filed as part of a link chain request (see Section 3.2.3).
92. See also Section 3.2.3 on the issue of lead time.
93. For brevity, I exclude more complex issues such as capital structure, debt service cover ratios, and so on, here.
94. Of course, there may be some 'scarcity' on the fringes of the allocation problem (e.g., regarding capacities between two possible steps of capacity extension) that require some sort of allocation (see Section 3.2.3 for the proposed allocation by optimization). But this certainly does not justify auctioning the full long-term capacity.
95. So instead of transporting gas from VP to VP with a single contract a shipper would require three contracts (exit contract, P2P contract on the exempted line, entry contract).
96. This would only be relevant if the TSO refrained from investing in the first place due to rate of return issues.
97. Where this cannot be achieved (e.g., on an EU border point where the adjoining non-EU TSO does not cooperate as required) some fallback balancing regime needs to be introduced (see also Section 3.4.2).
98. Based on the definition of system integrity in Article 2 (1) No. 9 of Regulation (EC) No. 715/2009.
99. Also termed 'virtual points' or 'VPs'.
100. Purely financial trades (or trades in physical instruments that are closed out before delivery) may be much higher though.
101. In this case it would have to be line-pack that is not required for transport purposes.
102. Consider an extra-hub that is located 'before' two European markets. It provides shippers with the opportunity to decide to which market the gas they buy at the hub shall be bought instead of always having to buy gas in one market and then transporting it to the other market.
103. Remember that in the MECO-S model every market has its own virtual hub, where trades can be effected.
104. I note that Article 2 (1) No. 11 defines TSOs as network users 'in so far as it is necessary for them to carry out their functions in relation to transmission'.
105. See Section 3.2.3.
106. See Section 3.2.2.
107. That is, measure (2) helps in implementing or gaining or increasing the benefits from measure (1), but measure (1) is not contingent on a prior implementation of measure (2).
108. Although the implementation of market coupling itself will help increasing the liquidity of spot markets. Therefore, the introduction of market coupling may help markets to close the gap to becoming functioning markets.
109. As opposed to legal instruments at the disposal of individual Member States.
110. By law or potentially regulatory decree.
111. By NRAs or lawmakers, depending on the respective powers of NRAs.

112. Including interconnection to storage and production and exits to final customers directly connected to transmission systems.
113. Subject to an allocation procedure if not all requests for capacity (link chain and non-link chain) can be fulfilled.
114. For the avoidance of doubt, this 'bundling' refers to individual intra-EU cross-market points. The string may (depending on the route chosen by the shipper) be made up of several such capacities and also capacities at EU border points.
115. This is required in order not to overburden (especially smaller) shippers with simultaneous auction procedures. Such procedures would also not help shippers in achieving a string of capacity they may be interested in because there is no guarantee that a shipper will be successful at all relevant auctions even if they take place at the same time.
116. Long-term link chain products are required especially on existing networks to underpin new long-term supply contracts signed by suppliers with the intention to sell (primarily) in certain (one or several) markets. Otherwise they would be forced to take a lot of (maybe too much) risk because they could never be sure to reach the markets they are interested in (e.g., because their consumption volume is large enough) with the gas they sign long term.
117. Taking due account of the required safety margins.
118. This does NOT prejudice the length of the balancing cash-out period, but only how the shipper communicates to the TSO the intended use of his capacity.
119. These harmonization items do not suffice to realize cross-border market areas (see other areas of required harmonization below).
120. Trading regions alone would require less harmonization items than listed below.
121. Such additional, fee-based tolerances would be an 'unbundled' network service with a price separate from transportation tariffs.
122. This helps to keep the trading region free of imbalances and therefore free of a system that deals with those imbalances. This is a special advantage in case trading regions are implemented involving Member States with differing currencies. On the other hand, a fully nominated trading region does not deprive shippers of anything they need, since end-user load balancing is taken care of in the national end-user zones. Settling of deliberate imbalances (e.g., caused by the shipper deliberately nominating entry and exit quantities in and out of a trading region that do not match) is also not foreseen by Regulation (EC) 715/2009 and generally not a reasonable application of a balancing system (markets should be used for that).
123. This is required to deal with unexpected interruptions of capacity that lead in and out of the trading region. Until the shipper has had the opportunity to re-nominate (in order to balance his account in the trading region) some imbalance may occur. This needs to be settled. Since such interruptions have a clear cause (the interrupting TSO) settlement can easily be effected between this TSO and his shipper.
124. For those capacity products for which auctioning is applicable.
125. This would be the case for any market–internal interconnection point between TSOs.
126. This is required in order to enable market coupling.

8. An American model for the EU gas market?

Sergio Ascari

1 Introduction – Why an American Model? What American Model?

Despite the MECO-S model advocated by Jean-Michel Glachant in Chapter 7 'A vision for the EU gas target model: MECO-S', the most natural reference for a target model for the European market is the North American model. Unlike any other theoretical model that may be proposed, this is a working model that has been developed as the result of a long historical process, and is widely regarded as a success story. It has delivered secure supplies at prices that have been generally lower than those found in Europe, despite objective supply costs (in terms of production and transportation distance) that have been roughly the same, at least before the shale gas boom of the last three years, when the gap has indeed deepened (Figure 8.1). The fact that innovation leading to shale development has been more effective in North America is not just chance; it is just another positive feature of the industry. Although it must be partly attributed to the peculiar US upstream regime where any underground production belongs to the land owner (rather than the state as in Europe), it also shows that the private sector is not afraid to undertake substantial investment in North America, as it knows that it will be able to transport the product to the market, and sell it.

Trading has developed in the USA and Canada far more than in any European hub[1] and the development of market centres based on hubs is playing a major role in the development of industry efficiency, in a way that is only starting to be faintly imitated in Europe.

Notwithstanding these undisputed positive outcomes, the American model is usually dismissed as not applicable in the institutional framework of the EU. Each observer from the Eastern shore of the Atlantic usually points to their preferred features of the American model as the reasons for its success, and complain that these are missing in Europe. For example, regulators usually mention the arm's length operations of pipelines and

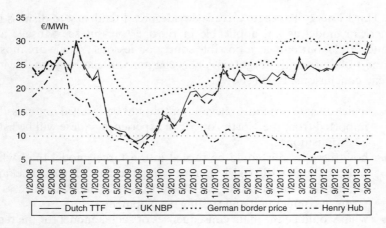

Source: Author elaboration.

Figure 8.1   US and European wholesale prices

supply, and the political unity of the USA. The gas industry focuses on the federal rather than state nature of regulation and its continuous reliance on distance-based tariffs, with Transmission System Operators (TSOs) notably underlining America's more generous rates of return allowed on transportation activities as the main triggers for its significant pipe-to-pipe competition, as well as abundant capacity that underpins its far more vibrant gas commodity market.[2] In any case, it would be wrong to take up only some features of the American model, which – although not perfect – draws its success and appeal probably from the combination of its regulatory choices rather than any single feature.

Leaving aside the discussions about the American 'preferred features' of the various stakeholders, there is widespread agreement that the EU market (even after implementation of the Third Energy Package) lacks the main institutional features that would allow it to imitate the American model. In fact, Europe is notably characterized by:

- no ownership unbundling provisions;
- no single continental regulatory authority;
- mandatory entry/exit rather than distance-based tariffs;
- mostly national or subnational TSOs rather than long-distance interstate pipelines.

Since these characteristics are clearly not present in the current market organization, and will not be found even after full implementation of the Third Energy Package, there is a widespread tendency to dismiss the American model as not applicable in Europe (on this see Moselle and White, 2011), but only as a possible source of 'lessons', which are mostly bound to be promptly forgotten.[3] This chapter will challenge such widespread conclusions. It will show:

- which lessons are most relevant and should be recalled and possibly imported from the North American experience – these will be listed as Propositions;
- how these lessons could be turned into a target model that, while fully abiding by EU legislation including the Third Energy Package, retains the main features that have fostered American success in terms of competition and trading development;
- what would be the main consequences of such a model for the regulatory framework of the EU, and in particular for the priorities of the European Network Code that should be developed and adopted according to the Third Energy Package.

For ease of discussion, the target model that will be developed is nicknamed the EURAM (European American Model). The meaning of any description of the EURAM should not be misinterpreted. It is inspired by the following:

Proposition 1   The target model is the structure that the gas market organization will assume as a consequence of the joint pressure of market and regulatory forces.

The North American liberalization experience, as well as the shortest European one, has shown that regulators, however powerful, cannot tailor the market to their own wishes.[4] Rather, the resulting market design is the product of different forces, which interact to yield a certain outcome. Thus, the optimal behaviour of public institutions should consider how industry (in its various sectors) and other stakeholders (finance, national governments, external market forces, end user representatives, etc.) may interact with regulatory efforts by National Regulatory Authorities (NRAs), the European Commission, competition regulators and security of supply authorities. The interaction of such forces occurs against the background of the industry's inherent features, which are worth recalling before starting to outline the EURAM.

2   Some Preliminary Analysis and an Outline of the Following Sections

The regulation of any industry is mostly based on its underlying economic nature. However, in the case of gas, some misunderstanding of (or disagreement on, whatever it may be) such nature is often the source of lasting disputes between regulators and industry. Considering the scope of this study, the most important part of the industry to be analysed is transportation, with some attention paid to services that are strictly related to it, like those of the LNG (liquefied natural gas) chain and storage, and to wholesale trading based on this underlying infrastructure.

To understand the main relevant economic features of gas transportation[5] it is useful to compare them with those of two other energy carriers, objects of a similar regulatory debate: electricity and oil. A synoptic view is provided in Table 8.1 and can be summarized by the following:

Proposition 2   The economically relevant features of gas transportation lie in an intermediate position between those of electricity, where transmission is a natural monopoly, and oil transportation, which is a mostly competitive industry.

The American experience reinforces this interpretation of the natural gas industry as located between electricity and oil. On the other hand there is a tendency to see the gas industry as more similar to electricity, which may be true for national and relatively isolated markets, but not for a continental market.[6]

Table 8.1 illustrates Proposition 2 by highlighting several features of gas transportation. It is less costly (per energy unit) than electricity (but more than oil), as a consequence of which it travels on a normally much broader scale. Its flows are predictable, like oil, and its storage is feasible at reasonable costs, though harder than for oil derivatives. Thus, its balancing requirements are less strict than for power and its logistics are also less demanding. In fact, the increasing share of LNG in gas transportation has increased the flexibility of trading arrangements, reducing the weight of fixed pipelines, with LNG playing the marginal[7] role. This role is often amplified, as it provides a competitive pressure fostering a more flexible use of pipelines as well. It is worth recalling that oil pipelines play a large role in oil transportation, yet their regulation is hardly needed, except in limited areas.

Flows are predictable in gas, unlike electricity: this avoids or sharply reduces the need for the complex arrangements that have been adopted in the power sector to either account for actual flows or to allocate their costs correctly and deal with network externalities, including the well-known

Table 8.1   Some economic features of three energy carriers and their regulatory consequences

	Electricity	Natural Gas	Oil Derivatives
Long-distance transportation costs	High	Medium	Low
Prevalent transportation range	Mostly national	Mostly continental	Global
Transportation flexibility	Low	Medium (via LNG)	High (via shipping)
Flow predictability	No	Yes	Yes
Weight of transportation in value chain	Low	Medium	Low
Transportation congestion	Common	Rare	Negligible
Storage	Very costly (pump)	Moderate cost	Low cost
Regulatory control	High	Medium	Low
Trading hubs	Agreed with regulators	Defined by market forces/ regulators	Defined by market forces

Source: Author elaboration.

ITC or 'Inter-TSO Compensation' mechanism. This greater flexibility entails important consequences for the ways gas markets are and should be organized (see Section 6).

The bearable, though high, costs of gas transportation and its predictability have led to the continental range of gas transportation, and an increasing intercontinental trade. Thus, as the unit cost of transporting energy over a certain distance as gas rather than electricity is lower, gas, rather than electricity, is normally transported internationally. Therefore, the share of transportation in the gas value chain is larger: for most EU countries relying on large imports the EU-based share of transportation costs is typically around 10–15 per cent of the wholesale price, higher than electricity's 5 per cent. Partly for this reason, gas transportation is a major source of competitive advantage and a field of entrepreneurial initiative and competition. Reduction of this to a centrally planned process would amount to losing a major share of the industry's efficiency potential. To sum up, as the American experience has widely shown:

Proposition 3   Competition in gas transportation is a major source of efficiency and should therefore be accounted for and promoted in the most suitable way within a target model.

In fact, even in Europe, competition between gas transportation routes occurs. For example, there are at least five projects competing to take gas across the 'Southern Corridor' from the Caspian production basin. Russian production aimed for Western Europe may use the existing Ukraine–Slovakia, Belarus–Poland routes, as well as the new Baltic and possibly a future Balkan way. Similar competition is developing for Southern Mediterranean gas, often from the same sources, as well as for North Sea gas. Most of these options are also competing with LNG terminals.

Originating from external sources and producers, but far from stopping at the EU borders, competitive routes extend well inside the EU. The choice of any of them entails important consequences for investment in EU pipelines and their interconnections, and affects their regulation. For example, construction of the Nord Stream has also required construction of two large pipelines (NEL and OPAL) to connect it to other major consuming areas. The availability of MEDGAS has triggered the development of more capacity between Spain and France. Any new major pipeline providing more supplies in South-Eastern Europe would probably require capacity reinforcement in the adjacent EU Member States. The way to address this issue has been rather different in the USA and in the EU so far, and will be discussed in detail.

Unlike in the USA, competition in transportation has been slowed down in Europe by the lack of 'interstate' pipeline companies, by limited (legal only) unbundling, weak regulatory enforcement of the unbundling rules (notably managerial and functional unbundling), and by regulatory practices that have privileged short-term price reductions to long-term investments (Correljé et al., 2009). In fact, most European TSOs have a national or subnational nature, and some even enjoy national monopoly rights under a licensing regime. However, this does not usually[8] exclude them from taking part in continental competition. For example, the historical transit systems of Central and Eastern Europe are at risk of losing their cross-border flows, possibly without being compensated by the national tariff revenue.

Thus, pipeline (and LNG) competition cannot be neglected. The challenge is how to include it as an essential feature of the target model. It is challenging, but necessary, to adapt the American-style (but also natural) pipe-to-pipe (and to LNG) competition to the European gas industry organization, based on national or even subnational TSOs. On the other hand, such competition should not be overrated: incumbent TSOs retain a cost advantage over competitors that may well discourage competition from newcomers, and such competition is (in the USA as well) a complement to rather than a substitute for regulation. This is more true the smaller the relevant market. Nevertheless, European market integration and the development of some infrastructure competition go hand in hand: neglecting it would reduce the pressure towards an efficient gas market.

As for limited unbundling, this has mostly allowed the retention of substantial integration between transportation and supply, with major investment decisions by TSOs often subordinated to the interests of sister supply companies.[9] In the last decade such integration, together with the regulatory uncertainty triggered by the successive 'packages', has certainly contributed to curbing investment and led to less capacity than a fully unbundled market would have realized. TSOs often had no incentive to develop capacity likely to be used by their parent companies' competitors, which in a few cases have actually put the brakes on investments. However, this season is probably over, as unbundling progresses under the pressure of both Third Energy Package implementation and market forces. The next section will show how this situation may evolve.

The development of competitive transportation initiatives under stronger unbundling rules is likely to further increase transportation capacity. However, even in the difficult first decade of market liberalization physical congestion has been limited – unlike in the power sector. It is likely that once new and effective congestion management practices have eliminated at least some of the remaining contractual congestion, and thanks to the competitive threat of new pipelines and LNG terminals, such capacity may further develop and cases of congestion will become even less common. Again, there is a profound structural difference with the electricity industry, where high transmission costs and loss of power limit the scope of long-distance trading and the price alignment between markets. The North American experience has shown that:

Proposition 4   Under a supportive, market-oriented regulation, gas pipeline capacity is normally abundant and not congested.

This does not mean that there is never any congestion, and we will see that some should be expected to remain anyway (see below, subsection 6.3.1). At this point, it is worthwhile pointing out that the North American system has delivered more capacity than the European system, for a number of reasons ranging from its federal regulation, its rate of return regulatory approach, its full unbundling and the private nature of TSOs (Correljé et al., 2009). The target model should consider this proposition as the basis for the definition of the regulation of pipeline capacity development and allocation, including the relative role of open seasons, auctions and regulated tariffs. This will be developed in Sections 4 and 5, with the latter devoted to the tariff problem, as the current entry/exit model followed in Europe may create some difficulties.

Finally, it is worth noting that the multidimensional development of competition has allowed North American regulators to rely on a less tight grip on the industry to pursue an efficient development of competitive markets. In fact, most of the trading arrangements and particularly the market design have been developed by the industry under regulatory control. In particular, hubs and the related market centres have experienced impressive development,[10] allowing them to take the lead in the industry's operations, including the main directions of resource allocation, dispatching, and the provision of services like balancing and storage. This development has generally followed rather different models from those of the power industry, in accordance with the different physics and economics of the carriers. To sum up:

Proposition 5   The location, services and role of organized markets are most efficiently defined by industry under regulatory control, rather than by central planning.

Section 6 will draw some consequences for the EURAM, focusing on the way markets will be organized, and how they will be connected. Finally, the chapter will examine the interactions between the various building blocks of the EURAM and their high-level consequences for the current process of outlining Framework Guidelines that will drive the development of the European Network Code.

3   Unbundling

Unbundling is certainly the issue that has received the largest media interest during the discussion on the Third Energy Package, and the related simplified views have often caused confusion. Several commentators have interpreted the outcome as if the EU had given up ownership unbundling, and expects most integrated gas companies to retain control over their networks, notably in the form of the ITO (Independent Transmission Operator) as described by Chapter IV of Directive 2009/73. In fact, the implementation of the Third Energy Package is currently (May 2013) far from over. Whereas several Member States (like France, Germany, Italy and others) have indicated their preference for the adoption of the ITO model, it would be wrong to think that the unbundling issue is over, and that the Third Energy Package will not have a substantial impact on the behaviour of the European transmission industry. The Third Energy

Package and the evolution of markets and industry organization are substantially modifying the incentive structure the industry will face. Yet, the outcome cannot be entirely predicted as some key variables have not yet been decided, notably on the regulatory side. To understand how the industry may evolve, it is worth noting a few points:

1. Several Member States have already opted for full ownership unbundling, or have in fact fully unbundled their TSOs: Belgium, Denmark, Hungary, Netherlands, Spain and the UK. These countries provide an important group of fully unbundled TSOs, which are likely to behave with the goal of maximizing profits from their independent business, rather than from continued quasi-integration of transmission and supply. Being subject to regulated tariff or revenue schemes these companies are likely to pursue the only way they can in order to grow, that is, by expanding their business and competing for further transportation services. Whereas a part of such growth is targeted at the faster-developing markets of emerging economies, another part of their efforts is likely to be devoted to Europe as well.

2. Financial markets have long expressed their preference for fully unbundled companies. The main reasons for such a preference are: (a) the regulatory risk that is pending on any company that may be suspected of abusing its market position, including the risk of a forced dismantlement by its national government or of measures taken by (or agreed under pressure by) EU competition authorities; and (b) the unclear rating to be attributed to integrated companies, with the low risk of the regulated business blurred by the much higher risk of a supply business involving substantial exposition to upstream events and price swings: this confusion limits the leverage capacity of the transmission activity and increases its borrowing costs.[11] So far, this preference has been often outweighed by the benefits of integration. However, such benefits are likely to shrink, as outlined below under (4) and (5).

3. A related issue is the increasing financing cost, notably in an era of tighter credit. Pressure to reduce debt burdens and the opportunity to accumulate financial power for more strategic business acquisitions is leading several major gas and power companies to divest regulated businesses. Less important assets have gone first, like tightly regulated distribution and power networks. However, debt growth and emerging opportunities may add another weight in favour of selling TSOs as well, notably if neutral owners (like pension or private equity funds) can be found so that the benefits of integration are not transferred to competitors.

4. Regulatory action by competition authorities, notably by the European Commission, has limited the scope for keeping markets tightly closed by under-investing in entry capacity.[12] This strategy is becoming even more stringent as the EU has introduced more effective congestion management provisions, and NRAs are increasingly requiring the adoption of open seasons – which reduce the integrated company's control on capacity growth – and auctions – which open up more existing capacity.

5. Regulatory pressure by NRAs will, of course, be strengthened by the implementation of the Third Energy Package, particularly in the case where the ITO option is chosen, which is unprecedented and therefore highly uncertain regarding its impact. It may be expected that the ITO will be in any case (a) less prone to the mother company's requirements; (b) under stricter regulatory control, notably as regards investment decisions, with competing stakeholders' needs taken more seriously; and (c) subject to heavier red tape burdens, through various programmes enforced by Third Energy Package implementing legislations and NRAs in order to secure more effective separation ('Chinese walls'). Moreover, even though in principle the tariff treatment of ITOs should not differ from those of fully unbundled TSOs, some regulators may in fact (at their discretion) allow higher returns and other benefits to TSOs that are freed from suppliers' control.

6. European energy companies have significantly changed in the last decades. In many cases, former state-owned, national, vertically integrated gas companies have changed in nature. They have been at least partly privatized, merged notably with power sector companies, and have lost their national focus in favour of an international dimension. Whereas the market share of large companies has been increasing, indicating a tendency towards more (though still low) concentration at European level, they have normally lost market share in their original 'home' base. For example, the top six companies' cumulative wholesale market share in the EU has increased from 64 per cent to 70 per cent between 2004 and 2009. However, the share of their sales achieved in their original home markets has decreased from 75 to 59 per cent: in other words, in their original markets incumbents have generally lost part of the market. A similar picture applies, although with a few exceptions, if a larger sample is considered. It is also interesting to note that the best performers (in terms of market share) are not companies that have taken a defensive stance in their original markets, but rather those that have moved more quickly towards new markets. Usually, those who have lost more market shares at home are also the overall winners. This shift in company strategy shows

that foreign markets are now more important than national ones, notably in terms of growth. A corollary of this attitude is the increasingly common decision by large energy conglomerates to dismiss low-income assets like regulated networks, as they need cash to buy others that are more strategic in terms of value: for example, upstream assets, components of the LNG chain, storage sites, or smaller competitors that may serve as bridgeheads in new markets.

All of these factors may foster the choice of ownership unbundling by companies, even though national legislation would allow them to continue with ITOs. Latest examples are the sale of networks by the main German concerns. Under full regulation, control of networks is less and less important for such companies, and regulated businesses tend to be purchased by institutional investors looking for safer though lower yields, like pension funds and insurance companies. Once free from the original owners' control, these network companies are more likely to consider international mergers with their peers, stimulated by the search for synergies and economies of scale.

Wherever ownership remains integrated, it is likely that a more independent TSO behaviour will emerge. Since at least some companies will compete for more transportation services, even integrated ITOs will be stimulated to fight back.

Turning to the original inspiration of this chapter, that is, the American model, it may be noted that even the USA falls short of full ownership unbundling. In some cases holding companies control both transportation and supply companies, though their operation is totally independent. After implementation of the Third Energy Package, the structure of the European gas industry may end up not so very different from North America's as far as unbundling is concerned.

For these reasons, by and large, it may be expected that TSOs in Europe will become more active in capacity development than they have been in the previous decade. This development may take several forms, the most common ones being mergers (as already implemented or attempted by transmission companies based in countries that have opted for ownership unbundling, like Dutch Gasunie, Belgian Fluxys and Hungarian MOL); and the development of special vehicles like joint ventures aimed at new projects: examples are UK Interconnector, the Nord Stream and its onshore branches (OPAL, NEL), as well as those proposed for Nabucco, South Stream and other Southern Corridor projects. However, as the interest in a renewed infrastructure business increases, full cross-border mergers should not be ruled out even for state-owned TSOs, notably as clear business opportunities show the benefits of such mergers rather than their political costs. After all, the same has happened with the important mergers that have characterized major energy supply companies in the last decade, leading to the sale of major 'national champions' to foreign interests.

A rather different, intriguing opportunity for TSOs in a future integrated gas market is to offer transportation financial rights, instead of physical long-term capacity, as has happened in some power markets (PCG, 2009). TSOs are in fact in the best position to offer this opportunity, which would be a hedging tool for shippers and provide a valuable alternative to long-term contracts. However, this option would be available to large TSOs controlling capacity over entire routes rather than to those with a merely national scope. Such opportunity may offer a further incentive to TSO merger and consolidation, although this is not for the near future.

These tendencies point towards the development of some European equivalent of the interstate companies that have borne most of the North American system, at least for action on incremental transportation needs. Even if these developments do not necessarily require integrated companies to sell their integrated TSOs, they increase the pressure on them, and may well further shift the balance that is already being affected by the above listed factors. The scope of such developments is, of course, related to the demand for new infrastructure to supply the European market, which is addressed in detail by the Ten-Year Network Development Plan (TYNDP) proposed by ENTSOG (European Network of Transmission Service Operators for Gas), the TSOs' official coordination body, as required by the Third Energy Package.

The demand–supply balance depends on a number of uncertain issues that are beyond the scope of this chapter, but have been analysed in more detail, for example, by Correljé et al. (2009) and IEA (2008). Among others, it is worth recalling issues like (on the supply side) the steady decline of EU production; the uncertainty about North African supplies and the increased costs of Russian E&P (exploration and production); the multiple difficulties of reaching Caspian and Middle Eastern resources; the uneasy development of European unconventional gas resources; and the expected cyclical tightening of the LNG market. And on the demand side, the strength of industrial recovery, and particularly the uncertain success of the sustainability policies and of the competing renewables and nuclear industries and of CCS (carbon capture and storage).

Overall, it seems that perspectives for transportation demand increases are substantial and justify the attitude of companies that decide to choose the best organizational, governance, regulatory and financial position that would prompt an aggressive strategy. It is now time to consider whether and how the European regulatory framework could make such endeavours succeed.

4   Long-term Capacity and New Infrastructure

4.1   THE RATIONALE FOR LONG-TERM CAPACITY RIGHTS

Reasons why long-term capacity (LTC)[13] should be granted to willing shippers derive from the market vision (see also CIEP, 2011) where, due to the decline of its domestic production and of its closer external sources, Europe is expected to consume more gas produced in increasingly remote or costly fields, including new gas sources within the EU (which may well become cheaper later but not at the start). All such gas must be transported by long-distance pipelines or as LNG, requiring huge investments that can only be depreciated over long time spans, normally in the order of decades rather than years.

Such developments often need new transmission infrastructure. However, even if sufficient gas infrastructures are available within the EU, both external and domestic producers should be reasonably sure that they can obtain access to the pipelines they need to supply their end customers. They should be able to contract access for a sufficient period of time and in conditions that are reasonably stable. They should also be protected from the behaviour of competitors seeking short-term opportunistic gains, for example by seeking control of some essential facility. And they should be safeguarded from opportunistic behaviour of regulators of end use markets or intermediate (transit) countries, who may be tempted to take advantage of their position (more on this in Section 5).

The reason why such LTC rights are needed by suppliers of natural gas and not by suppliers of other commodities (e.g., oil and its derivatives) is not related to the large size of the investments involved in E&P, but to the fixed nature of the infrastructure. For, if their gas cannot be transported by such pipelines, producers cannot redirect it to other markets, unlike producers of coal and crude oil and products, as a consequence of which TSOs or transmission system capacity holders could exploit the vulnerable position of the suppliers and such a risk would badly affect investment decisions, with adverse consequences for long-term supplies to the EU.

The problem does not occur to the same extent in the LNG market, as LNG can in principle be diverted to other destinations. However, the LNG market, despite a remarkable flexibility improvement in the last few years, is still far from the liquidity conditions that are typical of oil and coal markets. Any conclusions of the present section mainly refer to pipeline transportation but may also be applicable to LNG terminals to the extent that such markets still suffer from some rigidity.

Traditionally, the problems arising from the fixed nature of pipelines has been solved by reserving capacity on a long-term basis in either dedicated or shared pipelines. The reform of capacity allocation in most EU Member States has normally preserved all or a substantial part of these long-term transportation rights. In the traditional model, gas was sold by long-term commodity contracts associated with LTC rights, with the seller taking the price risk by means of a pricing mechanism based on prices of competing fuels (in the absence of any independent gas price setting). At the same time the buyer, which was normally an integrated company active in a net importing country, takes the volume risk, as it is required to pay the minimum contractual amounts anyway, under a 'take-or-pay' clause.

After gas market liberalization and in particular after the development of independent gas markets where gas prices are established as a result of trading, without direct reference to competing fuels, long-term contracting could be regarded as no longer necessary. If markets are liquid, any amount supplied by individual producers can be sold on them, and long-term contracts, though still useful, are less essential. Yet, they are likely to stay around, although on a smaller scale and possibly with slightly shorter durations, as shown by the experience of oil markets, as well as in the most liquid gas markets like North America or the UK (Lapuerta, 2011).

However, if the need for long-term capacity contracts is less pressing when markets are liquid, there remains a problem for the gas transportation industry. If it is no longer integrated with suppliers, this industry draws its income from the sale of capacity rights and cannot develop new infrastructure, or even ensure the maintenance of existing infrastructure, unless a reasonable share of its investment costs are covered by LTC contracts. This is another striking feature of the North American model, where liberalization has brought about a decoupling of commodity contracts and capacity rights. Whereas the use of long-term commodity contracts has declined substantially, long-term capacity rights have survived, supplemented by shorter-term transport products (Makholm, 2006).

In Europe, LTC rights have been criticized as a source of contractual congestion causing market foreclosure, notably if capacity could not be transferred to third parties. Yet, the right to use pipelines on a long-term basis to supply the market should not be confused with the right to leave the pipeline empty, even when other suppliers are willing to fill it with other, possibly cheaper gas. Hence, actions have been taken by competition authorities to free up such capacity, and lately the EC has given priority to congestion management, through an amendment to Regulation 715/2009.[14] The stronger the available congestion management mechanism, the more easily can LTC rights be awarded, with the ensuing capacity enhancement benefits.

It is worth noting that even countries at the forefront of the liberalization process, like the UK, have introduced the right to reserve capacity on a long-term basis (up to 16 years) at border points. On the other hand, TSOs fear that network users may hardly be interested in buying capacity long term, if they can reasonably hope to buy it later at lower prices.

To conclude, the vision underpinning the target model is a gas market where investment in upstream sources could and should be undertaken without any fully guaranteed market. Traders may still decide to opt for long-term contracts based on their preferred take-or-pay and indexation clauses, but these would be independent of capacity contracts. Consequentially, this vision underscores the right for, on the one hand, the suppliers to reserve capacity on a long-term basis, without seeing this right jeopardized at low cost, as it may happen if capacity were fully allocated through short-term auctions. On the other hand, it recognizes the related TSOs' right to sell their capacity long term to underpin the recovery of their necessary investments.

It is not possible to prove that such vision maximizes social welfare. It is rather a pragmatic intermediate stance, in between the wishes of producers who would call for secure markets and those of short-term traders who would call for full flexibility of supplies.[15]

Without any further discussion, it may be interesting to recall that a similar problem has been present in the discussion of the electricity target model, where the reservation of long-term capacity and its pros and cons has been discussed, and some interesting approaches have been proposed including the role of financial transmission rights.[16] It is too early to say whether such tools may take the role of physical LTC contracts. It may happen where TSOs have a more widely recognized independent role, so that they are interested (and can be trusted) to offer financial instead of physical capacity rights. The rest of this section discusses the related problems and the possible solutions.

4.2   ISSUES IN LONG-TERM CAPACITY ALLOCATION

There is clearly some overlap between the reasons for LTC allocation and the issues regarding new or reinforced infrastructure. After all, both the allocation of existing and the creation of new capacity address similar problems – shippers are interested in capacity. They are happy to book available capacity, but if this is found to be physically congested they should have the right to invest in its expansion by any relevant TSO on a level playing field with their competitors. This right has long been recognized, and several provisions have appeared in the various directives.[17] Yet, these have long been ineffective and the regulatory gap has been noted, notably concerning interconnections between transmission systems.

The process of building and booking capacity on new infrastructure may not be basically different from LTC allocation, although new capacity would have a certain lead time – usually of some years – before its definition and completion. This subsection focuses on long-term allocation of existing capacity, and will show how this process may interact with the development of new capacity, promoted by market forces and defined notably through open seasons.

In this respect a major issue must be addressed. In the current European legal framework, for reasons related to political fragmentation and particularly to the prevalence of imports from outside the EU, capacity reinforcement processes are not only driven by market demand, but also by long-term capacity planning, underpinned by a security of supply rationale, or by other political goals. For example, the process may be driven by the political will to supply new areas, or by an energy policy decision to promote gas consumption for environmental reasons. What is more, Europe increasingly relies on imports, including from politically risky areas, and has therefore adopted security of supply as a main pillar of its energy policy, yet market forces do not necessarily pursue such goals by their own initiatives. Moreover, policy-makers may want to foster new investment if they fear that TSO decisions lead to suboptimal investment, as they are too much affected by the interests of suppliers that have not yet fully unbundled their TSOs. It should be recalled that full ownership unbundling of pipelines is only found in a minority of Member States.

All of these factors suggest that in Europe, unlike in North America, the treatment of LTC allocation cannot be seen as a purely commercial process. The challenge is to set up a pragmatic mechanism where market forces and legitimate public concerns interact within a common and usually international decision framework.

The next problem of LTC is, of course, how long it should be. The longer the reservation, the larger the risk that capacity is hoarded by some strong players, including market incumbents and external producers, thereby reducing competition in the affected downstream markets. It is paramount that any LTC allocation should be strictly related to an effective capacity management (CM) procedure. It could be said that the longer capacity can be reserved, the more effective its release mechanism for short-term use should be, to be enforced whenever capacity is not used. Shippers (and the producers behind them) should be in a position to use their LTC, but cannot use such right to prevent entry by competitors that is based on cheaper short-term resources.

It is also clear, as stated, for example, in the European Regulators' Group for Electricity and Gas (ERGEG) Draft Framework Guidelines on Capacity Allocation, that only market-based solutions are considered acceptable for entry points into any Entry–Exit Transmission System (EETS), with the choice being restricted to either explicit or implicit auctions for physical capacity, and possibly to that between physical and financial capacity. This Framework Guideline does not, however, define that auctions should be used for LTC and other allocation processes, which is one of the tasks of the current discussion.

The duration(s) of LTC rights should be decided by market consultation – typical durations are up to 20 years – also by considering what is often done in the case of new infrastructure, where the rationale underpinning the LTC allocation is similar. Nevertheless, since the CM system may be only partly effective and the risk of capacity hoarding may be substantial, it may be reasonable to *cap* LTC, by setting a maximum percentage of total capacity to be auctioned, or (with the same effect) by reserving capacity to medium- and short-term allocation. A proposed (purely illustrative) structure could allow up to 70–80 per cent LTC, with at least 10–20 per cent mid-term (one to four years) and at least 10 per cent short term. The consultation may also consider intermediate durations (e.g., five, ten years), but the risk of straining the market by introducing too many regulatory decisions on durations and caps should be avoided.[18]

The most difficult problems, however, arise when the topology of gas transmission is considered. Whereas EU Member States have already used auctions for the allocation of LTC on individual entry points of a single EETS, substantial problems emerge whenever this process is extended to a few interconnected EETS. Shippers are normally interested not only in reserving capacity at each interconnection point, but also in booking capacity along several EETS at the same time. In fact they are often interested in supplying a market that is separated from the gas source by several intermediate countries and their EETS, where they may only partly (or not at all) be interested in supplying end users in those countries. Thus, they would like to be in a position to bid to reserve capacity on the entire route to the final (even the remotest) market of the chain, without being particularly interested in the intermediate exits.

It is worth noting that coordinated auctions on border capacity[19] along the route would represent a necessary condition for such capacity to be

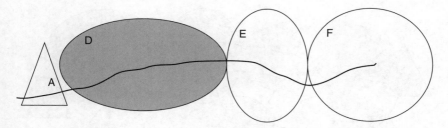

Source: Author elaboration.

Figure 8.2   Network topology type 1

booked, but not a sufficient one. For example, even with coordinated auctions, other shippers could outbid the first one on a limited section of the routes, possibly a single interconnection, and make its reservation at least partly useless. As in any poorly designed market, opportunistic forces would step in and secure control of bottlenecks, with a view to reselling them at higher prices. Therefore, joint allocation is necessary rather than simple coordination.

To understand the problem see Figure 8.2. A shipper (denominated 1) would like to supply mostly market F from an external source (e.g., a source in a non-EU producing country A), and therefore bid on interconnections AD, DE and EF on the pipeline connecting the markets. However, a shipper 2 wishing to supply mostly market D could outbid shipper 1 on the (congested) AD interconnection and make useless any reservation of DE and EF by shipper 1. A cascading auction design may in principle solve this problem, with capacity DE auctioned after AD, and EF after DE. However, it would fail to address a more realistic case.

Let us now assume that the system topology is closer to that of Figure 8.3, where six markets and three external sources are shown, located both 'east' and 'west' of the markets. This figure would be a more suitable representation of the problems occurring in the European transmission system, where gas is fed from all cardinal points as well as from inside the Union, and with the possibility of both commercial (backhaul) and physical (reverse) flows.

It is clear that if there are several sources, markets and interconnections, the potential number of combinations that shippers may be willing to reserve is potentially very high. No practical auction design could probably be devised for all of them to represent a reasonably transparent market, taking due account of the need for shippers to book capacity on routes comprising several neighbouring systems rather than individual ones. In Figure 8.3 there are at least 18 combinations if the possibility

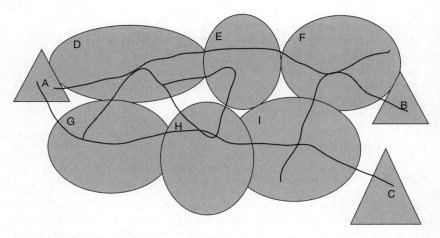

Source: Author elaboration.

Figure 8.3   Network topology type 2

of multiple routes is ignored, and there may be more than three times as many if these are included. In the actual European grid system, even with some consolidation of markets, hundreds of auctions would be required to address all combinations that shippers may actually be interested in booking. This is hardly feasible, and if implemented, would undoubtedly create huge transaction costs and uncertainty, for shippers, TSOs and regulators.

Further, even if such combinations could be auctioned, they would probably yield a much lower than optimal total transmission capacity, as the bookings would probably depend on the ordering of the auctions. As a result some interconnections could be neglected and others overbooked. On the other hand, it is hard to define a ranking for the auctioning of combinations. Two approaches may be envisaged to address this problem: single auctions and open subscription processes.

4.3   SOLUTIONS TO THE LONG-TERM CAPACITY ALLOCATION PROBLEM: SINGLE AUCTIONS AND OPEN SUBSCRIPTION PROCESSES

A first solution to the above-described problem may lie in the 'separate reservation' of interconnection capacity only. In such a case TSOs would simply auction interconnections (including entry points into the Union), and leave any other coordination effort to shippers. This would reduce the number of auctioned points to a more manageable level, in the order of a few tens. However, it would hardly provide the kind of LTC allocation sought by shippers, for several reasons.

The main problem is that, as already noted, shippers may need several adjacent interconnections, but may not succeed in reserving the same capacity on all of them. Therefore, the mechanism should foresee at least some possibility to downgrade the reservations, and would leave someone rationed. For example, in the Figure 8.3 example, with two shippers wishing to supply market H from source C, shipper 1 could win all capacity between C and I and shipper 2 all capacity between I and H. A bilateral bargaining would follow, with a substantial incentive to collude. Eventually, competition authorities may be flooded with requests to merge shippers like 1 and 2, driving a process of increasing concentration among the suppliers.

Auctions are a world where learning is essential. For example, after a certain outcome the bidders may 'be punished' by competitors if the bid was inappropriate. A single LTC auction defining capacity for a number of years does not allow for any such learning process and may therefore resemble a lottery rather than leading to a rational outcome.

A further complication potentially affecting any auction design, but particularly a single auction round for all interconnections, is related to speculators who may try to enter the bid for selected points with a view to reselling them at a later stage. Some countries have already limited this risk by requiring not only financial guarantees (which would not deter large financial institutions), but also the availability of long-term contracts for subscribers, which may be conditional on getting the LTC. This issue is not simple but it has been addressed with some success by regulators in Europe, like in Italy.

Thus, single interconnection point auctions for LTC are a possible but most likely not the best solution. Another solution could be devised by extending the experience of capacity reservation for new infrastructure, through 'open subscription processes'. The main steps of such processes are described below and could be seen as an extension and generalization of open season processes. At some point, several open seasons launched by TSOs may converge into a public open subscription process (OSP), but for the sake of simplicity and considering the existing differences these will be regarded as separate for the current illustration. In other words, the OSP does not exclude any other independent infrastructure project.

As stated above, the development of infrastructure by private initiative is a basic pillar of the American model, which should be preserved in Europe as well: in fact most of the European infrastructure has been developed by market-based initiatives rather than public decisions, even though in many cases developers were state-owned. The integration of market-based initiatives within (and to some extent channelling into) a public process is a variant aimed at addressing Europe's limited political integration, weak degree of unbundling and limited availability of local gas resources. The proposed OSP is (with the entry/exit tariff system, discussed in Section 5) the main divergence of the EURAM from the actual North American model, and is developed to allow for specific EU features.

From an economic perspective it could be argued that an efficient gas transmission system should not generate any long-term congestion, with capacity being increased up to the equilibrium level where willingness to pay for it equals its development costs, which in turn would be the basis of regulated tariffs. In fact even in the current, far from optimal organization physical congestion in Europe occurs in just a few cases. It is easily possible that almost all LTC requests could be satisfied at the regulated tariff.[20] The following proposal is based on that vision.

The process should be launched in a coordinated way. It is likely to last for several months, and should be repeated, perhaps every other year, with a view to offering capacity that may be released from the expiration of existing allocations,[21] or new pipelines. The OSP would be a process where private market players, as well as bodies mandated by public authorities, may take part. A platform would be established where all (private or public) stakeholders make binding capacity commitments, so that TSOs and others can finance and maintain or enhance existing capacity, or require the building of new assets. The following main steps could be envisaged:

Step 1 Technical capacity assessment
A first decision is related to the capacity that should be offered. In fact, available (firm) capacity at interconnection points is not independent of how other (parallel or converging) lines are used. The first step should therefore be the development of a common grid capacity model (the same basic requirement has been requested in the electricity sector).

The model should define not only total capacity to be offered, but also the implicit capacity usage at interconnections, which would be the basis for individual TSO capacity allocation and related rights and obligations, including for tariff purposes. Current ENTSOG work, including for preparation of the TYNDP, has already advanced in this direction.

It is worth noticing that the implementation of a single grid model, however time consuming, is likely to increase total available capacity with respect to what emerges from the sum of capacity calculated at single interconnections, due to the restrictive assumptions that must be made concerning capacity of interconnected pipelines.[22]

Step 2 Non-binding capacity market survey
Once the grid capacity model is available, shippers could be invited to state their (firm and interruptible) LTC requirements, in terms of source and destination (e.g., XX GWh/day from B to H). At this stage no auction process is envisaged: shippers would only state their peak capacity demand at the published regulated tariff for the required sources and destinations.

Any meaningful decision by shippers on how much capacity to request would in principle require that shippers know such tariffs for the whole duration of the LTC allocation. This is probably too long to ask of any regulatory process. However, considering the limited scope of capacity cost as a part of total gas value, it may be enough to require tariff updating criteria in line with the best EU practices. These involve regulatory periods where tariff updating criteria are defined in advance for periods of three to five years, linked to inflation rates and predetermined productivity improvements, except in special cases; and even periodical regulatory reviews involve some broad criteria for splitting of further productivity improvements between TSOs and shippers, but exclude any risk of sudden and groundless tariff change.[23]

Step 3 Capacity supply assessment
Once LTC requirements are fed in, TSOs would apply the common grid model and state the maximum available transmission capacity that can be offered. This calculation is performed with a view to satisfying the highest commercial transportation demand, without prejudice to the routing. It is not a path-based calculation, therefore it cannot be performed for any single TSO or even a subset of them. If any route or interconnection is congested so that the requested capacity cannot be offered, the concerned TSOs may agree and submit proposals for the reinforcement of the requested route. The process should be transparent, so that concurrent options may be proposed by competing companies or their groupings. It is expected that within such a process TSOs would also publish the indicative cost of capacity, notably in case investment is required or the current capacity tariffs are inadequate for any reason. In general such costs should be consistent with the tariff-setting criteria, but proposed tariffs would differ as new investment may be necessary.

Step 4 Binding bids
Once costs are known for all proposed links, market players are invited to submit their requests. This step is not basically different from the binding phase of an open season and would in fact be regulated in a similar way. Capacity contracts may be signed with the appropriate financial guarantees and ship-or-pay obligations. Such contracts could be defined for LTC rights to existing capacity as well as for new capacity.

Submission of bids and purchase of capacity should not be necessarily limited to commercial shippers. On the contrary, TSOs of systems located 'downstream', which have a legitimate interest in the availability of transit capacity, should be allowed to bid and reserve capacity, also 'on behalf' of their users. Indeed, an innovative, competition-friendly solution to reinforcing long-term capacity without too much appropriation by market players could be booking by TSOs of transit beneficiaries ('downstream' systems), paid by their regulated tariffs. However, its implementation may not be easy, as TSOs are not normally entitled to book capacity on other systems, and their regulators (or governments) should allow and instruct them to do so.

Where any such public service obligation is foreseen, TSOs (or other market players, for example, last resort suppliers) could also reserve capacity in transit systems, possibly at the request of governments, NRAs, or other authorities in charge of security of supply pursuant to Regulation No. 994/2010.[24]

The involvement of public authorities or of TSOs acting at the request of their regulators – and under a pact that costs of such capacity rights would be paid for by raising tariffs in the destination countries – poses a few problems. In principle, the public sector should bid first, otherwise a crowding out effect could arise. If markets know that government will raise taxpayer money or that regulators will charge users to finance investments, why shouldn't private sector operators just wait and see? Even the latest EC (2009b) proposals for a new infrastructure regulation confirm a limited, though increasing role for EC money, which could reach 9 billion euros out of over 200 expected investment requirements of the energy industry to 2020; however, much more is likely to be funded by national governments and regulatory decisions. Yet it would be no surprise if open season LTC auctions are deserted when private agents perceive that investments will continue anyway. In fact, the crowding out problem has already appeared, for example, in storage, in the case of the Hungary–Slovakia interconnector, and possibly in other open seasons.

This risk reveals two points. First, if private sector money is required for new infrastructure, as widely noted, private operators must be allowed private benefits in return. These could be exemptions in the limited cases where this is allowed, but preferably not in the case of inland pipelines to avoid creating a leopard-spots European network with a technically ineffi-cient lack of interconnections or a duplication of regulatory regimes. Most likely, it would be the award of LTC rights, tempered by appropriate and well-defined congestion management liabilities; or possibly the right to tariff discounts in return for early commitments and/or long-term ship-or-pay obligations. This takes us back to the step we are discussing.

Before proceeding, still another caveat should be emphasized. As noticed, in principle the public sector or TSOs acting on its behalf should state their commitment first, and let the private sector bid after them, to see if enough binding bids are available to justify the investment. In practice, conditions may change, including policy-makers' desires, therefore it may be hard to see what comes first. Politicians who strongly support a 'pet' project may well claim that changing conditions require stronger involvement. As always in economic policy, lack of predictability and credibility bear a cost: any such change would distort operators' and financing parties' perceptions and increase the cost of the projects. The latest proposal seems to go in the right direction as it foresees deadlines for the process. It could be useful to introduce periodical 'investment gate closures' to define timing of public and private interventions in the decision process, without prejudice to any fully privately financed initiative.

Finally, it is worth mentioning a special case of regulatory commitment. It has been proposed that open season bids should be accepted even if they cover less than 100 per cent of the costs, with regulated tariffs stepping in to match the difference. This certainly helps projects and could be based on past experience that shows that some more demand is likely to appear after the initial commitments. However, it is not in general a way to commit regulated money as a result of a proper, specific cost–benefit analysis. In any case, capacity contracts would be signed for all pooled interconnection capacity between the TSOs that are needed for the route required by the shippers, which would have requested capacity within Step 2, and be presented with bids within Step 3, as described above.

If a capacity enhancement is required, a by-product could be an auction of existing capacity, limited to the period during which capacity remains congested, with winners getting priority allocation in the ensuing increased capacity. Such an auction would concern the selected route to be allocated as a single (one stop shop) firm LTC service.

It is worth recalling that if caps on the LTC share are enforced, the routes are deemed to be congested if total capacity emerging from the optimal capacity model falls short of the required medium- and short-term margins.[25] This LTC capping requirement suggests avoiding too high reserve margins as this would increase the risk of LT congestion.

If TSOs or the relevant NRAs disagree on the choice of the routes to be up for auction, the Third Energy Package has a remedy. ACER (the Agency for the Cooperation of Energy Regulators) may make a decision according to Article 8 of Regulation 713/09. However, this article envisages long time scales for such decisions: up to one year after the time the NRA registers their disagreement. Whereas these implementation details are beyond the scope of the study it is worth noticing that such time scales would be too long for a swift decision on the meaningful auction. Any delay would be suffered by the upstream investment processes that the LTC allocation is supposed to foster, and eventually by the availability of competitive resources for European consumers. Thus, moral suasion could be used to select the routes to be auctioned, but it seems preferable to foresee a more cogent process as part of the Network Code capacity allocation rules, with an explicit role for swift decisions by the appropriate authority on the scope for auctions.

Step 5 Auctions for long-term congested routes
In the case that binding capacity bids do not reach the minimum size needed for the necessary capacity reinforcement, the interconnection or route could remain congested. This should be the exception rather than the rule, and should only happen in cases where demand exceeds maximum available capacity by only a small amount, which does not justify the investment. In such cases combined auctions may be held for the selected congested routes only. Since the whole process is likely to be repeated, possibly after a couple of years, it may be preferable to limit the auction to a relatively shorter time – or shippers themselves may prefer to book capacity for a shorter time (e.g., two years) if they know that the process will be repeated and they will be able to obtain LTC rights at a later stage, or seek another route. More on auctions is to be found in subsection 6.3.2.

4.4   CONCLUDING REMARKS

The outlined approach is based on TSOs normally acting to offer capacity to the market, as is the rule in North America. This should normally happen by decentralized action, based on market initiative. However, the still incomplete unbundling and the fragmentation of the European transmission system justify the proposal to integrate the capacity market with an open subscription period, where capacity for the necessary routes (from sources to sinks) would be offered by a centralized process based on a common, agreed flow model.

Moreover, the proposal acknowledges that capacity shortage should be an exception rather than the rule in an efficient system, which is the only meaningful basis for a target model. Therefore, if capacity is insufficient, a procedure to enhance it is the most logical answer. Auctions should be limited to the few cases where capacity is short and there is not enough demand to increase it, or where capacity cannot be reasonably increased due to technical discontinuities and environmental constraints.

The proposed approach also acknowledges that auctions are an excellent market-based solution in case of repeated allocations, as happens for short- and mid-term products, but not for long-term ones, as the prize would be too large and the learning process about the pricing terms would barely occur. Long-term capacity auctions for limited capacity bear a high risk of further capacity hoarding, which may not be entirely avoided even by congestion management procedures. This risk must be prevented and not just cured: in the long term, capacity should not be allocated but expanded if demand is there.

Therefore, the proposed approach minimizes the scope of auctions. Capacity should as far as possible be allocated at the regulated tariff (or tariffs in line with the regulated tariff criteria) to those who have a legitimate interest in it, excluding any purely financial interest. The use of auctions should be limited to special cases of congested routes, comprising several interconnections and offering virtual, non-path-based capacity, jointly offered by participating TSOs and consistent with capacity margins reserved by TSOs for mid- and short-term allocations. For the selection of such routes a transparent and relatively swift process should be devised.

The current work on the TYNDP has already provided significant building blocks for an effective open subscription process. However, the TYNDP is no decision tool. It is, of course, possible to envisage a totally new model where the development and maintenance of gas transport infrastructure would fall totally outside market criteria and be subject to decision by planning authorities, possibly preceded by informal market consultation and cost–benefit analysis. Under such models network costs would be mostly paid by end users, in analogy with the tendency to shift the cost of electricity transmission from generation to load in order to free generators from burdens and promote their competition. This model would be at odds with the basic assumptions of the EURAM, which underlines the possibility and opportunity of infrastructure development driven by market forces, though with possible integration by public authorities to address market failures.

A total network planning model would also probably not be desirable, extremely difficult to implement at EU level, and possibly against the legal framework of several Member States, recognizing free enterprise rights in gas transmission within the limits set by Directive 2009/73. The idea of a European network – or a strict coordination of smaller TSOs – with investment decisions taken at central level should be dismissed in that:

● the benefits of different companies or their groupings competing for different routes would be foregone for an important part of the gas value chain;

- it would be very difficult to properly allocate costs of investments not aimed at the national market (more on this in the next section);
- it would actually increase the politically affected part of the decision process, with the related risks of grandfathering and bureaucratization.

For all these reasons a total network planning model run by cost–benefit analysis and network repayment by end users is likely to either delay necessary investment, which would eventually jeopardize competition and security of supply, or to increase infrastructure costs due to inefficiency from lack of competition and political or bureaucratic interference.

In the EURAM view, the integration of private and public investment demand requires a common and transparent framework to avoid the dual risk of government subsidization of 'pet' projects and of free-riding by market forces in the hope that governments would intervene to pay for missing infrastructure. The TYNDP would remain an extremely useful building block and a benchmark scenario for decision-making by both private and public decision-makers, where the public role in decision-making is fully acknowledged and integrated.

Tariff regulation would remain. Transport market competition may be expected to appear for new capacity, and possibly for the allocation of LTC to existing pipes. But once the pipeline is built, regulation is necessary to protect network users from being exploited once they have invested in related supply infrastructure (exploration, production and upstream pipelines of LNG chains), which makes them dependent on the transmission pipelines. This justifies more in-depth analysis of tariffs in the target model, which is the subject of the next section.

Further, it should be emphasized that despite the availability of a common platform where LTC rights on the required routes could be booked, mostly at regulated tariffs or through binding bids, several market players may prefer to 'free-ride', or wait until capacity is developed at somebody else's cost, or possibly by public institutions, with a view to purchasing it later at auctions on a short-term basis. This is a typical 'public good' problem of common networks, as it may lead to under-investment. However, it need not necessarily be solved by public money. At least two regulation remedies may be suggested: (1) Any subsequent purchase of capacity may be subject to a reservation price, which would be equivalent to the regulated, cost-based tariff. This reduces the incentive to wait, as nobody could get capacity 'for free' or as a 'sale'. (2) Furthermore, TSOs may be allowed to apply an 'early bird' pricing principle, where capacity sold on a long-term basis is priced at a discount with respect to the reservation price of capacity sold in medium- and short-term auctions.

This would also stimulate LTC purchases and bids for new capacity by market players.

Finally, some might ask, what would be the role of exemptions in investment decisions taken within the proposed model? Exemptions are clearly not the favourite solution for pipelines across EU territory: in principle they are allowed only for LNG terminals and interconnectors. LNG terminals may be awarded exemptions if TSOs and other operators do not want to invest in them by taking the necessary risk to invest under Third Party Access, which is high as it is less easy to retain users with LNG terminals than with pipelines. On the other hand, in most cases LNG terminals enhance market competition, therefore their exemption – though awarded on a case by case basis – is likely to be justified in most cases.[26]

Interconnectors crossing the territories of other jurisdictions are more problematic. Their segregation from the host country system could entail a loss of efficiency and security of supply, and the same could be said of the virtual segregation provided by the exemption. Further, they would be totally excluded from the competitive market and may try to preempt competition, hence the doubts that have been often raised by NRAs against this tool (ERGEG, 2007, 2009). If a satisfactory LTC allocation mechanism is developed, investors and NRAs may well agree on using them as a more satisfactory tool than exemptions.

5   Network Tariffs in the Target Model

5.1   ENTRY/EXIT vs DISTANCE-BASED TARIFFS

Among the most remarkable features of the North American model is the regulation of interstate pipeline tariffs by a single federal agency (Federal Energy Regulatory Commission). Such tariffs are normally set on a point-to-point, distance-related basis. These are important features of the North American model and have been underlined as important for its success.[27] Yet, both of these features are apparently at odds with the European institutional framework, and are at the root of the common dismissal of the North American model as not suitable for Europe. Indeed, tariff-setting responsibility lies with NRAs according to Article 41 of the Gas Directive; and tariffs must be set separately for each entry and exit point.

Since, at first sight, the differences between the European and American tariff criteria and responsibilities are striking, it seems useful to analyse them in some detail, in order to understand if reasons for each approach are purely historical, and to understand whether they are really so different. From a theoretical perspective, the main reason for a 'federal' rather than 'state' (or national, in the EU) regulation of tariffs is clearly to avoid exploitation of transit flows by systems that lie between the main producing and consuming areas. It is clear that if transit flows dominate those heading for the local market, it is in the interest of intermediate systems to set tariffs well above costs, as the benefits of such behaviour for the transit jurisdiction would easily outweigh that of the highest impact of transportation tariffs on 'local' consumers.[28] A state regulator would be attracted towards such behaviour as well.

This problem can take more subtle versions than the pure exploitation of a transit location. NRAs of systems with dominant cross-border flows would be legitimately worried by cost swings that may occur in their systems as a consequence of falling cross-border flows, which they would not accept seeing on the shoulders of local consumers. It can be argued that this is a logical counterweight to the benefits that transit systems attain in terms of economies of scale, but this may not persuade the NRAs. This issue is analysed in more detail in Box 8.1 at the end of this section.

Whereas in principle the difficulties are the same on both sides of the Atlantic, solutions have been different. In the USA and Canada, the regulation of long-distance (interstate) flows has long been transferred to the federal level, so that no such exploitation of the geographical position of transit states is allowed. In Europe, where the regulatory power lies with NRAs, the Third Energy Package has brought about rather explicit provisions banning any such practices, which were in any case clearly against the spirit of the single market and could in principle (even before the Package) be pursued by more general EU single market legislation. These provisions are now included in Article 13 of Regulation 715/2009[29] and the main issue is how to implement them. Once this is done, in spite of the different institutional frameworks, the different responsibilities would be no reason to regard the European tariff system as fragmented, as compared to North America. Network users would rely on reliable tariffs based on fairly consistent principles, and any remaining difference between TSOs would be based on objective reasons and would probably not exceed those existing between (e.g.) US and Canadian tariffs, which have not prevented the organization of a largely integrated North American market.

It is worth remarking that, irrespective of any mandatory implementation of consistent and non-discriminatory tariff systems, European NRAs have shown a tendency to converge towards common practices, and network tariff setting is a rather consolidated business. Most differences can be regarded as minor, notably for the setting of allowed revenues, whereas more differences exist on tariff structures.[30]

The issue of tariff design, and notably the difference between entry/exit and distance-based tariffs, is less simple, as it is related to the technicalities of tariff setting. In fact entry/exit tariffs are a rather complex subject, particularly regarding the allocation of costs to entry and exit points. In short, the entry/exit tariff methodology can be seen as a generalization of the original point-to-point tariff system. It allows tariffs to adequately account for the multiple and often variable flows that are found in modern, liberalized systems, including the distinctions between physical and commercial flows.[31] In fact, entry/exit tariffs are often related to actual distance, with longer routes being priced higher than shorter ones. These tariffs tend to be similar to the 'special case' of distance-related tariffs in the case of mostly unidirectional flows, but tend to diverge in the case of uncertain flows, for example, with gas coming from various directions for technical and economic reasons. In such cases entry/exit tariffs are less distance related but tend to be 'closer' to 'postage stamps'. Now, a closer look at the European network shows that systems where transit prevails have mostly unidirectional flows, except in emergencies;[32] while the (usually bigger) systems with limited transit are characterized by mixed flows. The latter systems are often the 'final sinks' of the European network where most gas is consumed.[33]

Therefore, if tariffs are fairly and correctly determined, as required by the Gas Regulation provisions, they should in fact be very similar to distance-based ones for long-distance flows, which are mostly unidirectional as they are defined by the objective location of gas fields and markets. In other words, for long-distance flows including transit across several systems, a fair entry/exit tariff system would be extremely similar to a distance-based one. For shippers aiming to supply the big end-of-the-chain or 'sink' markets, such tariffs would work just like distance-based ones; they would simply add as many (import) entry and (re-export) exit tariffs as the number of intermediate systems used.

We can therefore conclude that, if properly implemented, the adoption of entry/exit tariffs at the level of each system (or Member State) does not preclude the capacity market to work as in the North American model, as far as long-distance transportation is concerned.[34] Thus, regulated tariffs should avoid any exploitation of monopoly power by TSOs, while at the same time fostering economic investment, and not excluding that, wherever possible, pipelines (or their groupings) compete for flows by selling their existing capacities at lower prices than the regulated ones, or by developing new capacity.

The rest of this section will be devoted to discussing how the implementation of such fair and effective tariffs could be monitored within the European institutional framework. Two special subsections will be devoted to the analysis of issues that deserve closer attention: (1) the case of tariffs for merged systems, which is important for those systems that may plan to merge – for reasons outlined; (2) the case of entry/exit tariffs in systems dominated by transit, which may raise special problems, which could, if not properly addressed, jeopardize the use, development and even the proper maintenance of such systems.

5.2   TARIFF HARMONIZATION ACROSS THE EUROPEAN MARKET

In the EURAM, cross-border trade would still involve the payment of an exit and an entry fee. However, in the case of auctions for cross-border capacity entry (and cross-border exit, once capacity is bundled) tariffs could be partly replaced by auction prices, even though the regulated tariffs should be retained as reserve prices. This would probably require the (up or downward) adjustment of exit tariffs, or the creation of an investment fund into which any positive difference between auction prices and regulated tariffs would be poured.[35]

The increased transparency and integration of the market could possibly trigger greater attention towards issues that have been relatively neglected so far, as network users have often been happy to obtain capacity without being able to fight much on its price. For other users, capacity costs were a transfer to a controlled transport affiliate, rather than a genuine outlay.

As unbundling and market integration progress, a greater concern for cost reflectivity and fairness of tariffs is likely to emerge. Moreover, as new congestion management procedures are expected to relieve contractual congestion problems, capacity becomes more abundant, and TSOs more independent of suppliers, cost awareness by shippers is likely to increase, as well as demand for closer monitoring of the capacity pricing behaviour of 'foreign' systems, even if regulated by their NRAs.

Since institutional responsibility for tariffs including cross-border flows lies with NRAs in the EU, any ex ante harmonization effort can only be based on moral suasion. This could be accompanied by monitoring efforts, which could be the basis for action in the case that the fairness requirements of the Gas Regulation were violated. In the current legal framework such action could only be taken by the European Commission, presumably after a request by affected stakeholders. However, a systematic monitoring, benchmarking and publication of tariff-setting criteria would greatly facilitate such tasks. This could include:

- costing criteria used for TSOs, including asset valuation methods, rates of return and their components, depreciation and operational expenditure, losses and fuel costs;

- cost allocation criteria between entry and exit points and between capacity, commodity and any other tariff driver;
- criteria for the updating of tariffs, normally occurring on an annual basis and by applying a multi-annual incentive scheme;
- transition provisions linking any two consecutive regulatory periods.

It is worth noting that if the resort to auctions is limited for long-term capacity (see Section 4), and congestion is not common, then the scope for deviations from regulated tariffs would be limited. On the other hand, if a substantial amount of capacity is sold long term and at regulated prices, it becomes important not just how tariffs are regulated now, but also the procedures for their updating, and even the process that is supposed to maintain regulatory stability, beyond the change of NRA personnel and national laws.[36] Although transmission tariffs are a relatively small component of the gas value chain, even a perception of unexpected and unjustified future tariff changes could represent a serious increase in regulatory uncertainty, and a blow to investment in new gas sources and transmission projects. Whereas national laws cannot be affected, an EU-level provision like the European Network Code could help reduce such risk.

The monitoring of tariff criteria could be included among current ACER responsibilities within the current legislation. It could be seen as part of the implementation of its responsibilities under Articles 7(4), 7(7) and 10 of Regulation 713/2009. Otherwise, monitoring could be promoted by the European Commission.

5.3   TARIFFS WITHIN MERGED MARKET AREAS

It has been suggested that market areas, identified by entry/exit systems, are merged, notably to increase market liquidity.[37] In the case of such mergers, a single tariff system should apply. Trading occurring at a virtual hub on the common network requires a single system of entry and exit tariffs in and out of the network, which is the physical infrastructure underpinning the hub. In pooled or merged markets some operational functions should be run by a common grid manager, acting as an Independent System Operator (ISO) in the sense used in American power systems.

Such a grid manager would allocate capacity or dispatch flows, including for balancing purposes, but it would not necessarily own and operate assets. Its cost share of the total would be very small, therefore the impact would be very limited for TSO revenues and their regulation. A large part of the assets and personnel would still belong to the participating TSO and could be regulated by the relevant NRA, as before the merger. It is, however, likely that, with the TSOs being joined into a common system, the respective NRAs and network users could be more sensible to any differences in the treatment of tariff components (like asset valuation criteria and rates of return), so that some further harmonization is likely to be promoted.

Much stronger is the expected impact on tariff design within the common market area. Allowed revenues of all participating TSOs should be pooled and the revenue raised by jointly set entry and exit tariffs. Therefore, tariff-setting criteria would have to be agreed among the participating NRAs, including (among others):

- how to define, bundle entry and exit points, and possibly regroup some of them as virtual ones;
- how to split revenue between entries and exits;
- how to allocate costs to each point;
- how to split revenue between capacity and commodity components, and recover fuel costs and losses;
- the length and timing of tariff periods and of their periodical updates.

Once these decisions have been taken revenues should be collected and split between participants, including the small share of the ISO. This could be named an Inter-TSO Compensation (ITC) mechanism, however, it would be far simpler and less controversial than what has been implemented in the power sector under this name. In fact, it would simply amount to collecting common tariffs and reallocating the revenue according to mostly predetermined shares. Tariffs related to lower-level pipelines could be directly left to each TSO.

The pooled tariff decision would obviously yield different rates than the present ones. In fact the whole tariff structure would be overhauled in the participating countries, with a potential impact on the tariffs paid by local customers. This is likely to become a major concern of NRAs, and a source of resistance against the merger by negatively affected parties (shippers, end users, NRAs).

Whereas it is relatively easy to assure revenue neutrality of the reform towards TSOs, the same may not be true for end customers. For example, customers near the borders of the new market area could experience some price increases, while 'central' parts could benefit. Fears of such changes could possibly slow down the reform process and the creation of larger market areas (or common trading regions). Nevertheless, the impact would in any case be very minor, as transmission tariffs represent only a very limited share of the end user price, usually less than 5 per cent.

BOX 8.1 TRANSIT TARIFF PROBLEMS

Transit is no longer a legal concept in the EU, yet it remains an economic reality, entailing a typical tariff problem. As a matter of fact, in several Member States or systems (notably among smaller ones), transit is larger or similar in size to domestic consumption.[38]

In such systems downstream demand swings may lead to sharp variations of transit flows, whereas the related costs are mostly fixed. The reason for the sharpest demand swings may be either that end use demand falls in the final destination markets, or competition, leading to usage of alternative sources, routes and infrastructure.[39] Such events may develop slowly, but nonetheless lead to potential unit cost increases within the transit countries.

The problem is normally related to fixed costs, as losses and fuel gas (also known as 'shrinkage') are usually covered as a separate item, in kind or as a variable charge. However, if these costs are covered by capacity-related charges the problem is exacerbated. In any case, costs would be borne by the remaining users. In the case of flow swings a tariff revenue risk arises.

Under a 'revenue cap' tariff, the TSO has a guaranteed revenue, but if transit falls more costs must be borne by domestic consumers, whose tariffs may notably increase. Thus, this solution is not usually supported by NRAs.[40] On the other hand, under a price cap, the risk would fall on TSOs, which may incur heavy losses: this solution is therefore opposed by the TSO itself. The problem has some consequences not only for the end users of the concerned transit countries, but also for the development and maintenance of existing pipelines. If the tariff system involves significant risks for its developers, its commercial development is less likely. For a fair analysis of this problem it should be acknowledged that host countries (and their TSOs) do benefit from transit in several ways:

- by the creation of jobs, profits, and land use rights for the local economy;
- by reduced transmission costs from economies of scale;
- if transmission cost allocation is not fair, some hidden cross-subsidies from transit to local consumers may occur, possibly supported by the NRA.

As noted, the cost allocation under entry/exit tariffs is a very technical methodology, with some differences in implementation across Europe. Monitoring by ACER and/or agreed guidelines may be useful to avoid discrimination, notably against cross-border flows: therefore such cross-subsidies should be ruled out in a target model discussion.

It is, however, useful to get some preliminary idea of the size of the economies of scale benefits, as the jobs, profits and land use rights are unquestionable remuneration of services rendered by the host country, including any nuisance from the pipeline. To estimate these benefits let us take a stylized representation of the Eustream system, the largest transit system in Europe, with an entry capacity in Eastern Slovakia (Veľké Kapušany) of over 12 mcm/hour, which carries gas of mostly Russian origin to the Western border of the country, with two exits into the Czech Republic and Austria, hauling gas directly or indirectly to several other destinations. The length of the system is about 500 km in Slovakia.

Now, as a mental experiment, let us assume that transit from Russia to Western Europe had originally followed different routes (e.g., through Hungary or Poland), leaving the Eustream pipeline for the service of the Slovak and Czech Republics only. In such a case, capacity unit transmission costs for these countries could be estimated at about 75 per cent higher, due to the loss of economies of scale. This can be named the 'standalone cost'.

The recent historical Eustream entry monthly load factor has been between 43.7 per cent and 91.4 per cent between 2004 and 2010, averaging 66.7 per cent (excluding January 2009, which was affected by the Ukrainian crisis). For example, if the average load factor were at its historical minimum the unit cost would be 50 per cent higher. Currently expected booked capacity for 2015–16 and 2019–20 would yield 50–65 per cent higher unit costs. It may be noticed that in such a case the unit cost, though higher, would still be lower than the standalone cost.

Under long-term capacity allocation with ship-or-pay clauses transit shippers bear most of the costs: the risk is largely transferred by transit systems to shippers, who in turn would probably move it further towards the end users of their supplied (downstream) markets. This point reiterates the case for long-term capacity allocation as a way of shifting some risk onto shippers.

However, not all capacity can be booked on a long-term basis. Shippers may prefer to keep some flexibility, as pipe-to-pipe competition (and LNG, new unconventional gas production etc.) may drive them to other infrastructure, and booked transit on existing pipelines may fall as a consequence. Further, allocation of too much capacity on a long-term basis could hamper the development of trading and spot markets and jeopardize competition, and regulators may well reserve some for short-term trading, as discussed in subsection 4.2 above. Congestion management provisions reduce the related risk, but also to some extent the appeal of booking long term.

It is also worth noting that similar risks are borne by larger countries or TSOs, but in such cases the risk is often spread over a larger public of domestic and cross-border TSOs, shippers and end users, and represents a smaller problem.

A typical solution is to limit the revenue cap to a certain guaranteed capacity component of costs, usually comprised between 50 and 90 per cent. The remaining revenue would be raised by a capacity- and/or commodity-related tariff, with risk falling on TSOs. Examples of this approach can be found, for example, in the UK, Italy, Poland, Hungary and Ireland.

A reasonable split between the guaranteed revenue cap share of costs and the risk falling on the TSO could be based on the standalone concept. Following this principle, tariffs of the transit country should never be increased beyond the level of the standalone cost, calculated on average historical flow, with any further risk falling on the TSO. A capacity- and/or commodity-related tariff would cover the remaining revenue, if flows occur, with the commodity tariff including fuel costs and losses.

The impact of the necessary transmission tariff reform would clearly be lower, particularly on small customers where the weight of distribution and retail price components is dominant. Moreover, some 'postalization' approaches could be applied to exit tariffs to smooth the impact, although this could create distortions and should be better seen as a transitional measure.[41]

6   Market Architecture

6.1   THE DEVELOPMENT OF GAS MARKETS IN NORTH AMERICA AND EUROPE

In commodity markets, the organization of markets is a business itself. Commercial ventures compete to develop market platforms and offer services that are used by market players. Liquidity is probably the best 'output' of a market and the main summary definition of its various actual products.

Markets have been usually developed where some objective conditions existed, mainly at the crossroads of commercial routes, or where abundant supplies attracted buyers. Gas has been no exception: markets have been developed mostly at junctions (hubs) of major pipelines and possibly near other important resources (production fields, storage sites, LNG terminals).

In the information technology era, the capability to organize markets has become a more important factor than physical locations where prices are set, with financial market operators often extending their reach to commodities (notably in the cases of New York and London). Oil is a typical example, even in Europe, with much organized trading occurring in the London Metal Exchange (LME), even if most products are related to deliveries at ports like Rotterdam.

On the other hand, electricity, which has much higher transportation costs per energy unit and a peculiar logistics that make it a comparatively shorter-range good (see Section 2), has developed a different market organization. Its limited long-distance trade allows for the development of many hubs, typically on a national basis. Since flows are hardly predictable, hubs are virtual rather than physical. Production (generation) is potentially less concentrated, allowing for a significant liquidity even on a relatively small market scale. Any expansion and cross-border integration of power markets has started from these specific characteristics.

As discussed in Section 2, gas lies somewhere between oil and electricity. Its production is only feasible where allowed by geology, therefore producers are often fewer than in electricity, like in the oil industry. Transportation costs are lower, however, than those of power although usually higher than for oil. Jointly considering these features, it can be expected that a lower number of commercial hubs will develop in a given area than in the power market, although possibly more than in the oil market.

If we look at North America, we can see an important number of hubs,[42] but four features emerge. First, these hubs have been developed by private industry rather than by governmental or regulatory initiative. Second, hubs are very different in relevance; an unquestioned leader has emerged (Henry Hub), with other medium or small hubs being used for local trading, with less liquid products. Third, the capacity products and related derivatives are mostly traded in financial centres that are often far away from the physical hub's location (which, as for oil, is mainly a pipeline node).

Fourth, market centres associated with hubs have expanded their services and have actually taken up several functions, which in the European organization are mostly TSO prerogatives. This has happened out of competitive advantage: for example, a hub where a large number of shippers have positions, with large pipeline connections, storage and possibly LNG resources, is in a potentially excellent position for the provision of services like gas parking, loaning, balancing, top-up and top-down and so on, which have developed as the modern, often virtual equivalent version of traditional storage services.[43]

It is likely that a similar pattern will emerge in Europe. A certain number of hubs, and possibly a ranking, will emerge, with the most liquid ones providing more sophisticated services than pipelines, and the latter providing the physical transportation, coordinated by the market centres. Whereas the technical pipeline dispatching may stay with TSOs, the commercial dispatching would in fact increasingly move to the market centres. Several gas companies in Europe are well aware of this perspective and have actively promoted the establishment of hubs and market centres.

Yet, the development of hubs in Europe has often been related to political intervention. Several governments have at least verbally pursued the goal of turning their country (or a specific location within their country) into a European gas hub. Whereas this is a legitimate ambition, it should be clear that it cannot be successfully achieved by all.

In fact, the organization of markets in Europe has so far followed rather different patterns (Jensen, 2007a; Jepma, 2011). In some cases (UK, Italy and to some extent the Netherlands) the preferred model has been closer to the electricity market, with centralized trading occurring both at the exchange and over the counter, although there have been no more attempts to establish mandatory pooling as in the original (but dismissed) British power market design. The innovation of the virtual hub, located on a transportation network, has facilitated this approach, with trade progressively moving towards the virtual trading point and away from the less liquid physical locations where it had previously started. In other cases, hubs have been developed mostly by industry with limited regulatory involvement. These have been based both on virtual points (as in Germany and France) and on physical points (as in Zeebrugge, Belgium and Baumgarten, Austria).

It should be clear that having a local gas hub is not necessarily the best policy option to get the cheapest gas supplies, notably if the local

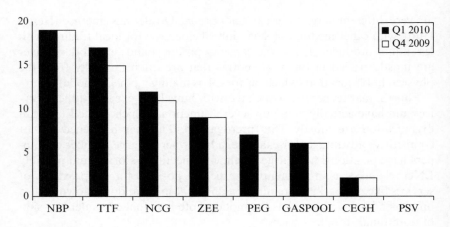

Source: ICIS Heren.

Figure 8.4 *Tradability rated out of 20 Q₁2010*

market cannot afford it. The risk is clear: governmental efforts to establish 'national' hubs may lead to excessive fragmentation of the European market, with too little liquidity in each hub, thereby strengthening the market power of (EU and external) suppliers. This cost adds to the investment and running costs of the hubs themselves. The North American experience also shows that several locations that are not hubs, but closer to cheaper hubs, enjoy lower prices than hubs located farther away from the cheapest sources.

In Europe, decisions about hubs should also take into consideration the opportunities to attain the necessary liquidity, which cannot be artificially produced (see Figure 8.4). Liquidity will appear where the suitable supply and demand conditions materialize, like pipelines, LNG terminals, storage sites and production and in the presence of sufficient traders and customers. Liquidity requires capacity, which can only be developed in the ways discussed above (Section 4) and – if available but locked by legacy contracts – made accessible by congestion management procedures. Shortcuts may be elusive.

6.2 CONNECTING MARKET AREAS

To understand the best options for European market design, let us see which ones are available. Some of the available options will be only summarized, as an in-depth presentation has been provided in more detail by the MECO-S model (Florence School of Regulation, 2011; see also Chapter 7 this volume). Whereas the basic options are similar to those outlined by the MECO-S, the analysis will differ.

Let us consider a market area, considered as a single entry/exit national or subnational area with one or more balancing zones. If such an area has few supply sources, poor liquidity and/or lack of competition, with the Herfindahl–Hirschman Index (HHI) displaying values above 5000, it is not likely to become a liquid and competitive market. To improve its liquidity, several remedies may be considered. Let us examine them in turn.

1   Boost supply competition

If markets are too small or do not have enough liquidity, it may be a matter of relatively tight and/or concentrated supply. Since Europe is surrounded by relatively abundant supplies, and the geographical position of most EU countries is hardly different with respect to such supplies, it means that either capacity is too limited, or is not available, or supply is too concentrated. Governments and regulators may then act to solve supply structure problems first, by increasing competition, for example by forcing industry splits or by a significant gas release programme, as some Member States did in the past.

It is beyond the scope of this study to discuss how this could be done. The promotion of competition by some form of gas release has been pursued by several Member States (UK, Italy, Spain) and to a lesser extent by competition authorities as a remedy for mergers (Germany, Austria), but results have been uneven. Nevertheless, for a small market, it may be inadequate to promote competition and foster liquidity by acting on market shares if access to different upstream supplies is simply not feasible. Thus, this is hardly a solution that could be recommended in general, but it may be useful in a few cases.

2   Reinforce import infrastructure

This may be the best solution, although it will not produce immediate effects due to the (increasingly long) lead times of new infrastructure construction. Furthermore, it runs the risk of causing large and inefficient costs, notably if it is decided on a national basis. We have seen in Section 4 how this could be done most efficiently through the joint participation of market forces and government institutions. If enough physical capacity is available but commercially congested and supplies are concentrated, any further capacity increase would be useless and inefficient: existing capacity should be freed first. Moreover, increasing capacity is sometimes a necessary but not necessarily a sufficient condition. It depends on which infrastructure is improved; for example, LNG terminals have recently provided access to relatively liquid markets, but in other cases the dominant positions of local as well as remote suppliers may actually be strengthened.

An important lesson of the North American experience is that relatively abundant capacity allows for easier competition. However, this capacity should be 'effective' and it should actually connect sources and markets. If this is not provided by interstate pipelines, like in North America, the solution lies in the definition of LTC on routes combining several TSOs, along the lines suggested in Section 4 above, rather than through initiatives by individual Member States, which may fail to address the necessary entire routes to sources.

3   Connect to a larger, more efficient and competitive market
This can be done by opening up existing but commercially congested capacity. This may be particularly effective for countries with relatively large but 'fully booked' interconnection capacity. The way to do this will be discussed below. This can be called the 'shopping mall' approach, as it recalls the option of citizens living in a smaller town where they cannot find the goods (or the prices) they would like. So, if they want better deals they can visit the shopping mall of a larger neighbouring city. If this is the preferred approach, the town administration's best policy may be improving connections with the existing neighbouring shopping mall, rather than promoting its own.

This approach has the disadvantage of losing some national independence,[44] but it is simple and can be attractive and efficient. In fact, a typical example of its application is the Irish Republic, which is in fact attached to the UK market through an abundant and flexible connection. In this way the Irish system can 'shop' in its biggest neighbouring market as much as it wants, while still keeping its own balancing and tariff system.

4   Merge with another market area so that the market size increases
This would presumably require the establishment of at least a common grid manager, operating like an ISO, with tightly coordinated gas day procedures and common balancing practices. It is most likely that in such a case an inter-TSO tariff compensation mechanism should be established, which is not technically difficult, but it may prove politically hard if some participants feel that they are discriminated against or if cross-subsidization arises (see Section 5.3).

For this option, different experiences have been reported. It has been noticed by Sisman (2011) that the recent merger of German market zones has entailed a reduction of total offered capacity. In France, the proposed merger of the Northern and Southern GRT zones would require substantial costs, which is just another way of raising the same point. On the other hand, E-Control, the Austrian NRA, has reported that coordinated operation of five Austrian TSOs has led to a capacity enhancement (Ascari and Cirillo, 2008).

Moreover, language and legal barriers may create coordination difficulties.[45] The implementation difficulties can be substantial, particularly between partners from different Member States. It is easier if a natural leader exists, for example, a larger TSO or an incumbent supplier, which is ready to act as market-maker in the new merged market, or as a balancing shipper in interconnections. In such cases, however, the risk is a limited competition improvement in the merged system. It seems that in both cases – and more seriously in the case of a full merger – a strong political will is necessary to overcome opposition by TSOs with a national rooting and by NRAs in charge of customers who may suffer from cross-subsidies.

If the expected impact of the merger is a more competitive market, and hence lower prices, the same resistance may materialize as against a gas release programme. The highly technical content of the merger makes such resistance easier. Yet, the prize for the merger could be the attraction of new suppliers and investments into the concerned countries, but this is often of more interest to consumers than to suppliers. However, doubling or tripling the market size does not always ensure an increase in its competitiveness, particularly if all competitors lean heavily on the same external sources.

A solution cannot be found for a general case. Depending on the conditions of networks, the pattern of gas supply, the availability of close or remote connections, and the political attitude towards national control over market development, a different choice may be preferred. From a European perspective, it is important to remember that in any case some hubs are bound to grow more and to become much more liquid than others. Indeed, a too large number of hubs may reduce overall liquidity, entail fragmentation and ultimately favour external suppliers. For example, there would be fewer arguments to move towards hub-based pricing and away from oil indexation of contracts, as a current but not easy path seems to be suggesting (Stern and Rogers, 2011). In other words, if the chosen market design entails a slower hub liquidity growth, the arguments of those who resist against switching to hub-based prices would be strengthened.

In North America, the smaller hubs survive for 'local needs' and players know that if price differences grow above certain thresholds they can (virtually) move their trading to the larger ones, where fixed costs of participation are more costly but prices (net of transportation costs) may be lower and products more flexible and tailored to the player's needs. Even in Europe, it can be expected that in the long run only a handful of hubs will survive, with possibly one or two continental leaders. In fact, the reduction in the number of hubs would be an indicator of successful market integration rather than the opposite.

An obvious question arises about the nature of hubs. Can virtual, entry/exit-type hubs have effective connections between them, as the typical North American physical hubs? Are future hubs all virtual, or is there room for physical ones?

The answer to the first question can be obtained starting from the discussion of entry/exit tariffs (Section 5). It has been noticed that for major, long-distance connections a properly designed entry/exit tariff is likely to be very similar to a distance-based tariff. Therefore, the 'cost distance' between hubs should be approximately the same as under a 'physical distance'-based tariff. In equilibrium conditions with reasonably good competition, prices should follow long-run marginal costs; they cannot be permanently below such costs if shippers must pay TSOs for transportation. Otherwise, sooner or later the TSOs would collapse. Only in the short term can prices get closer than transportation costs, as players may exploit already paid capacity and even the direction of flows between hubs may be uncertain. This has recently happened between adjacent virtual hubs of North-West Europe; however, this is not the case when hubs are significantly far apart, as the US experience shows (Figure 8.5), and cannot be the rule, as transportation costs must be recovered sooner or later.

As for the second question, it seems likely that trading will move from physical interconnections to virtual hubs, if the latter are available. This has happened in all markets where a virtual hub has been introduced. Furthermore, if interconnection capacity is bundled, 'flange' trading at borders would become impossible. Bundling has a technical rationale: in most cases border points have no technical or economic meaning, but are just a conventional point of a pipeline. It is perfectly rational if such trading disappears. The case may be different with regard to external borders and LNG terminals, but even in such cases trading has shown a tendency to move toward the more liquid, virtual hubs.

Whatever the basic liquidity, it will improve if several trading points are practically merged into one, as with the introduction of a virtual hub. Yet, it is worth recalling that, just as not all physical interconnections can become hubs, the same is true for virtual market areas. This does not preclude their possibility to obtain the best from the integrating European market.

In some cases, forcing hubs to be virtual and relating them to an existing or newly developed network may slow down rather than speed up the development of market hubs. For example, it may be difficult to replace the Baumgarten hub by a virtual one, as this would possibly require some kind of merger of neighbouring Member States' markets, which may be a lengthy process. Another example could be the Balkans, where a natural

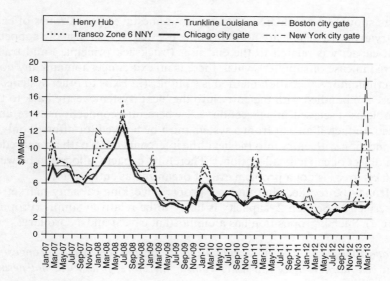

Source: Author elaboration, data from Platts.

Figure 8.5   US hub prices

location for a physical hub (outside the EU) could be in the Istanbul area, where several major pipelines interact near an LNG terminal and a storage site. Such hubs could benefit the neighbouring EU Member States as well, even though it would not be organized as an entry/exit market area.

6.3   THE RELATIONSHIPS BETWEEN HUBS AND MARKET AREAS

6.3.1   On Persistent Congestion

It has been taken for granted so far that, as requested by European legislation and summarized by ERGEG's definition, all market areas in the EU will be entry/exit zones, connected by auctions. Such definition is not at odds with the EURAM. As we have seen so far, entry/exit tariffs, if properly determined, would not hamper the development of the integrated market.

Usually the entry/exit system would also entail an entry/exit capacity allocation system. In such systems entry capacities may be allocated separately from exits. To understand if this is a problem, two types of exits should be considered: (1) Exits to domestic end user zones of each entry/exit area. These are normally uncongested. If (as it usually happens) exit capacity is related to the end user ('rucksack principle') and transferred in case of supplier switch, there is no exit congestion and any non-discriminatory allocation method is suitable. (2) Exits to other systems. If these are bundled with the entry into the 'next' system we are back to the problems discussed in subsection 4.2, where interconnections were analysed. In fact, if an exit from a system must be booked (or offered) only in connection with entry into the next, the interconnection path is restored as the object of capacity allocation.[46] Therefore, capacity allocation between market areas is not a problem even if organized as entry/exits.

It may be recalled that under a properly working capacity market, as described in Section 2, capacity is likely to be relatively ample (Proposition 4). Such a proposition has an important caveat and a corollary:

Proposition 4.1   Under economically efficient behaviour, congestion between market areas will never vanish; therefore, prices will not permanently align.

Proposition 4.2   If capacity is large, auctions would often be redundant: their outcome would yield zero prices.

To understand Proposition 4.1 the reader may want to consider Figure 8.6. Increasing capacity at any interconnection involves a growth in costs, presumably at higher than proportional rates. If at an early stage marginal capacity costs decline due to economies of scale,[47] this is reversed as economies of scale are exhausted. New pipelines are probably costlier due to increasing permitting difficulties and the unavailability of the easiest transit areas. Yet, more capacity has benefits through the reduction of congestion costs: for example, congestion reduces market liquidity and competition, triggering the 'deadweight' welfare losses of monopoly or other less than competitive markets (or even capacity rationing, in some cases). However, the marginal benefits of more capacity diminish as congestion is increasingly reduced. This happens steeply at first, and may even vanish beyond a certain level.

The economic optimum capacity is at the minimum total cost, which is where the marginal benefits of reducing congestion equal marginal capacity costs. If this equilibrium is achieved by market forces, the benefit of reducing congestion is measured by expected market price differences. In a market like North America, shippers would bid in open seasons to increase capacity if they think that they can exploit it by reaching higher-priced markets.[48] However, they would stop building capacity once the

price difference is small enough not to justify the costs. Hence, congestion would never disappear completely, and it is likely to appear, notably
in peak demand periods, through the seasonal cycle, as clearly shown in
Figure 8.5. Prices in Northern US hubs are well aligned to Southern ones
in summer, but far higher in winter when capacity gets congested.

If public authorities are allowed to enter the capacity market, as is
plausible in Europe, they could take into account the 'deadweight' (inefficiency) losses of reduced competition in their decisions. This would lead
to a higher valuation of congestion costs (in Figure 8.6, a higher and/or
steeper congestion cost curve) and hence to a higher optimal capacity.

Whereas the EURAM has suggested that public authorities could intervene into a single capacity market platform alongside private bidders, so
that a basically market-based mechanism is preserved, they may also intervene by including increased returns on investments, lump sum transfers,
capacity payments to national TSOs or other market players, and direct
investment, provided they are compatible with state aid provisions (which
is far from obvious).

Yet, congestion is most likely to remain at least during seasonal peaks
in mature systems. Moreover, the long lead times of demand and supply
adjustments in energy markets will easily entail situations where capacity
is 'too large' (as it was planned with a larger past or future market in mind)
or temporarily congested. Thus, price alignment would in general be
limited. Any assessment of the effectiveness of market integration should
indeed consider transportation costs.[49]

The corollary (Proposition 4.2) implies that, since capacity is likely to

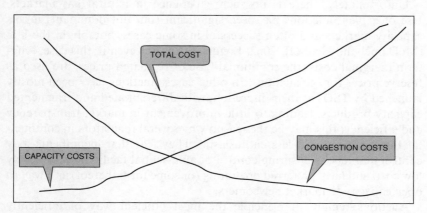

Source: Author elaboration.

Figure 8.6   Capacity cost and congestion

be abundant in most cases, auctions would likely yield zero prices. This may seem obvious, but it implies that auctions could never be a permanent way to remunerate TSOs. Otherwise, TSO revenues would end up coming mostly from exits and – since exits to other systems would be bundled to entries into (and auctioned with) them – these costs would fall mostly on domestic exits. This would be a problem for systems where a significant part of transportation occurs across the border (see Box 8.1 above) and may trigger serious protest from local consumers and NRAs.

For these reasons, the role of auctions would actually be limited in the EURAM – as it is in North America. TSOs would be mostly remunerated under LTC, with contracts granting them most of the required income, as discussed in Section 4.3. Normally such capacity would be paid by regulated tariffs, which should be cost-reflective.

6.3.2   On Auctions

Whatever the role of auctions in the target model, it is clear that in general they provide the best capacity allocation mechanism, wherever capacity is scarce. In the electricity sector, a long discussion has been held about the relative merits of explicit and implicit auctions (De Vries, 2004), and also about the different ways implicit auctions can be arranged, including market coupling (either organized as price coupling or volume coupling; market splitting; and locational marginal pricing). Some attempts have also been made to analyse the possible extension of implicit auctions to gas markets (De Joode et al., 2007).

Unfortunately, there is no such experience in natural gas markets. Use of explicit auctions has been significant (but not dominant) in gas capacity markets and often successful in some cases, notably in the UK (McDaniel and Neuhoff, 2002; Logue, 2010). But even in this case, long-term marginal costs, the traditional base of regulated prices, are used as reserve prices for the auctions. In other cases, auctions have been mostly launched by TSOs at their discretion, with differentiated and fragmented capacity products, leading to little improvement in market transparency and efficiency: this may be the reason why several regulators in continental Europe have been less enthusiastic. They fear that incumbents may control markets by ensuring control of an essential facility at a relatively low cost, and have preferred pro-rating (or some form thereof) as a way to open capacity to market newcomers.

Auctions remain in principle the most efficient way of efficiently addressing congestion, and are most useful as an essential feature of congestion management. This is extremely important in the practical case of present markets, although in the target model they are expected to play a reduced, mostly deterrence role. Under a market-based CM procedure, any unused capacity[50] would be lost (UIOLI – use or or lose it) or better, sold (UIOSI – use it or sell it) to the highest-paying bidders (in an explicit auction); or to the best bidders in the 'coupled' destination market (under an implicit auction).

The main theoretical advantage of implicit auctions as developed in the power sector is that capacity is automatically transferred to the best bidder in the commodity market, that is, to the supplier who is in the position to serve customers at the best price. This should automatically exclude the feared risk that any market player hoards capacity in order to supply the market at higher prices.[51]

The case for the introduction of market coupling has often been referred to by (1) lack of price alignment between hubs and (2) existence of adverse flows, which are gas flows from pricier towards cheaper markets, against economic logic (Neveling, 2011). In the current European gas markets, price differentials are often hidden: for example, several Eastern and Central European countries have higher prices than Western ones. Yet these are not formed in open markets, but through oil-indexed long-term contracts, for delivery by suppliers with large market power (or even monopolists). The lack of flows from the cheaper markets, leading to price alignment, is often attributed in part to the obligation stemming from take-or-pay clauses, and partly to difficulties in getting the (often virtual) capacity necessary for the implementation of (mostly backhaul) supplies from Western sources. The former problem is likely to be solved as demand grows and existing contracts are phased out, though it may be a long process. However, a clear tendency towards hub-based prices and away from oil indexation has been noticed (Stern and Rogers, 2011). As for the lack of backhaul capacity, this is in principle a relatively simple matter that regulation should be able to solve even without auctions, but as an essential part of the congestion management mechanism.

On the down side, implicit auctions involve significant transaction costs, particularly as they are new for the gas industry. For example, in power markets they are usually applied to markets with gate closure, whereas gas markets are accustomed to continuous trading. So any adaptation would be costly. Further, costs would be related to the establishment of the market offices in charge of arranging the coupling, by countertrades or other measures.

The physics of gas transportation is another reason why market coupling for day-ahead markets is less likely to play a large role in gas. In the power sector where market coupling was first applied, commodity trading focuses at day ahead because that is the optimal point to schedule generation. This is not the case with natural gas, which can take days to reach the markets from the original sources. Therefore, day-ahead markets in large continental markets may have a more limited role.[52] It may be worth reflecting on the fact that in the USA most market transactions involve monthly transactions and happen within a scheduled week every month, known as the 'bid week'. Accordingly, many pipelines require monthly balancing only. A forced restriction of continental gas market operation to the daily dimension may entail a loss of technical efficiency.

The main difficulty, however, is that market coupling and other implicit auctions require organized and liquid markets in all participating market areas, which is not necessarily the case everywhere, as noted above. Moreover, if only a handful of liquid hubs remained in Europe, the problem of allocating cross-border capacity would be different from that of connecting adjacent areas. Obviously, in the former case it would hardly be a problem, with abundant capacity allocated to applicants, as in the UK–Ireland case.

Others argue, however, that market coupling does not require liquid markets but may help to provide liquidity, quoting the example of some less liquid electricity markets (APX-Endex, 2011). However, market coupling can redistribute resources, but cannot create them. Liquidity can spill over to an adjacent, less liquid market if the former is 'very rich', so that it is not substantially 'impoverished' by ceding part of its resources to a neighbour.

To sum up, the costs of implementing market coupling should be traded off against the benefits of implicit auction. This trade-off may be represented by a picture like that presented in Figure 8.6, with resort to market coupling on the horizontal axis. Curves would have a different meaning. Increased use of market coupling would increase allocative efficiency, but involve some substantial transaction costs.

For these reasons it cannot be predicted whether implicit auctions will be used in the target model, even less whether they can be generalized. It is worth recalling that, whereas North America has been at the forefront of adopting and developing implicit auctions for the power market, it has so far refrained from extending them to natural gas.[53]

In any case, the contribution of implicit auctions would be presumably limited to day-ahead markets, where a small, though important part of trading would occur. An important role for market connection would also remain with other short- and medium-term auctions (for capacity products up to four to five years), where some problems similar to those of LTC allocations may arise. In particular, market players may be interested in multi-country routes (or link chains) rather than in single interconnections, and may fear bidding for a connection if they are not sure to get the 'next' one.

On the other hand, auctions for link chains clash with the problem of choosing the relevant links without unduly straining the market. Tentatively, such auctions may follow the same links chosen for LTC through steps 1–4 of the open subscription period suggested in Section 4. This is consistent with the natural development of capacity product auctions, where shorter-term products should be allocated after the longer-term ones, and using any capacity that is left from them. Auctioning of individual interconnections would then be available on a day-ahead basis.

However, in medium-term auctions, difficulties would be more serious than for LTC rights, where any possible conflict between sources could be eased by the development of new capacity. In the technical reality, capacities are not set by the size of pipelines and compressor power only, but may change depending on the interaction of pipelines. Interdependence may be high and agreement on the flow model used to define capacity may not easily be reached. The risk of disputes may suggest less ambitious solutions, like the requirement to coordinate auctions, possibly with prevailing downstream interconnections being offered after long-term ones; and to sell conditional products, allowing bidders to withdraw if they do not manage to win the necessary downstream capacity.

However serious these issues may appear in theory it should never be forgotten that markets will find their own solutions, alongside those suggested by regulators, as has happened in North America. Even in the relatively advanced and liquid North-Western EU market, the last two years have seen a much more effective capacity market, which has actually achieved remarkable price alignment without much regulatory intervention. Capacity has been mostly traded on secondary markets, and swaps and the diversion of LNG tankers between terminals have done the rest.

7   The Consequences of the EURAM for the European Network Code Process

The most important goal of the gas target model study is to provide guidance to the process of drafting the European Network Code, indicating its main priorities and how the various parts of the process would interact. This is important, particularly in the early stages of the establishment of the Framework Guidelines, which require the greatest involvement of NRAs, ACER, ENTSOG, the European Commission and assisting committees.

It is clear that the main requirement would be the integration and connection of market areas, which should not be confused with the establishment of hubs and organized markets centres. The connection of markets should at first be achieved by freeing up currently frozen capacity, mainly through congestion management procedures. These are not a fundamental feature of a gas target model, but they should still be present to play a secondary and deterrence role. However, congestion management is crucial for the transition towards the gas target model, as outlined in several points of the present chapter, which outlines a world where TSOs offer, ensure and manage capacity as their main and exclusive mission. In particular, congestion management (CM) should include the availability of backhaul capacity along lines with a prevalent flow. The discussion of how to organize market-based CM is out of the scope of this study.

Next to CM is the elimination of any further barriers that have in the past slowed down cross-border trade. This requires at least the harmonization of:

- cross-border allocation practices through the generalization of Interconnection Point Agreements and Operational Balancing Agreements;
- standardization of at least some capacity products;
- energy units;
- standard formats;
- the gas day and its main deadlines;
- any remaining interoperability issues.

Although these are often highly technical issues that may not raise political enthusiasm in the same way as unbundling, their speedy solution is probably just as necessary. Again, details go beyond this chapter, but a detailed scoping and roadmap should be defined within the ENC process.

A major way of connecting markets in the EURAM would be through the development of an efficient capacity market. This would be greatly facilitated by the development of TSO unbundling along the lines of the Third Energy Package and possibly through the choice of the ownership unbundling option, as several Member States have already done and financial markets would foster. However, this chapter has stressed that a generalization of full ownership unbundling is not necessary for the implementation of the EURAM. It rather emphasizes the push on a more competitive, transmission development-oriented TSO behaviour.

It goes without saying that this should be one of the NRA's main priorities, as an effective ITO regulation in combination with market forces could possibly trigger such behaviour, or even the sale of TSOs by market incumbents, and thus a reorganization of the transportation industry, with mergers and acquisitions, as has already occurred in the gas supply business.

The development of efficient infrastructure, as well as upstream (E&P, LNG and pipeline) investment, would also be greatly helped by the sale of bundled and coordinated long-term capacity, allowing shippers to ensure access from sources to markets. Given the current structure of European TSOs, it has been proposed to foster this process by developing a platform for LTC rights, to be structured as an open subscription period open to all market players as well as to other TSOs, including those mandated by public authorities for the fulfilment of public service obligations. Such a process would resemble open seasons rather than auctions; it could be repeated at a certain frequency (e.g., every two years) and lead to the development of new capacity if necessary, in addition to that fostered by normal market processes through TSO-driven open seasons. This would certainly require a significant effort by both the regulators and the TSOs. It would not be against the current development, but could be rooted in the experiences of the TYNDP, the Framework Guideline on capacity (which currently offers very little guidance on this) and the Guidelines of Good Practice on Open Seasons.

A further pillar for new infrastructure development, the maintenance of existing systems and its efficient use, would be the tariff structure. The Third Energy Package offers some detailed requirements on tariff methodologies. It has been shown that the entry/exit tariff model would be fully consistent with a continental and efficient capacity market, mostly based on regulated tariffs. Yet the risk of transit flow exploitation remains serious, as acknowledged in the Third Energy Package, and should be tackled.

A dedicated Framework Guideline is therefore probably necessary to define criteria for costing and tariff updating – even though some harmonization is already found thanks to the spread of best practices among NRAs – and for tariff design, which have not been very transparent so far. The Framework Guideline may define some general criteria (or Guidelines of Good Practice), which may be subject to systematic monitoring by ACER or the EC, without any loss of national sovereignty on tariffs and methodologies as confirmed in the Third Energy Package, but also with the identification of benchmarks where the EC may take action in case of discriminatory tariffs violating the provision of Regulation 713/2009/EC.

The European Network Codes in coordination with other important current processes (EMIR [European Market Infrastructure Regulation], REMIT [Regulation on Energy Market Integrity and Transparency]) may also define the criteria for a minimum playing field of market operators, and possibly a set of minimal products for market trading. However, the process should avoid any top-down definition of political or regulatory criteria on which hubs and organized market centres should be devised. As noted in Section 6, some of the main messages of the EURAM (taking up important lessons of the North American experience) is that price-making hubs will be very limited in number and that their detailed market design should be the product of market forces. Thus, a subsidiarity principle should prevail in hubs' decisions. The high risk of political interference would be in fragmenting liquidity, which would enhance the market position of (mostly external) suppliers vis-à-vis the European industry and its consumers.

Likewise, a strict subsidiarity principle should rule the way markets are interconnected, starting from the awareness that even if market zones can be organized as entry/exit systems, this does not mean that any of them could also become a liquid market. On the contrary, a decision should be made on a case by case basis, with a view to enhancing market competitiveness, on whether to connect markets by:

- expanding physical capacity to attach less liquid markets to larger ones and/or to new supply sources;
- merging the areas, possibly by pooling the higher-level part of their systems;
- linking the areas by auctions, including implicit ones, with market coupling as the natural candidate.

Again, current Framework Guidelines and the related ENTSOG work would be fully consistent with this approach. Auctions as a permanent CM tool would be needed anyway, and congestion is never going to entirely vanish. However, any solution has its proper costs that should be considered against the assumed benefits of greater integration. The analysis should consider in particular the contribution of market-based solutions, including swaps, LNG re-routing, and the secondary capacity market, which are likely to further develop as unbundling progresses, and could be fostered by appropriate measures. Further harmonization of technical rules and other CM provisions that are currently under discussion may greatly enhance the connection of market areas.

Finally, the balancing provisions, though more technical in scope, should be devised in such a way as not to foreclose potentially efficient market design options, consistent with the above considerations on hubs, market zones and their connections. For example, it should be possible to purchase balancing resources from other market zones and hubs. Market-based balancing should not be a way of devising a restrictive market design, nor of forcing mandatory pools.

It seems that in the target model devised by the current draft Framework

Guidelines, balancing responsibilities are significantly moved from TSOs to shippers. This would, however, require the availability of balancing services and resources, which cannot be in all shippers' portfolios – otherwise balancing may become a new essential facility, which gives market power to its holders. In the EURAM, as in North America, balancing services are often provided by market centres: this is just another reason to allow an efficient development of the hubs, and not an artificial one. Such tendency does not exclude that pipelines could still offer balancing services, but this option is increasingly less likely as TSOs lose control of the gas they transport, possibly including the line-pack. Yet, balancing requirements in the EURAM are a potential tool of pipe-to-pipe competition. Pipelines with adequate resources may well offer easier balancing conditions to attract customers.

8   A Summary and Comparison of the MECO-S and EURAM models[54]

The MECO-S (Glachant, 2011) model is based on three pillars:

- to enable liquid and competitive markets;
- to connect markets;
- to secure the operation of markets.

The three pillars are underpinned by the promotion of efficient economic investments.

In the MECO-S each entry/exit zone would also be a single price zone, where trading on a spot and forward basis would occur so that price signals are provided. If the market in a zone is not adequately liquid and competitive it should improve its liquidity by either developing new supply infrastructure or by merging with another hub so that a minimum market size and suppliers' abundance is achieved. The merger may be full (including for balancing and tariff purposes) or limited to a higher-level trading region, with balancing and retail trade left to lower-level zones.

Markets would be connected up to the point where either prices are aligned or the existing interconnection capacity is fully used. This would be achieved first of all by the introduction of enhanced supply and trading conditions, based on further harmonization of market rules, the gas day and its procedures, gas quality, and on reinforced congestion management provisions. Markets would be connected by auctioned long-, medium- and short-term capacity products. If pilot implementations are successful, day-ahead markets may be also connected by market coupling.

The enhanced trading conditions would also include the setting up of coordinated and conditional auctions for long-distance transport ('link chains'). Long-term capacity contracts would be allowed and could use the link chains. Moreover, in order to ensure security of supply, TSOs should be allowed to book and pay 'fallback' capacity in other systems, to be used in case they cannot use their usual supply routes.

All pillars would be underpinned by realizing economic investments directed at improving interconnections and overcoming congestion between and within markets. The MECO-S includes proposals for the definition of economic investments, based on open seasons and benefits from reduced price spreads between market zones.

The EURAM, broadly inspired by the adaptation of the US model to the EU framework, pursues three main objectives:

- the development of ample supply and transportation capacity;
- the development of hubs as allowed by market forces;
- the connection of market zones.

The first objective is pursued by promoting the most effective unbundling of TSOs from supply affiliates, with a view to fostering the supply of transmission capacity. This may require the establishment of a common European platform for long-term capacity, where market players and public institutions may bid through a multiple step process for the reservation of capacity on required routes, offered by TSOs on a competitive basis. Wherever capacity bids justify it, this process would also lead to investment. Due to their lasting relevance, harmonized tariff criteria would be set up and monitored at a European level. The share of total capacity that could be reserved long term would be capped so that medium- and short-term capacity trade may develop.

Hubs would be developed where justified by market forces, but not every market area would be a hub. Prices would be mainly defined in the emerging dominant hub(s), with minor ones related to them by regulated tariffs or auction prices.

Market zones would be connected, at first through effectively reinforced congestion management provisions and harmonization of market rules, the gas day and its procedures, and gas quality. Auctions (subject to tariffs as reservation prices), including implicit ones, could be used as an efficient way of connecting markets, but their use would be probably limited to cases where allocation at regulated tariffs and secondary trading would create congestion.

The main areas of agreements of the models are:

- the need for harmonized, enhanced trading conditions, including effective congestion management;
- the need to allocate capacity on a long-term and long-distance basis by providing linked chains to willing shippers, possibly with participation by foreign TSOs pursuing public objectives;
- the efficiency of connecting market areas by auctions, including implicit auctions if they can be proved feasible in gas markets.

However, the models have a rather different emphasis on how to ensure efficient investment. The MECO-S is based on objective criteria defined by regulators, while the EURAM privileges the promotion of a capacity market, with the possible participation of public bodies, or of TSOs on behalf of them. Further, auctions are seen as a generalized connection tool in the MECO-S, whereas the EURAM expects them to play a role limited to a minority of congestion cases.

As a consequence of this vision, although several aspects of the European Network Code could be the same, priorities would differ. The MECO-S stresses the need to develop and merge market areas everywhere. The EURAM privileges the connection of market areas between them and with hubs through abundant capacity, which may be sold at regulated prices if not congested. Under the MECO-S, NRAs would devote significant efforts to zone mergers wherever hubs are not liquid. Under the EURAM, they would rather focus on market rules harmonization.

Further, the MECO-S sees a mostly regulated or planned development of capacity, whereas the EURAM favours market developments integrated by public intervention, with a role for competition between infrastructures. At EU level, both models would start from the existing capacity allocation Framework Guidelines. However, the MECO-S would generalize the implementation of auctions and support efforts for the introduction of market coupling into gas markets. The EURAM would extend the capacity allocation Framework Guidelines to create a common platform for the capacity market, to be linked with the regulation of open seasons. Further, the EURAM would suggest drafting Guidelines of Good Practice on tariffs.

The models clearly disagree on several issues. In particular, the MECO-S regards any market area as being bound to become a liquid virtual hub or part thereof and denies that trading in a cross-border market may be a suitable option. The EURAM claims that few hubs may be expected to survive in Europe, supports the greatest efforts in the opening up of full access to such hubs by any other market zone, and warns against any political decision to develop inefficient hubs.

NOTES

1. The North American forward market is 2600 times as large as the European market (Makholm, 2011).
2. The predominantly national nature of production has also been noted. Whereas this is no reason for (e.g.) the Alberta-based producer to give in to US customers, the most competitive and market-friendly organization of import sources has helped to integrate it into a single market space, where this has been less easy with at least some of Europe's external suppliers.
3. A valuable attempt to draw such lessons can be found in Correljé et al. (2009).
4. See Makholm (2006, 2011) for an illustration of how it developed; see also Jensen (2007a).
5. In this chapter 'transportation' and 'transmission' have the same meaning. In EU legal language the official word is 'transmission', however its use carries the risk of neglecting the differences between gas and electricity transmission, which are stressed in this chapter.
6. This tendency can be clearly noticed if one considers that the regulatory framework defined by the electricity and gas directives in the EU is fundamentally similar. On the other hand, the USA and Canada have a much larger federal independent regulation of the gas industry, unlike power where regulation is mostly state/province based. Whatever the opinion on this difference, it is clearly consistent with the fact that natural gas travels on average much more than electricity, with some 60 per cent of gas consumed in Europe crossing at least one Member State border and nearly 30 per cent at least two, against about 3 per cent of electricity crossing one or more borders. Historically, the original development of European gas regulation in the UK may also contribute to explain such patterns, as the isolated UK gas market shares more of the electricity features than the European Continental gas market, with a far smaller transmission sector serving end users from mostly national and 'close' sources.
7. 'Marginal' is used here with the economics meaning of being the last unit that is delivered (or the first that is withdrawn) from a market in order to restore equilibrium (e.g., to achieve price alignment between markets).
8. The competitive pressure is not the same everywhere. For example, TSOs of large systems that are mostly 'sinks' rather than transit areas may feel a very limited pressure and develop in a relatively easier way, driven by national demand. This has been the case, for example, in Britain, France and Italy. However, new sources and streams can modify this reality: all of these systems are currently exposed to growing opportunities for providing cross-border services, which may well affect their business model if the opportunities are taken, and lead to strain if they are missed.
9. Communication from the Commission 'Sector Enquiry under Article 17 of Regulation (EC) No. 1/2003 on the Gas and Electricity Markets (final report)', COM(2006) 851.
10. Huygen et al. (2011, Section 3).
11. See, for example, Knight Vinke on Eni: http://www.knightvinke.com/media_centre/eni/; accessed 2 April 2013.
12. Action has been taken notably against GdF (later GdF-Suez), E.ON-Ruhrgas and Eni, leading to various remedies to reduce market control by large and integrated incumbents.
13. To avoid any further misunderstanding it should be clarified that within this study the definition of LTC is different from that in European legislation. In the latter 'long term' encompasses any capacity product above one year. In this study a distinction is introduced between long term, above five or more years, and intermediate term, which is between one and five years.
14. Commission Decision of 24 August 2012 on amending Annex I to Regulation (EC) No 715/2009 of the European Parliament and of the Council on conditions for access to the natural gas transmission networks; http://eur-lex.europa.eu/LexUriServ/LexUriServ.do?uri=CELEX:32012D0490:EN:NOT.

15. Yet, this approach is supported not only by the British experience but also by the wide support emerging for long-term capacity allocation rights in the recent call for evidence launched by ERGEG on the target model.

16. PCG (2009). In particular see slides 40–54.

17. The most compelling provisions are now found for ITOs in Directive 2009/73, Article 22. In the old Directive 2003/55, Article 21(2) reads 'Member States may take the measures necessary to ensure that the natural gas undertaking refusing access to the system on the basis of lack of capacity or a lack of connection makes the necessary enhancements as far as it is economic to do so or when a potential customer is willing to pay for them'.

18. Implementation could also consider delivering longer terms as strings of multiple shorter-term products, as already done in the UK: these details go beyond the scope of the present study. It is interesting to notice that a similar discussion is found in the electricity target model discussion: see PCG (2009, slides 38–42).

19. In this discussion any cross-border capacity is assumed to be 'bundled', that is, the same capacity is allocated on both sides of the border.

20. Possibly allowing for limited reinforcement (e.g., by adding compressors). However, technology requires that beyond a certain level a capacity increase can only be attained by doubling a pipe rather than by increasing compression, larger pipes or looping. But demand may not justify such a jump in capacity supply. This may be the source of remaining congestion in some cases.

21. Including legacy contracts. The GTM does not, however, discuss the treatment of such contracts, but it is assumed that there will be some.

22. This has been experienced on a smaller scale in Austria, where the allocation of capacity by a common grid manager has led to a capacity increase with respect to allocation by each of five concurring TSOs.

23. More on tariffs will be covered in the next section. The latest EC proposals on the definition of priority projects of common interest, though not limited to the gas sector, can be seen as a rather similar and consistent approach, on which the following steps may be rooted.

24. The participation of public institutions in an open subscription or open season process is not entirely without risk. Before investment decisions they may well offer subsidies to new infrastructure to attract shippers, with a view to increasing tariffs later when shippers are stuck to it. However, this risk is lower under an open process than in a less transparent and public decision mechanism.

25. For example, if LTC is requested for 60 GWh/d on a certain route and a cap on LTC at 75 per cent is enforced, the route is congested if it cannot deliver at least 80 GWh/d.

26. In the USA LNG terminals are now almost fully deregulated by the Federal Energy Regulatory Commission.

27. Makholm (2006, 2011); also, European TSOs have often shown their preference for distance-based tariffs, which are seen as the only cost-reflective type.

28. This happens even if tariffs are perfectly fair and do not discriminate between transit and internal consumption. In fact an entry/exit tariff structure may also discriminate against transit flows.

29. 'Tariffs [for network access] or the methodologies used to calculate them, shall facilitate efficient gas trade and competition, while at the same time avoiding cross-subsidies between network users. . .shall neither restrict market liquidity nor distort trade across borders of different transmission systems. Where differences in tariff structures or balancing mechanisms would hamper trade across transmission systems. . .transmission system operators shall, in close cooperation with the relevant national authorities, actively pursue convergence of tariff structures and charging principles, including in relation to balancing'.

30. Where, understandably the Gas Regulation requires NRAs to pursue convergence. A thorough analysis of European practices is provided by KEMA (2009).

31. In particular and notably on a medium-range scale, the liberalization of markets has

brought about backhaul flows, that is, commercial flows that go against the prevalent physical flows, and that should therefore be priced differently, as they contribute in some way to reducing the need for physical flow.

32. Examples of such systems are Austria, the Czech Republic, Slovakia, Bulgaria and (with a lower transit dominance) Belgium, the Netherlands, Poland and Romania.

33. Examples of such systems are: Germany, the UK, France, Italy, Spain and Hungary.

34. Commodity markets would, however, be organized in a different way, as entry/exit tariffs are naturally associated with virtual rather than physical hubs: these will be discussed in the next section. A different conclusion, although starting from similar concerns, is found in Hunt (2008). However, his proposals are not compatible with the Third Energy Package legal framework.

35. If market coupling is introduced (see below), the same could happen with the congestion rent earned by the administrative process from arbitraging between the markets.

36. A typical point raised by TSOs before regulators is: 'You are the best regulator in the world, but my investment cannot be recovered before your term expires. How can I be sure that your successor will be as good as you and respect it?'

37. Such mergers could also be limited to parts of the merging networks, for example, the main long-distance pipelines, as implicit in the 'trading region' option of the MECO-S model. See Glachant (2011, § 1.3.1.2).

38. See footnote 32 above.

39. For example, in the last few years a relative decline of Russian supplies to Western Europe, crowded out by cheaper Norwegian gas and LNG, has entailed a declining load factor of some large Central and Eastern European pipelines.

40. Moreover, if this amounted to increasing unit costs of transit, it could also further damage the competitiveness of the pipeline, triggering a vicious circle. However, this is probably a minor effect.

41. Postalization of exits amounts to setting a single national exit tariff, which implies some cost rolling. This has been implemented in France under an Energy Enhancement (EE) system. For more details and a simulation of the likely outcome of such merged systems, see Ascari and Cirillo (2008).

42. See Jensen (2007a, p. 119). For instance, Platts normally reports prices for six main US hubs.

43. Huygen et al. (2011, Section 3).

44. In the example the administration of the smaller town cannot, for example, decide the working hours of the shopping mall, but must accept those set by the larger city.

45. The MECO-S model has proposed the 'trading region' approach, which is a variant of the previous case where only the 'higher level' part of the network is merged and is used as the platform for the virtual hub, whereas balancing remains in the lower-level networks, known as 'end-user zones'. This approach requires less coordination than a full merger and may be technically easier and politically more acceptable.

46. This could be a single physical pipeline, or a virtual system of adjacent pipelines providing similar services, for example, connecting markets D and E in Figure 8.2.

47. In other words the second derivative of the cost function is negative with respect to capacity.

48. In no way could this decision be driven by short-term auction results. Short-term congestion is just a very limited indicator for bidders that must form price expectations over the long term as necessary to repay the investment costs.

49. For example, it can hardly be expected that in the long term wholesale prices would be the same in the UK as in Romania. Since willingness to pay is probably higher in the former due to higher per capita income, the proof of ineffective market integration would rather be the case where Romanian prices are higher than the UK's even though total supply costs to both countries is similar.

50. The discussion of how to define unused capacity is in practice very important and widely discussed at present in the EU, due to its efficiency as well as equity impacts, but its details go beyond the scope of the target model discussion.

51. In multiple power markets there is a further benefit: the algorithm would also track the best allocation of capacity among the nodes, which cannot be defined ex ante as it is driven by the physical laws of electricity transmission. This benefit would not be applicable to gas markets where capacity can be defined ex ante. This point was highlighted by Laurens De Vries in a private seminar.
52. This may not be the case in relatively small and isolated gas markets, relying on significant local resources.
53. Although it is hardly an economic rationale, it can be noticed that the much stronger European electricity industry has to some extent managed to extend its own paradigms towards natural gas restructuring, whereas in North America the primarily state-governed power industry has remained much weaker and is confined to a much smaller reach, notably after the Enron collapse. This is in contrast to the more federal-oriented gas industry, which is still linked substantially to the politically powerful oil industry.
54. The comparison is provided for readers' convenience, however, the summary of the MECO-S is solely the responsibility of the author.

Conclusions

Michelle Hallack, Miguel Vazquez and Jean-Michel Glachant

The definition of 'network activities' as regulated businesses is at the core of the EU gas market design. The EU gas industry has been opened to market forces in the last two decades and several activities of the gas industry chain have been reorganized under decentralized decision-making processes. To introduce competition in the gas sector, the rights of transmission network use have been unbundled from the network ownership. The owners of pipelines keep the property of their assets but they cannot use them any more as private carriers. Different players have the right to access gas consumers and suppliers by using the network infrastructures. Nevertheless, in order to give access to the same infrastructures to different users, one needs to define the conditions of usage in order to avoid 'commons dilemma' inefficiencies. These conditions of use and the corresponding investment decisions can be framed by a centralized management (a 'regulation') or by decentralized agreements ('contracts').

The organization around contracts was the choice of the liberalization process in the US gas sector. The EU restructuration process, however, has a markedly different path, guaranteeing the access to gas transport networks through a regulated framework. Most of the differences between both approaches can be traced back to this design choice. While the US gas sector uses agreements between network owners and users to organize network activities, the EU system opts for a 'nationally centralized' approach, which targets each European country network as a whole and defines the rules of gas network operation and expansion. So far, national regulatory agencies have had the responsibility to define pricing principles as well as the terms and conditions of services for gas transmission in the name of public interest. The need for defining rules for the use of a network under Third Party Access, however, does not tell what the required rules are. Our book shows a range of possibilities, as well as a range of potential problems associated with them.

Once the network is put under a 'centralized' organization of Third

Party Access, a critical issue concerns the definition of the 'commercial' network being used to trade in the commodity market. As this 'commercial' is always a simplified version of the physical network, bridging the gap between the two versions of the same network is always at the core of the market design.

The EU regulatory approach defining the use of networks is characterized by entry/exit transmission capacity contracts and tariffs, and local balancing zones with virtual hubs. Entry/exit regulation comes with the definition of a commercial network (being the network used to trade gas in the commodity market). Under this scheme, the need for bridging the gap between the commercial and the physical network arises. Short-term adjustment of shippers' portfolios is strongly based on the Transmission System Operator's balancing mechanisms. However, the use of balancing mechanisms to adjust the commercial and the physical network does not guarantee efficiency, as it frequently implies an inefficient use of the network and the socialization of its adjustment costs. The costs associated with a simplified commercial network are increased by the massive introduction of gas-fired power plants and LNG terminals.

This book has shown the growing challenges for the EU gas industry. Network usages have become more heterogeneous, while the new usages increase the value of gas flow flexibility. However, such flexibility is not traded as such in the commercial network. Thus, there are larger differences between commercial and physical flows, which in turn increase the need for short-term adjustments.

The definition of a commercial network closed within national borders is a challenge to EU cross-border trade. So far, the national TPA and entry/exit regulation approach has not been successful in creating an EU-wide market: could it be? As a consequence, the Third European Energy Package (year 2009 Directive) is establishing an agenda to design a set of EU-wide Network Codes to organize trade across EU countries. However, the existing national commercial networks are still working in abstraction of the physical flows, and hence a certain level of cross-subsidies among shippers. Whether there are significant cross-subsidies among network services inside a country (through national transport tariffs or a national balancing system), the cross-border trade tends to have a higher cost than within border. And this over-cost related to the cross border is an obvious barrier to EU-wide trade.

In order to develop an EU-wide gas market, these barriers associated with national borders should decrease or disappear. To do so, one may think of two contrasting solutions: (1) increasing the border limits or (2) decreasing the border limits till a purely nodal trade system is created. The first 'increasing' solution keeps the same entry/exit principle while increasing the size of the regions (to the limit reaching the EU level). The second 'decreasing' solution implies a commercial network that better reflects the physical network properties along the entire EU gas system. Both solutions, however, have drawbacks. On the one hand, increasing the size of entry/exit zones also increases the inefficiency of the network allocation and the scope of cost socialization among players. On the other, decreasing entry/exit zones opens a wider room to market power and players' strategic behaviour.

Decreasing the differences between the commercial and the physical network can be efficiently done by a combination of explicit and implicit capacity allocation mechanisms. But to do so, an efficient coordination among these mechanisms is strongly needed.

The two previous extreme solutions (EU-wide commercial network or the pure nodal) are not likely to be applied in the EU. The 'commercial' simplification of the network, on the one hand, facilitates the trade, while on the other increases the cost when the network has heterogeneous uses. The mechanism to be adopted should then allow the network simplification to facilitate trade but also to favour an efficient use of the network in real time. A coherent link between the explicit and the implicit allocations, thus, seems the key to getting a more harmonized while not too costly EU internal market. The explicit allocation should facilitate trade (especially in the long term), and the implicit allocation should allow network resources to be efficiently allocated (especially in the short term – down to intra-day). Furthermore, the set of explicit/implicit choices must allow players to adjust their portfolios while maintaining efficient economic signals.

The promotion of investment in network infrastructure is central for the development of an EU-wide gas market. There, a new critical choice arises: to 'centralize' the EU network planning activities or to rely on decentralized investment decisions.

A main difference between gas market models has to do with the organization of investment decisions. The achievement of the EU internal gas market will require adequate levels of interconnection among the existing national gas systems. The central question, in this view, is who is in charge of deciding on the adequate investments. One model builds on the 'central' planning of the European network, following the reasoning of a regulation of network activities. The alternative model is to look for inspiration in the US gas industry, where the development of the network is driven by market forces. The logic for that option is to take advantage of the potential information on network needs and the power to contractually commit being both in the hands of the shippers.

The debate between the EU and the US models of market building is open for a while. The repeatedly announced flood of shale gas should even keep it widely open. Our book only gives elements to understanding how we could build an EU-wide gas market on the existing institutional and regulatory European foundations.

Bibliography

Agency for the Cooperation of Energy Regulators (ACER) (2011a), *Framework Guidelines on Capacity Allocation Mechanisms for the European Transmission Network. Agency for the Cooperation of Energy Regulators*, Draft for Consultation, DFGC-2011-G-001.

Agency for the Cooperation of Energy Regulators (ACER) (2011b), *Framework Guidelines on Gas Balancing in Transmission Systems. Agency for the Cooperation of Energy Regulators*, Draft for Consultation, DFGC-2011-G-002.

André, J. (2010), 'Optimization of investments in gas networks', PhD thesis, Université Lille.

APX-Endex (2011), 'Market development and gas exchanges', FSR Specialized Training Course on Gas Markets, accessed 12 April 2013 at http://fsr.eui.eu/Home.aspx.

Artz, K.W. and T.R. Brush (2000), 'Asset specificity, uncertainty and relational norms: an examination of coordination costs in collaborative strategic alliances', *Journal of Economic Behavior & Organization*, **41**(4), 337–62.

Ascari, S. (2011), 'An American model for the EU gas market?', EUI Working Papers, No. RSCAS 2011/39, Florence School of Regulation.

Ascari, S. and M. Cirillo (2008), 'Towards a regional entry-exit system in the SSE gas market', GRI-SSE-OSS&EE Study, Brussels: European Regulators' Group for Electricity and Gas.

Baranes, E., F. Mirabel and J.C. Poudou (2009), 'Natural gas storage and market power', in A. Creti (ed.), *The Economics of Natural Gas Storage: A European Perspective*, Berlin: Springer.

Bartsch, U. (1998), *Financial Risks and Rewards in LNG Projects: Qatar, Oman and Yemen*, Oxford: Oxford Institute for Energy Studies.

Beckman, K. (2010), 'The great security of gas supply struggle', *European Energy Review*, 8 March 2010; accessed 21 March 2013 at http://europeanenergyreview.eu/index.php?id_mailing=47&toegang=67c6a1e7ce56d3d6fa748ab6d9af3fd7&id=1766.

Boltz, W. (2011), 'Vision for a conceptual model for the European Gas Market Workshop to discuss with academics', CEER Stakeholder Workshop on the Gas Target Model with Academia, 14 September, Vienna, Council of European Regulators.

Bonacina, M., A. Creti and A. Sileo (2009), 'Final remarks and policy recommendations', in A. Creti (ed.), *The Economics of Natural Gas Storage: A European Perspective*, Berlin: Springer.

Boot, A.W.A. and A. Thakor (2003), 'The economic value of flexibility when there is disagreement', CEPR Discussion Papers No. 3709.

Bourjas, D. (1997), 'Different options of underground gas storage facilities', in EIA (ed.), *Natural Gas Technologies: A Driving Force for Market Development*, Berlin: EIA.

Chabrelie, M.F. (2003), 'A new trading model for the fast-changing LNG industry', Discussion Paper, 1st Asian Gas Buyers' Summit, 24–25 March, Mumbai, India.

Clingendael International Energy Programme (CIEP) (2003), *The Role of Liquefied Natural Gas in the European Gas Market, Report 03/2003*, The Hague: Netherlands Institute for International Relations.

Clingendael International Energy Programme (CIEP) (2011), *CIEP Vision on the Gas Target Model*, The Hague: Netherlands Institute for International Relations.

Comisión Nacional de la Energía (CNE) (2008), *Informe 8/2008 de la CNE sobre la propuesta de resolución por la que se modifican las normas de de gestión técnica del sistema NGTS-06 'Repartos' y NGTS – 07 'Balance' y el protocolo de detalle PD 02 'Repartos en redes de distribución'*, accessed 21 March 2013 at http://www.cne.es/cne/doc/publicaciones/cne38_08.pdf.

Codognet, M.K. (2006), 'Analyse économique de la contractualisation de l'accès aux infrastructures de réseaux dans les réformes gazières', thesis, Université Paris Sud 11.

Correljé, A., D. De Jong and J. De Jong (2009), *Crossing Borders in European Gas Networks: The Missing Links*, The Hague: Clingendael International Energy Programme.

Creti, A. (2009), *The Economics of Natural Gas Storage: A European Perspective*, Berlin: Springer.

Crocker, K.J. and S.E. Masten (1988), 'Mitigating contractual hazards: unilateral options and contract length', *The RAND Journal of Economics*, **19**(3), 327–43.

Crocker, K.J. and S.E. Masten (1996), 'Regulation and administered contracts revisited: lessons from transaction-cost economics for public utility regulation', *Journal of Regulatory Economics*, **9**(1), 5–39.

Department of Energy and Climate Change (DECC) (2010a), 'Daily variation in electricity demand and the effects of the 2010 Football World Cup', accessed 9 April 2013 at http://webarchive.nationalarchives. gov.uk/20110123082441/decc.gov.uk/publications/basket.aspx?filetype =4&filepath=statistics%2Fpublications%2Ftrends%2Farticles_issue% 2F560-trendssep10-electricity-demand-article.pdf.

Department of Energy and Climate Change (DECC) (2010b), 'Feed in tariffs: government's response to the summer 2009 consultation', accessed 13 March 2013 at http://www.fitariffs.co.uk/library/regulation/100201FinalDesign.pdf.

Dorigoni, S. and S. Portatadino (2008), 'LNG development across Europe: infrastructural and regulatory analysis', *Energy Policy*, **36**(9), 3366–73.

EC (2006), *EU Energy Sector Inquiry 2006, Energy Sector Inquiry, Draft Preliminary Report*, Brussels: European Comission – Directorate-General for Competition.

EC (2009a), *Assessment Report of Directive 2004/67/EC on Security of Gas Supply. Commission Staff Working Document Accompanying Proposal for a Regulation of the European Parliament and of the Council Concerning Measures to Safeguard Security of Gas Supply and Repealing Directive 2004/67/EC*, SEC(2009)978, Brussels: European Commission.

EC (2009b), *Regulation (EC) No 715/2009 of the European Parliament and of the Council of 13 July 2009 on Conditions for Access to the Natural Gas Transmission Networks and Repealing Regulation (EC) No 1775/2005*, Brussels: European Commission.

EC (2010), *Communication on 'The Future Role of Regional Inititiatives'*, COM/2010/721, Brussels: European Commission.

Energy Information Administration (EIA) (2003), *The Global Liquefied Natural Gas Market: Status and Outlook*, Washington, DC: Energy Information Administration.

Energy Information Administration (EIA) (2007), *Electric Power Annual 2007*, US Department of Energy (EIA/DOE), Washington, DC: Energy Information Administration.

Energy Information Administration (EIA) (2008), *Annual Energy Outlook Retrospective Review: Evaluation of Projections in Past Editions (1983–2008)*, Office of Oil & Gas, US Department of Energy (EIA/DOE), Washington, DC: Energy Information Administration.

European Regulators' Group for Electricity and Gas (ERGEG) (2005), *Guidelines for Good TPA Practice for System Operators*, Brussels: European Regulators' Group for Electricity and Gas.

European Regulators' Group for Electricity and Gas (ERGEG) (2006), *Guidelines of Good Practice for Gas Balancing*, Brussels: European Regulators' Group for Electricity and Gas.

European Regulators' Group for Electricity and Gas (ERGEG) (2007), *Treatment of New Infrastructure: European Regulators' Experience with Art. 22 Exemptions of Directive 2003/55/EC – Interim Results of ERGEG Survey*, European Regulators' Group for Electricity and Gas.

European Regulators' Group for Electricity and Gas (ERGEG) (2008),

Status Review: Capacity Allocation Mechanism and Congestion Management Procedures for Storage, Brussels: European Regulators' Group for Electricity and Gas.

European Regulators' Group for Electricity and Gas (ERGEG) (2009), *Guidelines on Article 22 (Exemptions). An ERGEG Conclusion Paper*, 9 April, Brussels: European Regulators' Group for Electricity and Gas.

European Regulators' Group for Electricity and Gas (ERGEG) (2010), *Gas Balancing Rules on European Gas Transmission Networks – Draft Pilot Framework Guideline, Initial Impact Assessment*, Ref: E10-GNM-13-04, Brussels: European Regulators' Group for Electricity and Gas.

Esnault, B. (2000), 'La transition du monopole à la concurrence sur les marchés du gaz naturel en Europe: l'importance stratégique du stockage souterrain', dissertation, Université de Bourgogne.

Espey, J.A. and M. Espey (2004), 'Turning on the lights: a meta-analysis of residential electricity demand elasticities', *Journal of Agricultural and Applied Economics*, **36**(1), 65–81.

European Parliament (2009), 'Directive of the European Parliament and of the Council concerning common rules for the internal market in natural gas and repealing Directive 2003/55/EC', Directive 2009/73/EC, Brussels, 12 June, 2009.

Florence School of Regulation (2011), *Gas Target Model: The MECOS Model*, Pre-release version, accessed 12 April 2013 at http://www. energy-regulators.eu/portal/page/portal/EER_HOME/EER_CONSULT/ CLOSED%20PUBLIC%20CONSULTATIONS/GAS/Gas%20target% 20model/Tab1/20110404_Gas%20Target%20Model%20The%20MEC OS%20Model%20Version%203.7%20-%20pre-release_fin.pdf.

Frontier Economics (2011), *Target Model for the European Natural Gas Market*, report prepared for La Branche Infrastructures de GDF SUEZ.

Futyan, M. (2006), 'The Interconnector Pipeline: a key link in Europe's gas network', Working Paper No. NG11, Oxford: Oxford Institute for Energy Studies.

Gas Infrastructure Europe (GIE) (2009a), *GTE Reverse Flow Study, Report on Technical Solutions*, 21 July, 09GTE+209, accessed 16 March 2013 at http://www.gie.eu.com/publications/indexframe_plus_reverse. html.

Gas Infrastructure Europe (GIE) (2009b), *Preliminary GTE + Winter Outlook 2009/2010, Gas Transport Europe*, accessed 16 March 2013 at http://www.gie.eu.com/memberarea/purtext_plus_winter.asp?wa=pl us_winter&jaar=2009.

Gas Infrastructure Europe (GIE) (2009c), Storage Map Database, accessed 21 March 2013 at http://www.gie.eu.com/index.php/maps-data/ gse-storage-map.

Glachant, J.-M. (2011), 'A vision for the EU gas target model: the MECO-S model', EUI Working Paper No. RSCAS 2011/38, Florence School of Regulation.

Glachant, J.-M. and D. Finon (2010), 'Large-scale wind power in electricity markets', *Energy Policy*, **38**(10), 6384–6.

Glachant, J.-M. and M. Hallack (2009), 'Take-or-pay contract robustness: a three step story told by the Brazil-Bolivia gas case?', *Energy Policy*, **37**(2), 651–57.

Glachant, J.-M. and M. Hallack (2010), 'The gas transportation network as a "lego" game: how to play with it?', Working Paper No. 2010/42, European University Institute.

Gray, J.A. (1978), 'On indexation and contract length', *Journal of Political Economy*, **86**(1), 1–18.

Grossman, S.J. and J.E. Stiglitz (1980), 'On the impossibility of informationally efficient markets', *The American Economic Review*, **70**(3), 393–408.

Hallack, M. (2011), 'Economic regulation of offer and demand of flexibility in gas networks', PhD thesis, Université Paris-Sud 11.

Hartley, P., K. Medlock and J. Rosthal (2007), 'The relationship between crude oil and natural gas prices', Working Paper, Rice University, Baker Institute.

Hauteclocque, A.D. (2009), 'Long-term supply contracts in European decentralized electricity markets: an antitrust perspective', PhD thesis, University of Manchester School of Law.

Hauteclocque, A.D. and J.-M. Glachant (2009), 'Long-term energy supply contracts in European competition policy: fuzzy not crazy', *Energy Policy*, **37**(12), 5399–407.

Hayes, M.H. (2007), 'Flexible LNG supply and gas market integration: a simulation approach for valuing the market arbitrage option', dissertation, Stanford University.

Heather, P. (2010), 'The evolution and functioning of the traded gas market in Britain', Working Paper No. NG44, Oxford: Oxford Institute for Energy Studies.

Honoré, A. (2006), 'Future natural gas demand in Europe: the importance of the power sector', Working Paper No. NG10, Oxford: Oxford Institute for Energy Studies.

Hunt, P. (2008), *Entry-Exit Transmission Pricing with Notional Hubs: Can it Deliver a Pan-European Wholesale Market in Gas?*, Oxford: Oxford Institute for Energy Studies.

Huygen, A.E.H., C.F.M. Bos and M.V. Benthem (2011), 'The development of liquid trading hubs in the North-West European gas markets', in C.J. Jepma (ed.), *Gas Market Trading*, Netherlands: Energy Delta Institute.

International Energy Agency (IEA) (1994), *Natural Gas Transportation: Organization and Regulation*, Paris: International Energy Agency.

International Energy Agency (IEA) (2002), *Flexibility in Natural Gas Supply and Demand*, Paris: International Energy Agency.

International Energy Agency (IEA) (2007), *Tackling Investment Challenges in Power Generation*, Paris: International Energy Agency.

International Energy Agency (IEA) (2008), *Gas Market Outlook*, Paris: International Energy Agency.

International Energy Agency (IEA) (2009), *World Energy Outlook 2009*, Paris: International Energy Agency.

International Energy Agency (IEA) (2011), *Natural Gas Information 2011*, Paris: International Energy Agency.

Interstate Natural Gas Association of America (INGAA) (2001), *Backup Fuel Assessment for Natural Gas Powered Turbines Used in Electric Power Generation*, Washington, DC: INGAA.

Jarlsby, E. (2004), 'Lowering downstream entry barriers for natural gas: small scale LNG distribution in Norway', presented at the Energy & Security in the Changing World Conference, Tehran, 25–27 May.

Jensen, J.T. (2003), 'The LNG revolution', *Energy Journal of the International Association for Energy Economics*, **24**(2).

Jensen, J.T. (2007a), 'Gas pricing: North America', in Energy Charter Secretariat, *Putting a Price on Energy*, Section 4.2, accessed 2 April 2013 at http://www.encharter.org/fileadmin/user_upload/document/Oil_and_Gas_Pricing_2007_ENG.pdf.

Jensen, J.T. (2007b), 'LNG – natural gas – goes global: what does it mean for the Pacific Basin?', presentation at the 30th IAEE International Conference, Wellington, New Zealand, 18–21 February.

Jepma, C.J. (2011), *Gas Market Trading*, Groningen: Energy Delta Institute.

Joode, J. de, H.M. de Jong and L.J. de Vries (2007), 'Congestion management in meshed gas networks: can the electricity market serve as an example?', IAEE Annual International Conference, Potsdam, Germany.

Joskow, P.L. (1988), 'Asset specificity and the structure of vertical relationships: empirical evidence', *Journal of Law, Economics and Organization*, **4**(1), 95–117.

Joskow, P.L. (2003), 'Electricity sector restructuring and competition – lessons learned', Working Papers No. 0314, Massachusetts Institute of Technology, Center for Energy and Environmental Policy Research.

KEMA (2009), *Study on Methodology for Gas Transmission Network Tariffs and Gas Balancing Fees in Europe*, report to European Commission DG TREN, accessed 21 March 2013 at http://ec.europa.eu/energy/

gas_electricity/studies/doc/gas/2009_12_gas_transmission_and_balanc-ing.pdf.

Keppler, J.H. (2007), 'Security of energy supply: a European perspective', *European Review of Energy Markets*, **2**(2), 5–37.

Keyaerts, N., M. Hallack, J.-M. Glachant and W. D'haeseleer (2011), 'Gas market effects of imbalanced gas balancing rules: inefficient regulation of pipeline flexibility', *Energy Policy*, **39**(2), 865–76.

Klein, S., G.L. Frazier and V.J. Roth (1990), 'A transaction cost analysis model of channel integration in international markets', *Journal of Marketing Research*, **27**(2), 196–208.

Labandeira, J., M. Labeaga and L. Otero (2009), 'Estimation of elasticity price of electricity with incomplete information', Working Paper No. 2009-18, FEDEA-IBERDROLA.

Lapuerta, C. (2003), 'Brattle's assessment of the operation of the NTS', in *Gas Trading Arrangements: Reform of the Gas Balancing Regimes*, UK: Ofgem.

Lapuerta, C. (2011), 'Gas markets', accessed 12 April 2013 at http://www.florence-school.eu/portal/page/portal/FSR_HOME/ENERGY/Training /Specialized_training/Presentations.

Lapuerta, C. and B. Moselle (2002), 'Convergence of non-discriminatory tariff and congestion management systems in the European gas sector', The Brattle Group report to European Commission.

Ledesma, D. (2009), 'The changing relationship between NOCs and IOCs in the LNG chain', Working Paper, Oxford: Oxford Institute for Energy Studies.

Logue, C. (2010), 'Capacity auctions', ECRB Workshop – Gas Market Models, Vienna, 11 November 2010.

Lyon, T.P. (2000), 'Preventing exclusion at the bottleneck: structural and behavioural approaches', in M.A. Crew (ed.), *Expanding Competition in Regulated Industries*, Boston, MA: Kluwer Academic Publishers.

Makholm, J.D. (2006), 'The theory of relationship-specific investments, long-term contracts and gas pipeline development in the United States', accessed 2 April 2013 at http://www.nera.com/extImage/PUB_Gas_Pipelines_EN1038.pdf.

Makholm, J.D. (2011), 'Regulating gas pipelines. United States and Europe', accessed 12 April 2013 at http://www.florence-school.eu/portal/page/portal/FSR_HOME/ENERGY/Training/Specialized_training/Presentations.

Maupas, F. (2008), 'Analyse de l'impact économique de l'aléa éolien sur la gestion de l'équilibre production, consommation d'un système électrique', thesis, Université Paris Sud 11.

McDaniel, T. and K. Neuhoff (2002), 'Auctions to gas transmission access:

the British experience', AE Working Paper No. WP 0234, Department of Applied Economics, University of Cambridge.

Menon, S. (2005), *Gas Pipeline Hydraulics*, France: CRC Press.

Micola, A.R. and D.W. Bunn (2007), 'Two markets and a weak link', *Energy Economics*, **29**(1), 79–93.

Moselle, B. and M. White (2011), *Market Design for Natural Gas: The Target Model for the International Market*, LECG Report for the Office of Gas and Electricity Markets, London: LECG.

Mulherin, J.H. (1986), 'Complexity in long-term contracts: an analysis of natural gas contractual provisions', *Journal of Law, Economics, & Organization*, **2**(1), 105–17.

National Grid (2010a), Published BMRA (Balancing Mechanism Reporting Agent) initial demand outrun based on National Grid operational generation metering.

National Grid (2010b), 'System flexibility indicator', Operational Forum 26 May 2010, National Grid.

National Petroleum Council (NPC) (1999), *Meeting the Challenges of the Nation's Growing Natural Gas Demand*, Washington, DC: National Petroleum Council.

Neumann, A. (2009), 'Linking natural gas markets – is LNG doing its job?', *Energy Journal*, **30**(Special Issue), 187–99.

Neveling, S. (2011), 'Implicit auctions/market coupling as a possible element of a target model?', Gas Target Model Workshop II, Bonn, 22 February.

Nissen, D. (2004), 'Commercial LNG: structure and implications', presentation at the 14th Repsol-YPF Seminar, La Coruna, Spain, 26 May.

Nissen, D. (2006), 'The evolution of commercial LNG: optionality, security, and Coasian efficiency', presentation at the 29th IAEE International Conference, Potsdam, Germany, 7–10 June.

Nissen, D. (2007), 'The industrial organization of energy systems: a transactional approach', presentation at Dresden University of Technology, Germany, 20 June.

Offant, P. (2002), 'Convergence of gas and electricity market in the Southern Cone of Latin America', 17th World Petroleum Congress, Rio de Janeiro, Brazil.

Office of Gas and Electricity Markets (Ofgem) (2011), *National Grid LNG Facilities Price Control. Final Proposals*, 21 February 2011 accessed 21 March 2013 at http://www.ofgem.gov.uk/Networks/Trans/GasTransPolicy/LNGPriceControl/Documents1/LNGPC%202011%20Final%20Proposals.pdf.

Patrik, S. (2001), 'Fossil fuel flexibility in West European power generation and the impact of system load factors', *Energy Economics*, **23**(1), 77–97.

PCG (2009), 'PCG proposal for target model and roadmap for capacity allocation and congestion management', in *A PCG Report to the XVIIth Florence Forum*, 10–11 December, Project Coordination Group.

Platts (2009), 'PowerVision market', Quarter 2, 2009, accessed 13 March 2013 at http://www.platts.com/Products/powervision.

Porter, M.E. (1996), 'What is Strategy?', *Harvard Business Review*, **74**(6), 61–78.

Read, R. (2007), 'US LNG imports are expected to jump in the next two years', *LNG Journal*, 4–11.

Roques, F.A., D.M. Newbery and W.J. Nuttall (2008), 'Fuel mix diversification incentives in liberalized electricity markets: a mean–variance portfolio theory approach', *Energy Economics*, **30**(4), 1831–49.

Rosendahl, K.E. and E.L. Sagen (2009), 'The global natural gas market: will transport cost reduction lead to lower prices?', *The Energy Journal*, **30**(2), 17–40.

Ruester, S. (2009), 'Changing contract structures in the international liquefied natural gas markets: a first empirical analysis', *Revue d'Economie Industrielle*, **127**(3), 89–112.

Ruester, S. (2010), 'Vertical structures in the global liquefied natural gas market: empirical analyses based on recent developments in transaction cost economics', dissertation, Dresden University of Technology.

Ruester, S. and A. Neumann (2009), 'Linking alternative theories of the firm – a first empirical application to the liquefied natural gas industry', *Journal of Institutional Economics*, **5**(1), 47–64.

Saguan, M. (2007), 'L'analyse économique de l'architectures des marches électriques, application au market design du "temps réel"', thesis, Université Paris Sud 11.

Salama, M.M. (2000), 'An alternative to API 14E erosional velocity limits for Sand-Laden fluids', *Journal of Energy Resources Technology*, **122**, 71–7.

Saleh, J.H., G. Mark and N.C. Jordan (2009), 'Flexibility: a multidisciplinary literature review and a research agenda for designing flexible engineering systems', *Journal of Engineering Design*, **20**(3), 307–23.

Shaw, D.C. (1994), 'Pipeline system optimization: a tutorial', internal document, Houston: Scientific Software-Intercomp.

Sisman, N. (2011), 'Zone merger – learning from experience and developing an evidential based approach', ENTSOG presentation to the Target Model Workshop 3, London, 11 April.

Smith, H.T.S. and L. Trigeorgis (2004), *Strategic Investment: Real Options and Games*, Princeton, NJ: Princeton University Press.

Stern, J. (2007), 'Is there a rationale for the continuing link to oil product prices in Continental European long-term gas contracts?', Working Paper No. NG-19, Oxford: Oxford Institute for Energy Studies.

Stern, J. and H. Rogers (2011), 'The transition to hub-based gas pricing in

Continental Europe', Working Paper No.49, Oxford: Oxford Institute for Energy Studies.

Talus, K. (2010), 'Vertical natural gas transportation capacity, upstream commodity contracts and EU competition law', PhD thesis, Institute of International Economic Law, University of Helsinki.

Tirole, J. (1988), *The Theory of Industrial Organization*, Cambridge, MA: MIT Press.

UtilityWeek (2010), 'Gas is cheapest for baseload generation', 16 June 2010, accessed 13 March 2013 at http://www.utilityweek.co.uk/news/news_story.asp?id=163354&title=Gas+%27is+cheapest+for+baseload+generation%27.

Van Helden, G.J., P.S.H. Leeflang and E. Sterken (1987), 'Estimation of the demand for electricity', *Applied Economics*, **19**(1), 69–82.

Vazquez, M., M. Hallack and J.-M. Glachant (2012), 'Designing the European gas market: more liquid and less natural?', *Economics of Energy & Environmental Policy*, **1**(3), 25–38.

von Hirschhausen, C. and A. Neumann (2008), 'Long-term contracts and asset specificity revisited: an empirical analysis of producer–importer relations in the natural gas industry', *Review of Industrial Organization*, **32**(2), 131–43.

Vries, L.J. de (2004), 'Securing the public interest in electricity generation markets. The myths of the invisible hand and the copper plate', dissertation, TUDelft.

Williamson, O.E. (1975), *Markets and Hierarchies: Analysis and Antitrust Implications*, New York: The Free Press.

Williamson, O.E. (1979), 'Transaction-cost economics: the governance of contractual relations', *Journal of Law and Economics*, **22**(2), 233–61.

Williamson, O.E. (1985), *The Economic Institutions of Capitalism – Firms, Market, Relational Contracting*, New York: The Free Press.

Williamson, O.E. (1989), 'Transaction cost economics', in R. Schmalensee and R.Willig (eds), *Handbook of Industrial Organization*, Amsterdam: Elsevier, pp. 135–82.

Williamson, O.E. (1991), 'Comparative economic organization: the analysis of discrete structural alternatives', *Administrative Science Quarterly*, **36**(2), 269–96.

Winskel, M. (2002), 'When systems are overthrown: the "dash for gas" in the British electricity supply industry', *Social Studies of Science*, **32**(4), 563–98.

Zhuravleva, P. (2009), 'The nature of LNG arbitrage: an analysis of the main barriers to the growth of the global LNG arbitrage market', Working Paper No. NG-31, Oxford: Oxford Institute for Energy Studies.

Index